DEC 1 4 2012

HOW TO IMPORT WINE
AN INSIDER'S GUIDE

NAPA COUNTY LIBRARY
580 COOMBS STREET
NAPA, CA 94559

DEC 1 4 2012

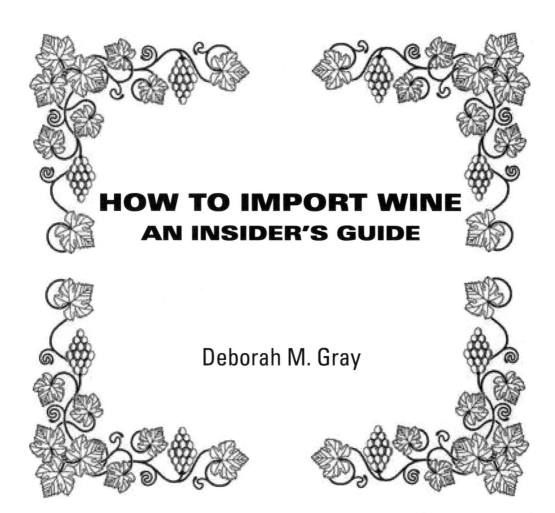

HOW TO IMPORT WINE
AN INSIDER'S GUIDE

Deborah M. Gray

The Wine Appreciation Guild • San Francisco

How to Import Wine:
An Insider's Guide

Text copyright © 2011 Deborah M. Gray

No part of this book may be reproduced or transmitted in any form or by any
means, electronic or mechanical, including photocopying, recording, or by
any information storage and retrieval system, without permission
in writing from the copyright holder.

The Wine Appreciation Guild
360 Swift Avenue
South San Francisco, CA 94080
(650) 866-3020
www.wineappreciation.com

Managing Editor: Bryan Imelli
Consulting Editor: Janeen Olsen, Ph.D.
Cartoons by Doug Pike

ISBN: 978-1-934259-61-0

Library of Congress Cataloging-in-publication
Gray, Deborah M.
How to import wine : an insiders guide / Deborah M. Gray.
p. cm.
Includes bibliographical references.
ISBN 978-1-934259-61-0
1. Imports—Handbooks, manuals, etc. 2. International trade—Handbooks, manuals, etc. 3.
Wine and wine making—Marketing. 4. Business logistics—Handbooks, manuals, etc. I.
Title.
HF1419.G73 2011
382'.4566320068--dc23
2011013539

Although all reasonable care has been taken in the preparation of this
book, neither the author nor the publisher can accept liability for any
consequences arising from the information contained herein,
or from use thereof.

*To Grant, Tyler and Zachary
and in memory of my father, Tony Gray 1921–1995*

TABLE OF CONTENTS

Acknowledgments

Writers write in solitude, but becoming an author never takes place in a vacuum. My heartfelt thanks to my editor, Bryan Imelli, who first gave substance to my publishing dreams, and to Wine Appreciation Guild publisher, Elliott Mackey, who brought them to fruition.

Thanks to my wonderful husband, Grant, and my boys, Tyler and Zachary, who always believed in my writing ability, even before they read anything I had written, and whose loving support has meant everything to me.

I am so fortunate to have three sisters who would do anything for me, but my sister, Catherine Gray, has to be singled out for going above and beyond to carefully edit my drafts, despite enormous professional and personal responsibilities of her own. My mother, Mary Gray, would not be happy unless I acknowledged her, just for being my mother, but truthfully her unwavering belief and encouragement is always appreciated.

My father was the inspiration and the guiding force behind my wine career and for that I will be eternally grateful. Not only has it provided me with an amazingly interesting, challenging and entertaining profession, but brought me into contact with remarkable people, resulting in enduring friendships.

This would not be complete without a shout out to the writing community of AW and especially my Purgatory friends, who have unselfishly supported me on this journey, kept me sane and become great friends in the process.

Foreword

If you are passionate about wine and love to travel, you have undoubtedly encountered many special wines that made you dream about introducing your intriguing discoveries to others back home. However, the realities of wine importing are daunting and complex. For those of you who dare to pursue this dream, this book is an invaluable resource.

In today's wine market, plenty of room remains for you to become a wine importer. Globally, wineries are looking for representation in the expanding US marketplace. Periodically, well-known and established brands need new importers. More often, new wine regions emerge onto the scene and catch consumers' fancy. Hundreds of little known varietals are awaiting discovery. Everyday around the world people are starting new wineries. The opportunities are abundant for creating a unique portfolio of sought after wines.

Passion for wine and an ability to find rare treasures in a world of exciting wines are not the only key factors that will ensure your new importing business will flourish. You must acquire knowledge of importing and have keen business acumen to succeed. Importing and selling wine is a competitive business involving a vast array of regulations and technical issues. Those fledgling entrepreneurs who do not devote the time and energy to learning the ropes will not succeed.

Deborah M. Gray succinctly walks the reader through the vital steps of the process, from finding suppliers and brand creation to acquiring distribution and building market support. The reader will learn the many intricacies of setting up an import business, including licensing, shipping and logistics, and navigating wine's complex distribution channel. This book is a product of her rich and extensive experience as a world-class wine importer, and it is filled with examples of both her triumphs and failures. Anyone wishing to launch such a venture would do well to take advantage of the wisdom in these pages.

—Janeen Olsen, Ph.D.
Professor of Wine Business, Sonoma State University

Introduction

Much of life is about timing. In the mid 1980's my father, Tony Gray, embarked on an ambitious plan to export wine to the U.S. He would be considered both foolhardy and a visionary in his lifetime and this venture was no exception. The 1980's saw the introduction of a few, mass produced Australian brands into the U.S. with some success, but very little of anything from small, family-owned, single vineyard estates. Not only did Tony intend to take on the American wine buying public, but he had the temerity to call his wine brand Australian Gold. No quirky aboriginal dialect, no quaint vales or estates. This was guerrilla marketing positioning. *Let's take on all of America with something that embodied the best of Australia.* It was a bold idea and a progressive label.

Unfortunately, in this broad brush approach, he had not considered some of the more imperative aspects of export, such as appropriate importation, distribution and a little matter of payment.

Through phone calls and faxes, he did find and secure an importer in California, a very short-lived arrangement that lasted until the importer's warehouse and all its contents was seized by the IRS for back taxes. In a protracted legal battle the wine mysteriously disappeared. Tony lost both a container of wine and any hope of reimbursement.

Undaunted, he tried again. This time it was a better researched, small importer in Florida, who was very enthusiastic and seemed to be a good fit. Tony made the trip over, met with the gentleman and sealed the deal with a handshake. Within six months of arrival of the first container, the importer had gone out of business, over 500 cases of Australian Gold were still in storage, the new importer was behind on payments and once again any hope of recovery was gone.

My father, perennially optimistic and determined to find a way to crack the elusive U.S. market, turned to me for help. Which brings me to timing.

I had no experience in the wine business, and incidentally a demanding career, but the opportunity was irresistible. Here was the chance to help my Dad, represent my family's wine, and educate Americans about the Australian wine industry at a time

Figure I.1   Australian Gold Poster

when most people didn't even know we grew grapes. I was living in Tampa Bay, Florida and heard about a restaurant that was opening up nearby with an Australian theme. What better place to start.

It was easy to get a meeting with Tim Gannon. It was his first restaurant and he was personally involved in its physical creation. He hadn't yet been to Australia, but there were boomerangs on the wall, an Aussie themed menu and the partners were applying their previous corporate restaurant experience to a new concept on their own. The year was 1987.

Tim was gracious, and receptive to my proposal. The timing was perfect. But timing, however serendipitous or cosmically aligned, is only as good as one's preparedness for the situation. I presented a beautiful label, a brand name to fit their theme, terrific pricing and a soft, fruity wine to complement the food and the prevailing palate. But the varietals, Semillon and Sauvignon Blanc, were unfamiliar and unpronounceable and I had nothing in my limited repertoire to convince him otherwise. I thanked him for the meeting and left.

That restaurant was Outback Steakhouse. Today, according to Fortune 500, Outback Steakhouse has over 900 restaurants across the U.S. and many other countries, with revenues of $4 billion by 2009. If I had possessed the knowledge and experience during that most propitious of meetings, I would have had answers, options and alternatives that may have laid a foundation for a long, successful business alliance, propelling my father into the U.S. wine business far ahead of the curve. My subsequent, intermittent efforts around Tampa Bay were insufficient to sustain my father's dream and he withdrew from the U.S. It wasn't until 1992, when I established my own import company that he decided to tackle it again.

Yes, timing is everything, but in the wine industry timing has to be backed up with a plan. And never has this been more essential than during the difficult economic challenges we face today in a congested wine brand field overrun with players.

Most people, gazing longingly across the fence at the wine business, seem to have their rose colored glasses perched firmly on their noses. When I tell people, with a sigh, that I have a stack of wine in my office for my palate to wade through, they mock-commiserate with me. "Oh, poor you," is the not uncommon response, which really means, "Wouldn't I love to have that problem." But, as you will discover in concrete terms, the tasting and enjoyment of wine is just the tip of the iceberg.

Years ago, when I started my import company, the only bit of advice anyone gave me was "don't do it." It was proffered by the head of a wine distribution company, and I've never figured out if he really thought it was a bad idea or was just afraid of the competition. Needless to say, I did not heed his warning. Since this was the only advice I received, I plunged blindly in and several years of trial and error ensued as I made my way up my own steep learning curve. Fortunately, this training I received in the trenches will alleviate much of it for you, and provide far more than a basic understanding or academic treatise on the importing and distribution of wine into the U.S. It is an exciting, rewarding, fascinating field if you know what you are doing. I really do want to reach back with a helping hand to those who are entering the field now. Each person shouldn't have to reinvent the wheel.

A plethora of wine books can be found on any bookstore shelf, with subjects ranging from the nuances of regions, tastes and food pairings by notable authors, to bicycle treks into bucolic countryside and in-depth texts on wine making and wine marketing. Until now, there has been nothing to compare to this comprehensive step by step guidance through the importing process, from portfolio composition through distribution, presented in a practical, easily digested format.

Drawing on the author's nineteen year's hands-on career as a wine importer, this book's primary purpose is to *demystify* importing wine into the U.S. For anyone considering such a professional move, regardless of prior experience or education, this book will lay out specific guidelines and instructions for setting up and running a wine import business from the perspective of someone who is actually importing and distributing on a day-to-day basis.

I'll share stories with you of actual experiences, advice on how to streamline your journey, alongside the more enjoyable aspects of successfully representing a product that brings people pleasure and enhances social settings. The prospective importer enters a world where tasting wine is part of business and business is often conducted under the olive tree overlooking rolling hills of trellised vines, or with a gourmet meal at the cellar door restaurant. But it is still a business and one that must be approached armed with the right tools.

In other words, this is a career choice from which you can derive much satisfaction and an enviable lifestyle. But first, you must do your homework. Or it may become akin to the oft-repeated boater's lament "a big hole into which you pour money."

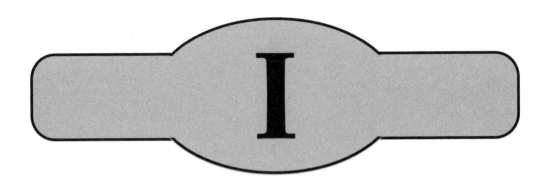

1

INITIAL CONSIDERATIONS

You may have picked up this book as a curiosity, considering what it might take to be a wine importer, or you may already have decided it's definitely for you. But, like any business, it's an entrepreneurial pursuit and takes a certain type of individual. Let's look at why you are considering undertaking this endeavor before we plunge into the nitty-gritty.

- Do you have wine industry experience?
  - o this could be anything from retail to wholesale, or working in a winery; any of this can bring experience or knowledge to your venture and be very helpful, but be careful not to romanticize your experience or consider that one type of background prepares you fully for another.
- Have you been in some other form of perishable goods import business?
  - o any type of importing prepares you for the technical aspects of container management and logistics, but perishable goods—such as food and drink—extend this knowledge into the arena of FDA, understanding product movement in a timely manner and budgeting.

- Does it seem fun and exciting?
  - o not exactly an experiential reason, but one which will instill the necessary enthusiasm and desire to learn more about the business that will benefit you; just don't allow yourself to get carried away with the idea that it is fun and exciting and forget about the real world work and perseverance that will be necessary for the business to succeed.
- Have you made money in an unrelated venture and now wish to invest?
  - o this can be a great reason, but the same caution as above can apply and that is to consider that an investment will only pay off if you have done your due diligence; this is not a hobby, or a business for the dabbler, unless you are only the investor and will surround yourself with knowledgeable, experienced people.
- Have you always wanted to be an entrepreneur?
  - o not a bad reason, but be prepared to back it up with capital, a willingness to learn and an understanding that being an entrepreneur—unless you have considerable funds—does not mean being the boss and delegating everything to subordinates. It also means donning a variety of hats, including secretary, filing clerk and delivery person if that's what it takes to get the business off the ground.
- Are you looking for a part-time or full-time operation?
  - o there is no reason not to approach this enterprise from either perspective, but recognize the ramifications and commitment of each before you proceed.
- Is this a passion?
  - o this is very often the reason many people enter the wine business—from the perspective of loving wine and wanting to become more involved in the process—and I applaud this motive, as long as it is combined with the real world considerations outlined above.

All of these may be legitimate reasons and ones which will serve you well, depending upon your goals. If you are looking for a part-time occupation, be prepared to downsize your idea of number of brands and area of distribution. On the other hand, be aware that economies of scale when it comes to office set-up, license fees, travel and other expenses will not become cost-effective until you are at a certain volume level. If you don't have the experience, reading this book will put you far ahead of the game. At the very least it will form the building blocks from which you can create your own wine import structure. A couple of other points to consider:

- Do you have the basic self-discipline for a business that requires adherence to deadlines, such as state reporting, brand registrations and payment of fees and taxes in a timely manner?
- Are you a big picture person or detail-oriented (you must be both!)?
- Can you happily multi-task?

In other words, be prepared for coordinating container consolidation, submitting applications for label approval, keeping up with multiple license renewals, following government regulations regarding every aspect of wine, communicating with distributors, maintaining inventory levels and more…all at the same time.

But most importantly, if this is something you feel excited about, if your dream is to blanket the country with the next *Two Buck Chuck,* or source the unsung, artisanal finds of the wine world and lovingly hand sell each bottle, this may happen. Who's to say it cannot? Certainly not those who would seek to discourage you.

Portfolio—Options and Building

You may have uncovered that rare gem on a trip to Bordeaux or the Loire Valley and would love to make it available to wine devotees back home. Perhaps you have a passion for Argentine Malbec or Roussanne from the Côtes du Rhône and want to rush out and build a niche portfolio with all the nuances of your discoveries, but there are far broader, and narrower, considerations in selecting and building your portfolio beyond the initial catalyst that triggers you to consider a career, or adventure, as a wine importer. It would be helpful to examine that impetus within the framework of the various factors that can absolutely mean the difference between a financially viable, commercial entity and an expensive assortment of wines to add to your own cellar.

Let's say you have already decided exactly what type of wines you want to bring in and their origin, based on favorite vacations, palate preference or wines you enjoyed representing when you sold to retailers for a state distributor. There is nothing wrong with this approach. It is the way many highly profitable companies began. First and foremost, you should be excited about what you represent, just as in anything you undertake in life. Without passion, this will not be much fun and there is far less likelihood of success and fulfillment. But let's drill down a bit deeper and examine factors that may help you make alternate decisions, expand your thinking, or confirm your own choices, as you put together a workable portfolio.

Sourcing Options

Some of these considerations would be:

- **A small collection of large brands, or a large collection of small brands**

  When considering the overall makeup of your portfolio, the number of brands isn't necessarily the first decision you will make, but normally one brand does not generate sufficient interest from your prospective customers, nor sufficient income for you. Unless, of course, you have the great fortune to stumble upon a situation that proves to be the exception—a large production winery with many desirable wines, great reviews and impressive pricing. Or a high volume brand with established U.S. distribution that is looking for a new importer. Otherwise, this is all about how you want to spend your time, what interests you most and in general terms what you want your portfolio to look like. Sourcing small production gems from remote vineyard regions may be right up your alley, whereas someone else is all about landing a couple of big brand potentials and concentrating on building them towards large scale national distribution. This speaks somewhat to your personality and your long range ambitions as well.

- **Specialization in one country—what does that represent to you**

  If you choose to focus on France, e.g., because elegant and restrained old world wines appeal to you personally, should this be limited to one of either Burgundy, Bordeaux, Loire Valley or Alsace, or encompass the whole country? Would you be able to find sufficient production from each region to complete a well rounded selection? Are vintages in that one area so unpredictable that it is unlikely you will be able to procure adequate wine each season to make this a going concern? Undoubtedly, your endeavor should be a passion, you should represent what you believe in and enjoy, but presumably your ultimate goal is to build a thriving business as a successful importer.

- **Appreciation for the wines from that country, its regions and its classifications**

  Using France, which although a particularly rigid example, could certainly apply to other countries, do you comprehend the vineyard designations, the *Appellation d'Origine Contrôlée* (AOC) or more commonly known as *Appellation Contrôlée* (AC) and their strict compliance laws regulating everything from vineyard to label specifications? Are you familiar with vintage conditions, relevant *terroir*, varietal and style that typify the finest offerings of the region? These would all be important considerations in successfully selecting, pricing and representing wine from that, and any other, locale.

- **What about one hemisphere?**

  This can be a portfolio specialization decision and, additionally, can help defray travel or container consolidation costs in putting together various brands. It also helps you with the warehousing issues. Sourcing from "new world" or "old world" will tend to differentiate the wines as representative of particular styles. Not that either hemisphere produces one-dimensional wines—far from it—but it can be useful as a way to characterize the make-up of your portfolio, if that's your goal.

- **Should it be made up of many countries or both hemispheres?**

  This is really another way to look at the previous issue and is a personal decision based on the same factors and how you wish your portfolio to look, elements of travel, where you warehouse, and perhaps adding another item to that, what is being offered to you that you feel you cannot pass up.

- **Are you familiar with the up and coming or "hot" regions?**

  Entering the market with product that is starting to gain considerable attention or recognized as a "must have" for a wholesaler's book may be a way to jump start your sales and achieve faster distribution, as long as you recognize what the current expectations are of that region, pricing, styles, etc.

  A few years ago Chile was all the rage, and remains popular, but they were so successful at marketing themselves at the lower end of the price spectrum that they are having difficulty raising the price bar. Argentina, on the other hand, which is one of the "hot" areas as of this writing, recognized their niche—full-bodied Malbec at great prices—but has managed to diversify their varietal offerings and price levels. Where is the next "hot" region? Can you be there ahead of the curve?

- **Conversely, have you become aware of what country origins may be over-saturated, ebbing in fashion, or no longer considered good value?**

  Australia is the first example that comes to mind, again as of this writing. During earlier days of less globalization and travel (pre internet) and a fascination with Australia from afar, it was exotic and romantic. Like Chile, it entered the market with inexpensive wines, mostly blends—familiar sounding varietals combined with unfamiliar names. Savvy vintners blended Chardonnay with one of the most widely planted (but unfamiliar) white grapes at the time, Semillon, and combined Cabernet with the most widely planted (but also unfamiliar) red grape, Shiraz. Consumers recognized at least one grape in each of the red and white and, priced at a retail of $5.99, were prepared to take a gamble on the wine. As bright, accessible wines reminiscent of California, these soon found a loyal consumer base and opened the door to other wines, and slightly higher price points.

  However, it was not until the *Wine Spectator* end of year issue of 1995, that Australian wines were firmly established at the next level. In that issue, Penfolds Grange, which sold for $100 a bottle, was featured on the cover, named *Red Wine of the Year* and awarded 98 points out of 100! Suddenly, Australia was anointed as a world class wine producing country and able to introduce wines to the U.S. consumer at every price point, with considerable acceptance.

  The upward trend continued until the exchange rate, massive planting, and over-proliferation of brands, particularly the "critter brands" (cute animal labels) that followed Yellow Tail, resulted in consumer fatigue with the crowded category. This is not, by any means, to say that Australian wines are unfashionable. They remain a very feasible addition or area of concentration in the portfolio and most distributors would recognize it as an essential category, but an understanding of its current positioning will help you with your decision. France is another example of waxing and waning popularity, but even during less popular times there are plenty of excellent examples of fine French table wine and sought-after Bordeaux. It requires, however, due diligence to identify those wines from well-represented regions that still offer great quality for good value, at any price level, and identify trends within the industry that do not depend upon region, but more on style, blend or character. Ultimately great wine is great wine.

- **Do you see a niche for esoteric wines that makes financial sense?**

  What do I mean by that? You may, for example, love Moldovan Cabernet, or Mexican Carignan, and those would certainly represent a niche, but would a

Figure 1.1   Example of Australia's Unique Vineyard Ecosystem (Courtesy of Whistling Kitie Vineyard, Riverland, South Australia)

portfolio based on these wines, or these particular countries, be economically feasible? At this time, probably not. On the other hand, if you recognized a region or wineries of South Africa that produced fabulous Pinotage and you saw little of it in the market, then this could be a good starter niche. Not something perhaps on which to build your empire, but South Africa is continuing to build a reputation for wines such as this that are not yet fully realized in this market. Obviously, research on your own, and current wine publications, will tell you more about the likelihood that Pinotage, or any other grape finds, have either overtaken the market at the time you read this, or already fallen out of favor.

- **Are there wines that are so new they are likely to be misunderstood, or have not yet reached sufficient critical mass to be in demand?**

This overlaps somewhat into the previous area, but relates more to varietals, blend, style or packaging that is completely unfamiliar to the consumer, or may be too confusing for the consumer to appreciate. This can be overcome, as Chile and many others have done, by simplifying the label and westernizing it, if the winery agrees and it seems appropriate. Otherwise, make these wines, if you love them, a small part of the portfolio or a hand sell passion. If you plan on building your success around them and are just starting out, it's difficult to be at the vanguard of change and innovation.

- **Will you have difficulty securing sufficient wines from this region or these brands?**

  Something to consider when you've fallen in love with those fabulous dessert wines and discover that they are only made in vintages where botrytis occurs naturally, which the vineyard owner tells you averages every four years. Or the vines are never irrigated and the yields are so low that occasionally there isn't enough to sell. Or vintages all over the appellation are so variable that it is unlikely that you will want to bring in wines each year, because quality is not acceptable. You get the picture.

- **Will you encounter a language barrier?**

  This is certainly something that can be overcome, through the use of agents, brokers, trade organization, and people in the family or area who could serve as interpreter, but I only mention it to cover all those variables that can realistically come into play and may end up being a factor you would prefer to avoid.

- **What impact does or will the exchange rate have on your purchases (based on historical, current and anticipated global trends)?**

  Presently, the Euro and Australian and New Zealand dollars are all trading high against the American dollar. Does this mean you should stay away from all of Europe and most of the Southern Hemisphere? Of course not. This will change as the global currencies wax and wane. But be prepared to factor in fluctuating or increasing exchange rates into the price, or choose a region that represents the best value or most stable currency to you. Nothing can erode a margin—and your profit—faster than the exchange rate.

- **Must each wine in each brand represent a superlative quality level, or are you more concerned with representing a region or country?**

  This is a subjective decision and not one based on what is correct or advisable. It speaks to branding, to some degree, which we will address later. It also takes into consideration your own preferences—country, palate, lifestyle, etc.

Can you recommend something pronounceable?

Figure 1.2 © David Pike

QPR—Quality Price Ratio

This has become a key element in wine selection, representation and consumer decisions. To compete with, and rise above, all the brands from around the world already on the shelf, and all the brands on the horizon, your wines must be able to represent really good value. Even better if it can "over deliver." In other words, the sort of wine that makes the distributor or retailer say, "wow, I expected this to be a lot more money." The sort of wine that compels consumers to announce on internet message boards and to their friends, "you should check out what I just came across."

This becomes easier to find these days with markedly improved winemaking techniques, modern facilities and knowledgeable vineyard management. Which means wines of comparable quality are also available to everyone else in the field, and it becomes important to determine if your wine represents the best quality for the price *at each level*.

Packaging

Another key element in the brand selection is packaging, and it cannot be ignored (see Figure 1.3). Although numbers vary depending upon the survey, it has become evident that the vast majority of retail wine purchases are made by women and very often their choice of an unknown wine will be on the basis of overall visual impression. They may have narrowed it down to red or white, price or origin, but given the dizzying array of prospects—over 65,000 SKUs (stock keeping unit), with hundreds introduced every year—it often comes down to packaging or label.

Irrespective of gender, consumers will also often have a preconceived notion of how a wine should taste, based on packaging. Items that will influence, even subliminally, are:

- bottle shape
- bottle quality—weight, feel, punt, etc.
- label graphics
- name
- back label story
- capsule
- quality of label
- cohesiveness of design and overall package

First and foremost it must be eye-catching and not, as one distributor told me years ago when he declined one of my brands, "shelf recessive." In other words, not only did it not stand out on the shelf, it actually receded from view.

However, this does not mean eye-popping, garish and discordant. It cannot just demand attention. It has to be *meaningful* attention. Does it say fabulous at $5.99, but

Figure 1.3   Example of Package Design

it's actually a $40 retail wine? Are the label graphics artfully blind embossed with gold leaf on linen weave, on a high shouldered bottle with a deep punt, at a retail of $5.99? Doesn't that sound more like the $40 wine? Aside from the expense involved (I exaggerated the example for the sake of making a point) consumers want any one or a combination of fun, bright, quirky, edgy, trendy and daring at $5.99. They also want a pronounceable name or at least a memorable label that's easy to describe when they return to the wine store and say they'd like "another bottle of that wine I got last time." Consider Rosemount's ubiquitous diamond label, Rex Goliath's *47 lb Rooster* or in the case of the name, *Fat Bastard.* The latter is now one of the best selling wines from France, originally because of the shock value of the name. It doesn't hurt that the wine, in each case, is sufficiently enjoyable to keep coming back for more. In fact, it is essential.

You will find that some wineries will be wedded to their dreadful label and cling to it as they would to a cherished family member. I have heard, and more:

- It's been in the family for generations.
- It's the ancestral crest.
- The Europeans have been behind it since we introduced it to the UK and Switzerland in 1988. (Translated as "it was old-fashioned then and it's now hopelessly out of style".)
- We just spent considerable money redesigning the label and absolutely love it.

More importantly, do you love it? Can you see it working in the U.S. market? At the risk of painting with too broad a brush, European labels have traditionally been more, well, traditional. Americans have embraced innovative and out-of-the-box for some time, almost to an extreme, and what works in Europe is no indication of what will work here.

The label must simply be something *you* feel can work. You don't *have* to love it, but the majority of those you show it to should at least like it. It can follow trends without necessarily being trendy. It can start its own trend even. As long as it's understood, enjoyed and seems to fulfill a reasonable expectation of price point and quality.

The exception to this would be the high end wine that has garnered enough accolades, awards, ratings and cult status they can pretty much do anything they want. The followers of these wines just want the wine.

Branding—Not about the Wine

Branding usually does refer to the wine, or collection of wines under a brand, so the discussion begins there. A brand owner's ultimate goal is to be recognized and synonymous with something that makes it more desirable than other wines of its ilk, thereby making the job of selling wine that much easier, with the benefit of image and prestige.

It could be the best of its appellation or varietal, the most food-friendly, the greatest value, the highest rating, the first from that region, the most highly touted. It can be identified with a name: Baron Philippe de Rothschild or Francis Ford Coppola. It can be the first New Zealand Sauvignon Blanc to rate above 90 in *Wine Spectator*. All these things sell and, if the brand continues to do its job, will sell on the basis of those identifiers for a long time to come. It will even sell through variable vintages and wine quality that isn't quite up to scratch and ratings that occasionally disappoint. As long as the image remains intact and it can consistently perform to a certain level, or a perceived level. Possibly because of the confusing selection of wines on restaurant lists or retail shelves, it's an area to aptly apply the old maxim, "there's no such thing as bad publicity." I've seen people seek out wines long after their star has faded—quality has deteriorated, because grapes are sourced instead of formerly estate grown, the winemaker has left, or the price has gone through the stratosphere—simply because of name brand familiarity.

Branding, for the purpose of this section, refers to you or your portfolio, or both. Are *you* the expert on Petite Sirah, Riesling, Viognier or Malbec? Can you be? Do you want to be? Can you become the go-to person for esoteric, well made varietals and blends? Wines that individually are not going to make up a successful wine business, but collectively start to build gravitas for your portfolio and you, as the acknowledged, savvy source of such wines.

Cool climate wines could be a branded portfolio specialty, or wines from around the world under $10, or ratings over 90 points in major U.S. based magazines. Broad selections or great quality finds from Austria or Eastern Bloc countries or a concentration on small islands (Tasmania, Waiheke, Kangaroo Island, Sardinia, e.g.). Make up your own category, but continue to research and ask questions. It may seem like the best idea since sliced bread to you, only to find out that no one really cares if you're an expert on Eiswein.

But if you truly want to stand out, then branding might well be the way. It's an option you can explore down the road, but it can also become a goal as you put together your first portfolio.

Balancing the Portfolio

Even if you've decided on specialization—wines rated above 90 points in *Wine Advocate*, e.g.—it would be difficult to stock your offerings with only wines above $30, or all Cabernet Sauvignon. A balanced, diverse portfolio can still be a specialized one that aims for branding, or limits its scope to certain regions.

If a distributor is looking at your price list and sees all wines of a particular price point or certain varietal, or too similar in style to differentiate, then you are effectively competing against yourself—cannibalizing your own portfolio. They will not, no matter how desirable or highly rated each wine is individually, buy them all. If that were the case, then they would be asking their sales people to do the same thing—present wines that compete against one another. It's not cost-effective and it wastes time. There is no time to waste in today's wine business.

Summary

Bearing in mind what you want to represent and accomplish, aim for an exciting portfolio that offers a range of diversity to the distributor, both in style and price point. Specialize in New Zealand if you wish, but by including Sauvignon Blancs from

Marlborough, Pinot Noirs from Central Otago and Martinborough, dessert wines from Waiheke, organic wines from Gisborne and Bordeaux blends from Gimblett Gravels you are giving your potential customer an intriguing and well considered range of wines from which he or she can choose a broad selection.

My Story

I will remind you occasionally of my early days as a new importer to illustrate a point and occasionally as a means for you to understand how easily one can make many different rookie mistakes I am hopeful you will avoid.

One of the first shipments I brought in was an entire container of bone dry, moderately expensive Hunter Valley (Australia) Semillon—around 800 cases. If you think bone dry, moderately expensive Hunter Valley Semillon might be a difficult sell now, consider 1992. I believe it retailed for around $20. My motivation was this:

- Extended terms of payment (very attractive for a new business with limited resources).
- A winemaker held in high esteem who consistently won national awards and gold medals for his wines.
- The wine's exceptional quality.
- Varietal characteristics that exemplified the grape.
- Introducing to the U.S. a varietal that was synonymous with the Hunter Valley (Semillon was one of Australia's two most widely planted white grapes).

What could not be overcome was this:

- Americans still *talk dry, but drink sweet*, but even more so back then, and this wine was almost devoid of residual sugar.
- A price point that was way beyond anything the US consumer was accustomed to paying for Australian wines in general and Semillon in particular.
- No reference in the consumer's experience with the grape, and unwillingness to embrace it.
- Lack of knowledge of Australian regions.
- Unfamiliarity with Australia's icon winemakers.

I sold three cases to a couple of local Atlanta restaurants, and the rest returned to the vineyard, after collecting warehousing fees for several months. Doing my due diligence in *this market* could have averted this disaster.

2

BUILDING A BUSINESS MODEL

At this point, take a deep breath and look at this as a business, because to make it a success will require an investment of money, time and physical resources, and before you consider bringing in your first bottle you must build your foundation. First, decide what sort of an entity you will be.

Company Structure, Personnel, Partners

The initial decision regarding the structure of your business must necessarily be yours. Whether an LLC, sole proprietorship, C Corporation, Partnership or S Corp will be up to you and, if you have them, investors and partners. Several good books are devoted entirely to the subject. So, I'm not going to attempt to advise you on this. But they *are* decisions that have to be made with considerable forethought. If you have partners and investors, who owns the majority share, and what is the delineation of roles? Even a "silent partner" often wants their say.

Based on my own experience, if you bring an investor as a working partner into your own endeavor, please make sure they have either been in the wine business or have more than a rudimentary understanding of how it operates. Many of the tried and true business principles from the corporate world simply don't apply here, much as the successful CEO of an unrelated company might want to apply them. Additionally, the wine industry has changed dramatically in a relatively short time and you must be flexible and continue to change with it. Someone who has worked within the industry will recognize this and be willing to make those adjustments with you, instead of trying to impose their own, unrelated, experience on your business model.

If a shareholder has over 50% stake in the company, they have, if they desire, *all* the say, not just a majority of the say. Should they wish to go down one path and you another, you lose. If they decide to bring in too much wine at too high a cost, spend money on staffing you don't need, guess who prevails? If you have confidence in your partner/investor and they bring so much to the table that you are happy to give up control, so be it. But make sure this is your carefully calculated decision beforehand, and not a shocking reality once you are in the midst of your venture.

Naming the business should take into consideration what you will become, not what you think you are now. To name it Joe's Fine Wines from Argentina is pretty limiting, even if you think you'll only ever want to represent anything from Argentina or never give up ownership. Similarly, calling yourself Hot Wines from Hot Regions may sound as if you have a handle on trends, but trust me, trends change in this arena too.

Office Requirements

It is entirely possible for you to conduct your business from an office in your home, at your discretion. The bulk of the wine will, by necessity, be stored elsewhere and, as this is a wholesale operation, there will be no retail traffic or surprise visitors. Just be sure it has privacy, a door to close, sufficient room to accommodate two people, and doesn't share space with the kid's game room or any other function of the house. It will be disruptive to you, and home noise will bleed over into professional conversations. It is one thing to have an office at home, quite another to let your suppliers and customers know they are competing for attention with the dog and X Box.

Initially, in a small enterprise, it can all be handled by one person. Part-time assistance, at least, is very helpful, especially if you are out of the office or traveling, but it is feasible to start alone if finances or personal inclination dictates. In either regard, the size of the office can be reasonably small. The equipment you'll need will comprise:

- File cabinets—this is not a paperless business. You must keep physical records in the event of a local license office audit, signed contracts, signed and approved label applications (COLAs), tasting notes and so on.
- Computer—either one laptop to take with you when you travel or one PC that remains in the office for personnel and one laptop for you.
- Dedicated phone line for the business—even if it's just you in a home office in your bunny slippers, you must sound like a professional company and have the phone answered with the business name. It also enables you to select a feature to forward calls to your cell phone if no one is in the office.
- Copier and Fax—both are necessary, but can be combined in one machine. There are extremely efficient, inexpensive laser machines available today.
- Programs—Word, Excel and Quick Books, Adobe and Microsoft Publishing—Adobe and Microsoft Publishing are purchases that can be held off for a short while, if need be, but are extremely helpful in both creating and editing labels and POS (Point of Sale) material.
- Wine racks.

Wine racks? Didn't I just say the wine is stored elsewhere? Yes, but you need to organize the samples you'll receive to evaluate, and those you'll have shipped to you (by the 12 or 6 bottle case) from the warehouse to send to prospective customers and for publication review. Have a system to organize the cases that aren't in racks, from which you'll pull to replenish the racks or send out directly. Generally, have at least a case of each new item or new vintage sent immediately to you from the warehouse upon container arrival.

Figure 2.1   Bottle-necker

If you decide you can't work from home, are planning for the future, or when you expand your operation, office space that can realistically handle even large-scale national distribution can be conducted in office space comprising:

- Reception—(entry, waiting room or working space)
- Two cubicles in a general space—one for compliance and one for invoicing/bookkeeping
- Conference room—doubles as meeting space and tasting room
- Your private office
- Storage room for wine samples

Geography Decision: National or Regional

It's a good idea to consider what you want your business to look like, both to you and your potential supplier (the winery).

Do you intend to bring in wine just for distribution in your own state? Are you planning on blazing trails through all 50 states as soon as possible? The Federal Basic Permit (your import license) entitles you to import as an exclusive agent for the entire country. It doesn't require you to differentiate to obtain your license.

However, how you intend to operate impacts your business model. It could also impact the goals of the winery or vineyard you choose to represent (or have approached) and this should be communicated to them at the outset.

For instance, a winery may already have an importer for New York and New Jersey, but wish to broaden their distribution and add only a region, say Ohio, Indiana and Kentucky. That may work well for you, but in general you'll feel constrained by this arrangement, since Illinois is so close and you have contacts there, or because you intended to represent all brands in your portfolio for the whole country. And, by the way, national importing is the norm rather than the exception, but this is sometimes at variance with the understanding of other countries. If you really believe in the brand, always keep the lines of communication open. The importer covering New York and New Jersey may go out of business, fail to deliver on their sales or decide to give up the brand because it conflicts with something else in their portfolio. It happens all the time.

Resources—Time and Money

The answer to how many resources, how much time and money cannot be arrived at through one formula. There are many variables to consider, and should be evaluated as part of the whole picture. To a great extent it will depend upon your personal aspirations, plus time and capital constraints. My goal in this book is to sincerely assist you, with as much expertise as possible, in the decision making and implementation required in setting up a viable import business. I hope it will read in a straightforward and easy to understand manner, but I would be remiss if I made it sound simple to execute and something to be undertaken as a frivolous diversion.

Therefore, I would suggest that importing is not necessarily something to be considered as a part-time occupation, unless you are doing this in conjunction with a wholesale operation. That is, if you are importing wine solely to sell within your own local wine distribution company. There are too many licenses, logistical considerations, volume of wine, warehousing and other considerations that require *some* economies of scale, however minimal, to derive a profit from simply importing part-time. I believe you can be a part-time broker, distributor, retailer and salesperson, because all of these can be limited in all the ways that importing cannot. Limiting your business and limiting your scope is well within your purview, but if you truly wish to become a wine importer, treating it as a hobby or something in which to dabble will, in my opinion, result in poor results. Among many other considerations, alcohol is a heavily regulated industry and requires attention to reporting, license renewals, an understanding of laws and payment of necessary duty and taxes. These activities become second nature to someone who is actively engaged in a flourishing wine company, but become onerous to someone who only occasionally has the time to devote to the pursuit.

There are still many other options for the aspiring importer. If you work well with others, then putting together a team of like-minded people who each bring value to the table, and perhaps needed capital, will spread the responsibility to the extent that your position may be occupied in a somewhat part-time fashion. The downside is that your share of the profits will most likely reflect this diminished role, unless the team you put together is utilizing *your* capital and you remain a majority shareholder.

Irrespective of the number of individuals running the company or occupying certain roles, or if you are doing it all yourself, there are certain overarching constants under consideration in your initial and ongoing financial outlay:

- volume of wine on each container
- freight, duty and taxes
- quantity of wine to be stored
- warehousing fees
- licensing and brand registrations (varies by state)
- salaries, commission and taxes
- office overhead

- travel
- sample usage
- marketing and promotion
- insurance
- furniture, fixtures and equipment
- domestic freight (air, ground)

These are constants to the extent that they will exist; the dollar amount, the breadth of the expense, will be up to your business model, your aspirations and possibly your limitations.

Some items will be reduced considerably by your desire or budget, but to some degree they will be required. Preparing a business plan and budget incorporating these items will give you a much clearer picture of the financial outlay you can expect at the outset and moving forward.

Warehouse

Again, a decision affected somewhat by variables, covered below, and a decision to be made sooner, rather than later. This will determine where the container will arrive for paperwork, what licenses you need, and to factor into pricing.

> **Geographical area**—if your licensed premises (your office) is on the East Coast and your immediate area of distribution will be New Jersey, New York, Connecticut and Pennsylvania, then warehousing at a licensed, bonded facility in New Jersey, where wine from various sources is stored, becomes a logical first choice for you. Containers regularly dock at Port Newark/Elizabeth, e.g., unload and truck a short distance to area warehouses, minimizing transit time, cost and handling. Your distributors will be familiar with the warehouse location, able to pick up less expensively, can consolidate orders with others at the same warehouse and replenish quickly when they run out. You won't have to wait as long for samples as when

shipped from the West Coast and, if desired, can visit the warehouse to interview the principals or for periodic physical inventory.

Alternatively, if you live on the West Coast, or a nearby state, warehousing in Northern California makes sense. Oakland is a shipping gateway to this region. Again, you select a licensed, bonded warehouse where distributors are as familiar with the name and location as they are with their own. They presumably have trucks going out to Napa or Sonoma once a week or every two weeks to pick up other wines stored at the same warehouse, and are well acquainted with the warehouse routines and requirements.

If you live anywhere in the mid or southern regions of the country, the decision can be dictated by where the majority of your distribution will take place or which wine region you source from, but should, in my opinion, be limited to a coastal choice (see Figure 2.2).

Wine sourcing regions—where you intend to source your wine from will likely have a bearing on where you warehouse. In addition to your own geographical position, if your imported wines all come from Europe or South America, both of which are closer to the East Coast, it is cost-effective to warehouse there. The transit time is shorter and less expensive. If the wines are from the Southern Hemisphere (Australia, New Zealand, South Africa) they are closer to the West Coast and for the same reasons it makes sense to warehouse there. Decide on the basis of both economic feasibility and personal choice.

Business model—if national distribution is your aim and you are building up significant business in states on both coasts, then warehousing in two places, one east and one west, could make sense for you, but this may be phase two of your plan. If you live on the West Coast and have a contract with a national chain with strong store business up and down the Eastern seaboard then you may choose to warehouse on the East Coast. The other alternative is to use that national contract, and a volume commitment from the chain, as a compelling argument to persuade distributors in each state to warehouse the wine for you, since they will have to ship directly to the chain's stores anyway.

Fees—nothing can eat up a margin faster than unanticipated expenses. All warehouses charge monthly storage, by the case. In addition, there will be a minimum

Figure 2.2 Groskopf Warehouse and Logistics, Sonoma, California

charge each month—the "floor"—regardless of number of cases stored. This can be significant and require a large volume in storage at all times just to make this minimum, or your per case charge can go from affordable to exorbitant.

There are many other fees, including container unloading, in and out (when wine comes in or goes out), bill of lading, repackaging, rush orders, sending samples via UPS or FedEx, including a charge for the box and inserts, and other services that may be offered on demand, such as applying special labels to bottles (UPC codes, e.g.) or repackaging partial cases.

Final Questions—Determine if the warehouse has a policy regarding returned goods (from the distributor), whether they accept responsibility for breakages, incorrect vintages shipped or mistakes in general and how they handle them. Good, experienced warehouses will have online, private access for the importer to check inventory levels, shipped invoices, pending shipments and many other useful tools for you to manage your warehouse business.

Contact other customers for references. This is one of the most important of your relationships and it should be an enduring one. It is far too expensive to store all your wine at one facility and have to move it to another and incur those charges all over again. I have warehoused at the same facility since 1993, and the hallmark of our relationship is trust, respect and give and take. No relationship is perfect and the one you forge with your warehouse, by virtue of the volume of transactions, will be fraught with frustration, the occasional misunderstanding and mistakes. But everyone has them and it's the combination of realistic rates, quality of service, resolution of the missteps and how they treat their customer that counts.

Summary

Aspects of the business that initially do not have anything to do with wine require deliberation and planning to effect a positive outcome for your business model. No one way is the right way. It has to suit your style and your circumstances. Making the most practical warehousing decision early on can actually keep the sales momentum going. Whichever option you choose, the warehouse should be affordable, responsive, on either coast, and readily recognizable to the wholesalers and truckers who will be coming to pick up your product. It should be licensed according to the laws of that state and bonded in the event you need to put goods into customs bond.

My Story

I established my first import business in Atlanta, Georgia. Not having a clue as to how to proceed, I began by seeking out warehouses in Atlanta. Having secured one, I alerted my first two distributors, one in New Jersey and one in Georgia. The Georgia distributor was delighted because they could send a local truck to pick up small amounts whenever they wished, generating multiple invoices, incurring unnecessary charges at the warehouse for me, and it did not require the distributor to make a long term commitment. The New Jersey distributor was horrified, as was every other distributor who followed. If they wanted my wine—and fortunately for me, this was an era of great interest in Australia and very few brands—they paid for the privilege with the inconvenience of diverting an entire truck to Atlanta solely to pick up my three or four brands, and sacrificed some of their margin, or increased the price of the wine. In turn, my margin was shrinking by paying more for a small, local warehouse and for the container to be trucked overland from California. I quickly learned that to remain financially viable and geographically competitive I had to choose a warehouse that met the criteria I've stated above.

3

LICENSING, PERMITS, AND DEFINITIONS

With all the detailed instructions and tips I have included, this section may appear overwhelming at first and have you chomping at the bit to get to the less mundane aspects. If you break down each piece in order, you'll find it will flow easily for you. You are building the foundation brick by solid brick, until you have a sturdy importing business structure on which to start layering your own individual design and flair. We simply have to remember that alcohol is a heavily regulated, closely monitored industry and adhering to these regulations allows us the freedom to do the part we really care about.

The Importer in the Distribution Chain

I felt it was important to introduce this subject before we go any further, because so often to the uninitiated the term "importer" becomes indistinguishable from "distributor" and some use it interchangeably. In the U.S., the titles are as different as vigneron from importer or distributor from retailer, and must be understood from the outset.

That's not to say an importer cannot also be a distributor—under certain circumstances—but to understand an overview of the roles, we must look at them in their discrete form.

Importer is the term used to define the licensed person or company who directly liaises with the winery (in most instances) and is the only entity authorized to import alcohol into the U.S.

Distributor is the licensed company in a given state which is authorized to buy alcohol from an importer and sell it to a retail store, restaurant, hotel, grocery store, casino or chain within their state boundaries. They are also known as a wholesaler or wholesale distributor.

Retailer and restaurant refers to the commercial enterprise that sells to the consumer. This covers all customers of the distributor including hotel, grocery store, casino or chain.

This is what is known as the **three-tier system** (see Figure 3.1), which operates in the United States and was written into law after the repeal of Prohibition.

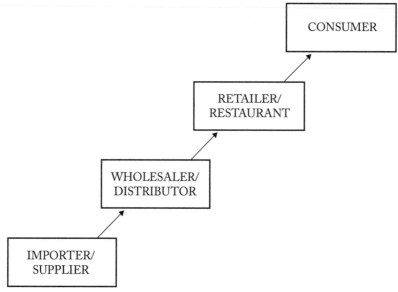

Figure 3.1   The Three-Tier System

The definitions are true no matter what the circumstances, but can be diluted or multiplied in a business model in different circumstances. For example:

- In Control states (discussed later) this model becomes more of a two-tier system, in that the State is both wholesaler and retailer. Although again there are variations on this, depending upon the state.

- National wholesale chains may appear to circumvent the laws of individual states, when in fact they are adhering to it by establishing brick and mortar businesses in each state in which they do business, and operating as licensed entities within the framework of that state's three-tier system.

- A distributor may choose to import one or more of their products for several reasons, mainly to have more control over a brand in their portfolio, to realize a double margin on a sale, (i.e. importer > distributor and distributor > retailer), or even because they were approached by a winery to import their wines exclusively in that region. Normally, their distribution business takes precedence over the importing aspect, because they choose to limit their importing to their local area. In this case, it will be understood up front with the winery that there is limited sales potential for their wine, to the extent of the limitations of the individual distribution area.

- An importer can choose to distribute their own products in their state, by applying for the correct licenses and establishing an office, warehouse and distribution system—i.e. sales and delivery mechanism—and paying the appropriate taxes. Generally, an importer will choose to distribute for some of the same reasons as the wholesaler, but the focus will be the inverse of the wholesaler who chooses to import, because national or regional distribution will require the greater attention. If they have agreed to take on and import a brand for national distribution, expectations would likely be higher that they would be making inroads into multiple states.

  In California, for example, an importer can be all parts of the three-tier system and more. An importer may apply to the ABC (Alcoholic Beverage Control) for a retail license to sell from a bricks and mortar store, if they meet the state requirements. Additionally, or separately, an importer can sell over the Internet, with the appropriate retail license. So, in effect, an import company can be its own self-contained entity from winery to consumer.

- Tied-House Laws relate back to England and laws that were put into affect that regulated the sales of alcoholic beverages in bars, pubs and taverns, where the ownership of the entity was "tied" to a specific supplier of alcoholic beverages.

According to Wikipedia:

> *Under the current post-Prohibition, alcoholic beverage regulatory regime, tied houses are generally illegal in the United States. Tied-house restrictions have been construed as forbidding virtually any form of vertical integration in the alcoholic beverage industry.*

This is no longer true. There have been numerous challenges to the Tied-house laws and some legislation has overturned these rules as recently as 2009 in Washington State. There will no doubt be more to come as the climate of the wine industry, the business models and the available technology continue to evolve at rapid rates. It would therefore be reckless of me to set out more than a general overview of these laws and allow you to go to the individual State's websites for the most current legal requirements.

Since this is a book about importing, I am leaving out wineries, which have greater leeway in many states and licenses that operate differently.

Necessary Licenses and Other Licensing to Consider Now

EIN—Employer Identification Number

This can be completed and submitted online at www.irs.gov and is a prerequisite for your import license. It is also essential for opening a bank account as any entity other than a sole proprietor, for which you can use your social security number. Obtaining an EIN is an easy, fast process.

The Federal Importer Basic Permit

This is the first of the industry licenses and the most important, but at this stage it feels a bit like putting the cart before the horse. TTB (Alcohol and Tobacco Tax Trade Bureau) at www.ttb.gov requires that you identify a winery willing to export to you

before you can apply for a license, described as Contract or Letter of Intent with Foreign Suppliers (see Figure 3.2). It's a relatively new provision and very general, so it's
possible to still be in discussions with a winery that may not ultimately sell to you and
yet request a letter from them to enable you to obtain your Permit. It does not obligate
them to export to you, nor obligate you to purchase their wine, but simply a stated
intention. TTB just wants to know you're serious and intend to operate as an alcohol
importer within a reasonable period of time. There are no examples on the website,
but I have included a perfectly acceptable, simple format. It should be on letterhead
and signed by the winery or vineyard principal.

TTB's site is straightforward and easy to navigate. Instructions, forms and Q&A
are readily found under the Importer tab. The primary application is 5100.4, covering
wine, beer and malt beverages, and requiring documentation of business structure (C-
corp., LLC, etc.), financial sources, personal data. They will conduct an extensive background check and will take the processing of the license and subsequent issuance seriously, so be prepared to answer fully and truthfully and line up your sources of funding,
even if it's a loan from Aunt Millie or the proceeds from a home equity line of credit.

Processing of the application will take about 60 days. Although it may be faster, there
is no route to expedite the process. Incomplete applications will not be processed at all.
It's best to start it as soon as practicable, in the event of delays or unforeseen obstacles.

One Mile Winery

June 2, 2011

To Whom It May Concern:

It is our intention to supply Mayflower Wine Imports with wines from our company, One
Mile Winery in the U.S., pending all approvals.

Should you wish to verify this statement or request any further information, please do not
hesitate to contact the undersigned.

Sincerely,

Pierre Marchand
Managing Director

Figure 3.2   Letter of Intent with Foreign Suppliers

An agent will call you to conduct an in-depth interview regarding your understanding of your enterprise, industry legal requirements and anything else they feel they need to ask to determine your readiness. Take this interview seriously. They can and will delay or deny your application if they feel there is cause. On the other hand, this can be a comfortable, friendly experience if you are ready with appropriate, candid answers and look upon the process as necessary and non-threatening.

The Federal Basic Permit is required to clear samples, as well as containers; therefore, well before you organize your first shipment, this becomes critical when requesting new vintages or first wines from your prospective wineries, vineyards or foreign brokers.

If you intend to sell domestic wines or wines you did not import, you will also need a Wholesaler's Permit. Both can be applied at the same time on form 5100.4. There is currently no fee for the initial application.

The Basic Permit licenses your entity and *place* of business. Therefore, if you move or your company configuration changes, i.e. from a sole proprietorship to a partnership or you form a corporation, you will need to apply for and obtain a new license.

COLAs Online

When you receive your Basic Permit, you should immediately apply for access to online submission of your COLA (Certificate of Label Application) at www.ttbonline.gov. It's a simple one page form, costs nothing, approval takes about 30 days, and it's ready for you when you have labels to submit. Access to online label submissions is the only sensible way to submit applications. The technology has been available since 2003 and I was among the first to jump on the bandwagon, making my life instantly easier. Prior to that, submissions were hand-written on a paper form, to which you glued actual labels or legible, full color label graphics and sent snail mail. Unless you incurred additional (unnecessary) expense sending each application via FedEx, you were left wondering whether TTB (or BATF at that time) had received it and what happened to it. Believe it or not, some people still do it this way, but I can assure you that online label submissions are the only way to go. I don't want to get ahead of ourselves by discussing label approvals at this stage, but it is the correct timing to register for COLAs online.

POA—Power of Attorney

The Basic Permit is the common element to each license and regulation, so you can see why it is such a crucial first step (well, literally after the winery/vineyard letter). Samples sent to you from any country will have to be cleared through customs using your authority to clear under your Basic Permit Number. I am not recommending any particular company, but I personally find that DHL www.dhl.com and FedEx www.fedex.com are the most common carriers and it would be useful for you to contact them as soon as you have your Permit to complete paperwork that allows them to clear for you—the POA. They will also require a copy of your Basic Permit and State license. Once this is through their systems (and you have to be patient; they don't all seem to talk to one another within the same company) it will expedite any shipments you receive. Otherwise, important samples may be held up indefinitely at customs and even returned to sender—not a good way to begin a relationship.

Home State Licenses

Each state has wildly disparate state licensing requirements, so much so that they are not variations, but appear entirely unrelated. The state in which you are federally licensed will be the state in which you must also comply with their particular regulations. Contact details for each state licensing agency, including links to each of their sites, are available on the TTB site. This is not only a helpful resource for your own state, but for all the states in which you seek to do business, which will be discussed further later. The hyperlink is http://www.ttb.gov/wine/control_board.shtml or simply search on the site for state control boards. Although not all state board links remain up to date, it is helpful to have them in one list as a resource. Going to a link that is defunct will usually direct you to the correct site and likewise the phone number. I find it easier to do this than to search the individual state by liquor licensing body, as the link on the TTB website will usually get you to the appropriate section, whereas a Google search can result in arriving at a state home page from where you must often navigate to the correct area.

California State License

If your product is stored on the West Coast, you will be licensed by the California ABC (Alcoholic Beverage Control) to import into and warehouse in the state (Type 9 and 17), irrespective of where you live or where your licensed premises is located. Application processing takes about 90 days. It is important that the warehouse you choose is also licensed (Type 14).

New Jersey/New York License

Only the Basic Permit is required to meet regulations for East Coast facility storage for sale to distributors. If your licensed premises are also located in the tri-state area, and you wish to distribute your own wines (sell to retailers), a separate wholesale license is mandatory through the respective New Jersey or New York agency in the state in which the warehouse is located.

Other State Licenses

This is presumably the launch of your enterprise, or you are just getting established and have limited distribution. Perhaps you are further along, but seeking advice on how to take a grassroots distribution enterprise to the next level. Regardless of your situation, *do not* go out and start getting licenses in every state, nor even in every state in which you wish to do business. This is not a case of *build it and they will come*. It is unnecessary and costly and ultimately a frustrating time waster. We will get into state licensing, brand registrations, outsourcing compliance vs. doing it yourself and related topics later in the book, but suffice to say, at this stage you should have only the essential licenses to begin to import and distribute your first container.

4

PORTFOLIO—SELECTION AND DECISIONS

Throughout this section and the rest of the book "vineyard," "winery," and "vigneron," will be used interchangeably, to mean the supplier from which you purchase the wine. Now that you've conducted your research, settled on specialization or broad scope and identified the appellation or multiple appellations, you are ready to start selecting actual wines. There are a number of alternatives to assist you with this process.

Narrowing the Field

On-Site Selection

If you regularly vacation in a country where you discovered an appealing selection of wines from a particular vineyard, you now have an owner with whom you can talk about exporting his wines. This establishes that you enjoy the wines of that region and appreciate the level of quality, so you might consider asking the vigneron if he or she has neighbors who could also be interested in exporting, ask for an introduction and an opportunity to try their wine. Driving to adjacent areas to expand your search could

Of course, here in Australia we have to learn to contend with vineyard pests that are unique to our locale.

Figure 4.1   © **David Pike**

also prove fruitful and will broaden your familiarity with the region's topography, *terroir*, and other features that you will use in marketing your portfolio.

Family or close friends in the country of origin could assist with identifying and providing you with resources or set up appointments, so that you can optimize your time spent in the country when you do visit and meet with vineyard representatives personally.

Wine Industry Experience

Employment with a distributor or retailer will have brought you into contact with wines and even specific brands that you would enjoy representing. I do not consider it good form to try to poach from another importer's portfolio, but this could give you the inside track to a brand who is already leaving (or being dropped by) an importer and in this case an acceptable opportunity. The ideal situation is if the brand already enjoys broad market distribution. However, it is unlikely that they would choose to go with a new, untried importer unless you have established a strong, long term connection to them, or they can secure a financially guaranteed commitment from you.

Don't be turned off by a brand that was not the one taking the initiative to end the relationship with their former importer. The importer may have a conflict within the portfolio, made a commitment to a new, larger brand that will compete with the prior brand, it might not be a good fit for their personalities or the direction the portfolio is taking. One of the most successful brands I ever represented was previously with another importer, who voluntarily gave up the brand, right on the cusp of greatness. Two years later, one of its wines was the highest rated wines ever reviewed in the *Wine Spectator* for the price.

On the other hand, it may signal a deficit in the brand or a difficult personality and you should certainly take a hard look at this aspect.

Alternatively, you may find that your area of preference has been honed through years representing a particular country and while the actual wines you enjoy are taken, their neighbors may be available.

Agents

What if you are unfamiliar with the country, its logistics, language and customs? What if you don't know how to find available wines? Do you travel all over the globe? Do you phone vineyards and introduce yourself over the phone, before finally discovering they are too small for export or already represented? Different approaches are dictated by your inclination, time, knowledge, capital and resources.

There are agents or export brokers in all countries who can assist you in your search, or who already have a stable of brands for which they are looking for homes. This is their bread and butter after all, and they make their money either through commissions from the wineries or adding a commission or markup to the wine, in a price quoted to you. This adds yet another layer to the price structure (and the layers can start to add up), but they can often be worth it.

- An agent is very familiar with the region and available brands, thereby saving you the trouble of excessive travel and the time commitment.
- They are fluent in the language (where applicable) and presumably have an established reputation or relationship as an export broker/agent. Even English-speaking Australia, South Africa and New Zealand have their distinct customs, idioms and idiosyncrasies and a broker/agent may well be an advantage if you are unfamiliar with the country.
- They can be contacted initially via phone and should be agreeable to sending samples for you to evaluate.
- Agents/brokers are also often much more familiar with the U.S. requirements than the wineries and can be your intermediary in explaining the situation to them.
- They are in a position to convey expectations from you to the winery and vice versa.
- Agents may even be able to negotiate a better price for you, based on their relationship with the winery/vineyard or familiarity with comparable wines and market conditions.
- The agent will presumably have experience with freight forwarders and shipping companies, which ports to use and even container consolidation of wines, thereby relieving you of the headache of such arrangements.

The important point to take away from this exercise is to weigh the added cost of the agent and the distance it can create between you and the vineyard, against your time, resources, familiarity and ability to source the same quality—or any wine for that matter—through other means. As with anything else, there are good and bad agents, which should become readily apparent in the early stages of your association. There are also those who are just plain insecure and will try to be the buffer between you and the winery, out of fear you will do an end run around them and cut them out when you've established the brand. Never do that. It's not ethical. But do make it clear that you also wish to initiate your own relationship with the winery. The closer you are to the supplier, the more opportunity you have to influence their supply, styles, labels and any other crucial aspects of your business. If they know and like you, they will be more concerned with your needs and building a long-term relationship.

Trade Associations

Most countries from which you would be likely to import have trade associations established in the U.S. designed to assist with the marketing and exposure for their products, which often includes indigenous or manufactured items of that country. Most of them are based in New York and often have regional offices. Some have their own independent organizations to promote food and wine under the auspices of their country's embassies.

It is important to note that foreign trade associations vary significantly in their involvement in active promotion and should not necessarily be viewed as the best or likeliest avenue for import opportunities. However, they most certainly can provide an understanding of their respective country's regions and wines and may help you narrow your focus by understanding the most popular and, conversely, the up and coming lesser known areas. Some of them also actively seek importers for their winery clients, or retain a data base of wineries seeking representation. These organizations may not be acquainted with the wineries or their principals, but are seeking to broaden market share for their country's products in general.

They are definitely worth contacting and a potentially valuable resource. They should be happy to assist you, since your success is their success. They will also enable you to be in the loop of any trade shows, organized winemakers trips, or special events you may wish to attend.

Trade organizations go by varied names, depending upon what the respective country wishes to call it, but will most often have the words Trade Commission in their name. A wonderful resource is the Wine Institute at www.wineinstitute.org. Its intent, as stated on their masthead, is to be "the voice for California wine," but there are many other helpful sections for all importers, wineries and exporters, including some trade organizations, listed as "external links" under the "Press Room" tab. Additionally, it is a resource for state shipping laws, recent legislation and more.

Personalities—A Relationship, Not a One Time Purchase

This is the stage where that big funnel filled with so many choices and decisions, narrows down to specific countries, then regions, then vineyards, then brands and ultimately wines. You are at the point of discussing the representation and importation of wine with specific individuals and this becomes a very personal exercise.

"It's business," some will say, but it's so much more than that; it's a relationship. There are many more relationships you will develop throughout the importing and distribution of your wines, but this is clearly one of the most important.

In thinking about your commodity, you must consider the source. Wine is made from grapes, which are a harvested farm crop. Unless you happen upon the acquisition of wines from a large, international corporation, you will most likely be buying from someone who has tilled the soil, planted root stock, tended the crop, prayed for rain, prayed for sun, harvested, pressed, fermented and waited years for the fruits of their labor. Their journey may have taken them through local sales at cellar door, to national distribution to international sales … and then back again. This could be their first vintage or their one hundred and first. They could be naively embarking on their first venture or been burned with the demise of their last importer. There are countless permutations, but whatever their personal circumstance, they are looking for a representative—particularly someone from another country—to whom they can entrust their product with the hope, or the expectation, that it will become almost as important to you as it is to them.

On the other hand, you cannot afford to allow this to cloud your judgment. This part *is* business. Remember your trips to Napa or Tuscany? The romantic chateaux, the charming cellar door experiences. How it was some of the best wine you had ever tasted, so good that you bought a case and had it shipped home? At home, it was still thoroughly enjoyable, but was it really the *best* you had ever tasted? Did you really need *that* much Sangiovese? Ambiance has a great deal to do with the perception of our experiences, and wine may be one of the most compelling examples.

You will often find, as you sit on the terrace in the vigneron's backyard, surrounded by rose bushes and perhaps savoring aged cheese and homegrown olives, that you really want to represent these wines, you want to love them as much as your host does.

Figure 4.2   Creed Wines 2007 Mataro (Mourvedre) Aging in French Oak

You particularly want to be able to come back to this spot and experience the same thing again. This individual is happy to see you, will introduce you to the local bistro, café or watering hole and truly want to entertain you and make you a part of an extended family. Not all the time, to be sure, but often enough. You are a potential purchaser of their product—and contributor to their livelihood—and these farmers, winemakers, landowners, will be strongly motivated to make sure that this *does* become a relationship.

Your job is to separate perception from reality and make decisions regarding the taste, selection, viability and all those aspects discussed in the previous chapter. It will also, let me tell you from experience, behoove you to be sure you can work with them. The effort you will put into developing the brands of your portfolio is not designed for a quick purchase and one time sale. A lot of the time and labor is front end loaded when you select, introduce and promote a brand. Building on the initial order is where you have some economies of scale, and where you can guarantee continuity to your customers and the assurance that the work *they* put into your portfolio is not misplaced.

Consider your own personality. Are you:

- Driven
- Goal oriented
- Focused
- Detail oriented
- Opposed to deadlines imposed by others
- Workaholic
- Responsive to requests
- Laid back
- Communicative
- Collaborative

This would be the time to consider whether you can work with the autocratic, new vineyard owner who retired from a vice presidency with SONY and cashed out his stock to start an expensive project on prime land, using state of the art equipment, having hired the local hotshot winemaker. He still wants to get his hands dirty (that's part of the appeal: "getting back to the land" after a lifetime of corporate sterility), he knows he has become a farmer, but he's going to be the best darned farmer in his hemisphere, producing wine the likes of which the world has never seen. And maybe he is. Are *you* the retired or cashed out IBM exec who understands exactly how he feels and is a perfect fit? Do you understand his need for detailed graphs and regular reports on your progress, his confidence that he has done his due diligence on the market and knows exactly what his pricing should be, and his expectation that he can contribute a good deal to your enterprise including a semi-annual trip to work the market?

What about the local hippie winemaker, who makes wines utilizing what the *terroir* gives her that vintage—and it's very good—but doesn't know a graph from a graft and really isn't interested. She wants to make her 800 to 1,000 cases of wine—depending upon the year—and find good homes for them. If you don't commit to the wine quickly enough, it may be sold elsewhere, because with her it's *the quick or the dead*, and she most likely won't come over to visit, because she can't afford to and the dogs would miss her. But she's not going to compromise on quality and she will supply you with whatever you need, *as long as you speak up quickly and without equivocation.*

These might sound like extremes, or caricatures, but I can assure you I know people exactly like this, and about fifty other different, but equally quirky, challenging, interesting, entertaining, frustrating and ultimately extremely rewarding people that populate the wine industry, and whom you will inevitably come across. The issue becomes whether you can work with a particular personality type and who best suits your style. Can you modify yours and theirs and meet somewhere in the middle? Occasionally, it's not so much about the style, as the character traits. If the individual is purely ego driven, greedy and untrustworthy, it doesn't matter how good their wines are, whether they are male or female, market savvy or blithely naïve. Inevitably, this will become a nightmare and you will regret the decision to override your gut.

Contracts

Personally, I have rarely had a contract with a winery, but this is a product of starting my own import business in 1992 when contracts were not common, and because this has traditionally been an industry of handshake agreements. However, based on experience, and that of others, I *do* recommend a contract of some sort—a simple, but comprehensive, agreement that covers responsibilities and expectations—the salient points of your working partnership. I would be careful of prolonging the process, and possibly delaying getting started, with a league of attorneys taking weeks to construct a document that takes weeks for each side to decipher.

Quite frankly, I believe it protects you, the importer, more than the brand owner, although it would depend upon their idea of an agreement and their own individual expertise or experience in the matter. They will want assurances that you will pay them, of course, and available recourse in the event you do not. Most significantly, it defines, in written form, the areas you have already agreed upon and leaves less to subjective interpretation. I am not an attorney, and would not presume to advise you as such, but simply put: it should include what you intend to do for them and what they agree to provide for you. More of this will be expanded under the expectations section ahead, so that you have a clearer picture of just what that should be. Some expectations on either side do not have to be more than verbal acknowledgments, clearing the way for more discussion, but it allows you to incorporate those points that are most meaningful to you, and give both sides a measure of confidence moving forward.

I also believe it should also afford you some protection in the event the winery decides to change importers after you have built the brand's sales and distribution to a measurable degree of success. This has been accomplished through your considerable time and expense. Nonetheless, the brand owner is always just that—the brand *owner*. You have agreed to be their agent in the U.S., but at no time do you own the rights to the brand and its supply and distribution. It can be taken from you at any time, irrespective of your understanding. Therefore, some compensation for future earnings, at a level you both agree, is reasonable. And I stress *reasonable*. The beginning of this relationship should ideally be on a congenial footing, and one in which each party feels they are being justly represented by the contract.

Expectations—Yours and Theirs

Irrespective of style and approach, it becomes imperative to establish, in the early stages, what the expectations are on both sides. Leave no aspect to chance and assume nothing. Without this caveat, you would be surprised at the extent of time, energy and resources that can be spent on securing a particular brand, only to become aware of a deal breaking requirement on their part, or an assumption on yours that was never addressed. Some of these would be:

- National vs. regional appointment
- Terms
- Which wines
- First year volume
- Allocation
- Sample allowance
- Payment currency
- Price increases
- Long term goal
- First purchase

National vs. Regional

As discussed earlier, since national and regional importing are so different, and critical to the future of the brand, it is in your best interests to determine, from the commencement of your business, which model to choose. However, if the brand you fall in love with belongs to someone who only wants national distribution through one importer, or, alternatively, multiple importers, this should be discussed in the beginning either to avoid misunderstanding, or perhaps early enough to change the mind of either party.

Terms

They vary, but common U.S. terms for wine purchase are anywhere from 60 to 120 days from B/L (Bill of Lading), FOB (Freight on Board) port of origin. In other words, the winery gets the wine to the port nearest to them, or the one nearest to them that ships to the U.S., and the date on the B/L provided by the shipping company is when the clock starts ticking. This lessens the time where wine is sitting at the dock waiting for a ship.

It is not necessarily customary, but not unusual for a winery to want to have the first shipment under LC (Letter of Credit) to ensure payment. This requires a guarantee from you, through a letter from your bank, to ensure sufficient funds will be on deposit to pay the invoice at the close of terms.

Which Wines

You would be surprised at how often the vineyard owner, with a quiver full of varietals produced on their property, will automatically assume you will take them all. It doesn't matter what they are, or how many—if you agreed to bring their wines to the U.S. you agreed to bring them *all*. Just like children—no favorites! It is up to you to explain, as diplomatically as possible, that whilst they are all lovely in their own inimitable ways, the ones you feel best equipped to begin with, based on market research, style, price, or whatever the reason, are, e.g., these three wines. You will necessarily need to start slowly, to establish the brand carefully and not overwhelm distributors. Fostering a warm and collaborative relationship is crucial, but this is your business and you have to purchase according to common sense and fiscal constraints.

It may not be the conventional varietals that win over the esoteric or funky. It could be that *that* style of Merlot from Australia won't sell, or the Bordeaux blend from New Zealand will be too difficult at that price point. They may be beautifully made wines, with structural integrity and recognizable grape names, but if it doesn't appear to be the right time, then don't do it. Find at least two wines from the brand (unless they only make one) that will complement one another and provide the best entrée into the market. They don't have to be red and white, or even both table wines. It could be a Tawny Port and a Sparkling. Just make them "best foot forward," as you see it. You can always add later.

Figure 4.3   Mark Creed of Creed Wines

First Year Volume

This is a critical element. It is not uncommon to reach an accord with a vigneron on all levels, only to discover that this individual thinks that 5,000 cases for the first year would be a perfectly reasonable "starting" volume. After all, there are over 300 million people in the United States. That paltry drop would be absorbed in no time. That's when you groan and try to explain (again) that of those multi-millions, only a certain percentage drink wine, of those a smaller percentage drink regularly, a number of people only drink *Two Buck Chuck*, or wines of a certain country…and on it goes. Yes, U.S. wine drinking percentages are increasing in both number and annual per capita consumption and the right wine, marketed properly, can certainly succeed. But add to the mix the sheer volume of international imports, America's own thriving wine production, increased plantings everywhere and the consolidation of wholesalers and you have a situation that requires a skilful, savvy approach. Which is where you come in and why they need you. For your sake, do not promise something you can't deliver on, or commit to wine that puts you out of business. It's far better to set conservative expectations and exceed them, to the delight of your supplier, than find yourself backpedaling or—worse—being confronted by an angry vigneron who, having bottled and labeled all his production just for you, is in financial ruin!

On the other hand, if you have reached an agreement with Trader Joe's or Whole Foods to supply wine to all their stores, that's a different story. But not usually the way it goes out of the gate.

First Purchase

I'm now referring to the actual first container commitment, from any and all sources, as opposed to the volume you are tentatively committing to over the first year to an individual vineyard. As with everything else, a good deal of thought should go into the size and composition of this first container. Unless you have lined up some large preorders, you are at the starting gate, hoping your horse is a winner, but not actually sure how he's running that day.

There is no one right way to launch and manage your wine import business, but there are certain considerations that make the difference between success and failure, or profit and loss. This is one of them. Aside from the obvious failure I outlined in Chapter I—the 800 cases of high priced Semillon—there are other ways in which wine will languish in the warehouse.

Let's assume you have put together an appealing group of brands from one country. Even if you are immediately importing from several countries, or decide to branch out later, you can only fill the container at one port. After that, it's sealed and on its way.

Unless you are starting with a big budget and expect to hire a full complement of sales people as soon as possible, my recommendation is to estimate how much you can sell within a three month period and this is the approximate quantity you should put on the first container. Any more and you have mounting warehouse fees for wine already paid for—but not sold. Any less and you run out before a new container arrives. If it moves faster than expected you can always order more, but wine that does not sell quickly also runs the risk of not selling at all, because you have overestimated the demand, or time works against it in vintage change expectations.

I have always started out slowly with wineries, explaining that this is the "test" shipment. Throw it against the wall, see what sticks and proceed from there to build an increasing, but manageable, volume. I'm actually more diplomatic about it—after all, these are all wines they are proud of and expect to sell well—but essentially that's the bottom line.

Allocation

Although the early stages are all about lowered expectations and conservative commitments, you still want to know how much the vineyard is willing to allocate to you for either your region, or the entire U.S. They may have an almost limitless supply and allocations are not really an issue, but what of the special place of old vines that produces only 300 cases of each wine in a vintage? You will need to know whether you can have 290 cases or 50 and whether this is a fluid allocation or static. If the wines garner amazing press or achieve cult status you will want your allocation protected and if you are splitting the country you will need to know that the wines are split equitably with the other importer. Make sure the winery does not confuse allocation with *commitment*, unless you want it to mean the same thing.

Sample Allowance

A significant consideration so often ignored, but one which can have a major impact on your net profit and your ability or willingness to utilize samples to increase sales.

In my opinion, any supplier of wine—vineyard or winery—should provide a sample allowance, even if their production is small. The smaller they are the less wine they produce and they may be resistant to the concept. But the smaller they are the smaller the sample allowance, and if they understand the importance of sample usage at all stages of their brand development they will willingly acquiesce.

Samples are used for many purposes, but comprise at least the following:

- Publication and competition submission
- Prospective distributors/wholesalers evaluation
- Trade shows
- Prospective chain buyer evaluation
- Wine dinners
- Wine tastings
- Distributor's sales meetings
- Distributor's sales staff for sales calls

Some of the uses are expanded later in the book, but for purposes of discussion with the supplier, these are all viable reasons for a sample consideration.

There is a good deal of the subjective about this, but is usually expressed in a percentage discount off the invoice. Whilst generalities are helpful to a degree, I recognize it is the specifics that will be important to you on this subject, so I offer a series of suggestions and from that you can distill what feels comfortable to you, or what works for your supplier. These are all examples of allowances that I have worked with in the past:

- 5% on the first container and 2% on subsequent shipments
- 3% across the board on all shipments
- 2% across the board on all shipments, but a free case of each new wine to be reviewed by press
- 5% on all new vintages, 3% on shipments of the same vintage
- 5% on new and old vintages, until a satisfactory sales level is reached
- 2-5%, based on cost and rarity of wine, and varying with the shipment
- 2.5% across the board, and free cases of new wines for *you* to evaluate and pre-sell

There are other variations, but these give you the necessary springboard and I can assure you they are all realistic examples. I have encountered resistance on several occasions, usually from very small or inexperienced vineyard owners, but once I explain the scope of sample usage and their absolute necessity, this resistance lessens, if not disappears. I also let them know that this is not just their investment; I send out and use far more than most sample allowances and they are helping me defray costs and giving me far more latitude in utilizing samples to secure and increase sales.

Sample allowances are not to be confused with incentives. This is a separate discussion to have with the winery and whether or not they are in a position to build this into the price, wherein they offer periodic deals and incentives to affect price and stimulate sales. Although it is a topic that can well be broached during these first negotiations, I have saved this for a later section of the book, where the incentives can be illustrated within the relevant framework.

Payment Currency

The question of currency in the payment of invoices should be raised, but there are no hard and fast rules on this. If you feel the currency of the country of the wine's origin is stable, the exchange rate is very good and unlikely to fluctuate, or you can build in sufficient margin to allow you a degree of comfort, then it's not a problem.

One option is to build in *forward contracts* on currency, where considerable fluctuation is already taking place, or the prevailing feeling is that it will likely increase. This demands speculation on your part and, although you have stabilized the currency for the foreseeable future, it stipulates a specific date, specific quantity of currency and at a rate you agreed to at the time of the contract. It locks in the rate at the current value, but requires considerable insight on your part into your future needs.

The winery may have its own preference. I have known suppliers with personal or business ties to the U.S. who prefer wires into their U.S. bank accounts. Not uncommonly, a supplier with no U.S. connections will quote in USD because they feel it keeps their wine at a specific price, such as retailing under $10 or under $20 (both important price levels), but since they don't set the price over here, this is a topic for the next chapter.

Whatever your choice, or the winery's, factor it into your pricing and you will be better prepared in the event of changes in exchange rate and market conditions.

Price Increases

As a rule, price increases from the winery should not be automatically triggered by each vintage or the start of a new year, but there are certainly circumstances that do precipitate an increase—e.g. a lower introductory price for the first shipment, unexpected costs of doing business or the winery's USD currency choice eroded by a devalued dollar.

The winery cannot anticipate some of these events, but can address, at the outset, whether they intend to increase pricing on an arbitrary basis, or as a conscious decision. It is not the most critical aspect of your early negotiations, but one I mention to keep you informed as to what may be customary and some of what to expect.

Long Term Goals

My emphasis in this section is on the winery's goals more than your own, although you may have very specific and easily articulated ambitions, which will be important for the winery to hear. If you do, be sure you can back them up and that you haven't sent them happily running out to buy more French oak barrels at $900 a pop, based on your unsubstantiated projections.

Some wineries only want to know you will do your best and will take as much wine as you can sell and see where it goes. This gives you a certain peace of mind at first, but does not guarantee supply in the long term. You may find yourself in the fortunate position of rapid growth and the winery cannot keep up with demand. This leaves you with dissatisfied customers and lost sales and momentum.

Others want to determine how much you can purchase over a five year term, down to the last case. It is very difficult for you to make any projections based on no historical reference. I find myself in this position all the time and I do understand the motivation behind each person's request for this information. After all, their own long range plans—and perhaps the livelihood of their entire family—hinge on what you anticipate the sales and growth will be over time. However, I don't want to be put in a position of committing to something on which I can't deliver, based on information I just don't have, and neither should you. I think it is reasonable to explain that you want this to be an honest and successful *long term* partnership and you will be in a better position to give them your anticipated needs and objectives after the first few months or the first year.

You will at least want to ensure that your first few months can provide you with sufficient wine to back up the first orders, but don't let them think they should have the wines all labeled for the U.S. requirements, ready and waiting for an order. If they find this more cost-efficient, then by all means, but otherwise the advice I have just given should dictate how they will approach the beginning stages of this endeavor and that is: *softly, softly*.

References

It would be helpful to line up references, if at all possible, from within the wine, banking and professional industries, to offer peace of mind to the winery, who will be across an ocean from you and their goods. It is understood you are new, but if you are funded by or partnered with someone with an established reputation, or if you come from a successful financial or corporate background, this will be helpful in establishing credibility. It then just takes one winery or vineyard who has taken a chance on you. Assuming you have performed well for them, and paid on time, they can become the reference to which you turn when looking to secure the next brand.

Summary

From the time you start speaking seriously with your prospective supplier is the perfect time to establish the ground rules, expectations, commitments and the framework of the working relationship. But never forget that it is a relationship and that this will be the true foundation of your collaboration. The tone you both set will see you through good times and bad, through misunderstandings and through the inevitable time when, if you are successful, someone will come along and promise your supplier a better import experience through *their* company!

My Story

I had not usually found the absence of a contract to be an impediment in doing business, but about six years into national representation for two brands owned by the same person—an ego-driven man who was dissatisfied with the level of U.S. sales—I was abruptly told that he was switching to a New York importer, because he thought New York was *the* place to be. These brands unfortunately represented about 45% of my portfolio at the time. The owner flew to the States, met with me for fifteen minutes to give me the news before flying on to New York and that was that. I had no contract and therefore neither notice nor compensation was required and none was offered. It was a significant blow and although I did recover from it, it was not without extreme difficulty. Others in the same position have not.

The ending for this story is that the two brands did very poorly with the new importer and disappeared from the States, and the owner went bankrupt after defrauding his creditors in the amount of 60 million dollars. Some satisfaction, but I would have preferred the notice and the compensation to allow me some time to replace the lost sales and income.

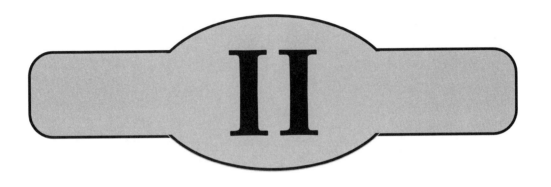

5

PLANNING, PREPARATION AND PREPAREDNESS

There are several tasks that should be undertaken pre container shipment, some of which are required and some that could be considered advisable. They will all save you time—and possibly money—by taking care of them at this stage, assuming you have reached agreement with wineries, vineyards or agents for specific wine to be bought and transported in the foreseeable future.

Purchase Orders

Before a winery is ready to commit resources towards U.S. compliant labeling, allocating wine to you, and all the logistical considerations they will embark on, they understandably will want a commitment from you in the form of a purchase order (see Figure 5.1).

A purchase order also protects you in the specificity of its content and should contain the following:

- Purchase order number (for tracking)
- Date
- Terms
- Price (identifying where it will be shipped from and in which currency)
- Currency of payment
- Shipping point
- Vintage
- Consignor (the supplier, with contact details)
- Consignee (your contact details)
- Quantity
- Sample Allowance

QuickBooks has an example of a purchase order that can easily be modified to suit your needs. Much of this is self-explanatory and easily understood. However,—and you will be glad of this advice—be sure that you stress that the vintage must be strictly as ordered. Too often, without any ulterior motive, a winery will ship wine to you that you neither ordered, nor ultimately will be able to sell.

Imagine that you tasted a particular wine, learned that it was a gold medal winner and loved the particular style that vintage produced. You order it and receive the previous vintage. Huh? No gold medal, different taste and a tough sell. The winery, in their defense, may have thought you were aware that they would ship you the vintage they were currently working through, not the one they were releasing in two months. They could also have a difficult time selling this vintage domestically, but don't think it will be a problem to move such a small quantity in the vast United States. Either way, it could be devastating to your sales.

Imagine that you were expecting the latest Sauvignon Blanc release—fresh, lively, aromatic and just released, everything the U.S. consumer is expecting. Only the winery still has 150 cases of the previous vintage in stock and, since your order was for 250 cases, it made sense to them to deplete the previous vintage and make up the differ-

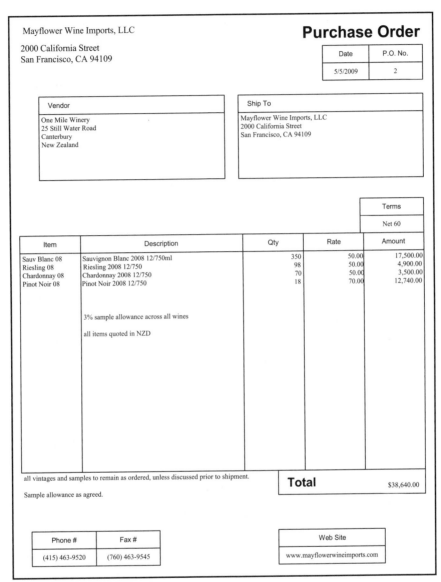

Mayflower Wine Imports, LLC

2000 California Street
San Francisco, CA 94109

Purchase Order

Date	P.O. No.
5/5/2009	2

Vendor	Ship To
One Mile Winery 25 Still Water Road Canterbury New Zealand	Mayflower Wine Imports, LLC 2000 California Street San Francisco, CA 94109

Terms
Net 60

Item	Description	Qty	Rate	Amount
Sauv Blanc 08	Sauvignon Blanc 2008 12/750ml	350	50.00	17,500.00
Riesling 08	Riesling 2008 12/750	98	50.00	4,900.00
Chardonnay 08	Chardonnay 2008 12/750	70	50.00	3,500.00
Pinot Noir 08	Pinot Noir 2008 12/750	18	70.00	12,740.00
	3% sample allowance across all wines			
	all items quoted in NZD			

all vintages and samples to remain as ordered, unless discussed prior to shipment.

Sample allowance as agreed.

Total $38,640.00

Phone #	Fax #
(415) 463-9520	(760) 463-9545

Web Site
www.mayflowerwineimports.com

Figure 5.1   **Example of a Purchase Order**

ence with the new. But now, instead of 250 cases of the current release, you have to list two different vintages on your price sheet, submit both to publications for review and presumably deal with the concern of having everyone choose the new over the old—U.S. tastes and expectations being what they are.

The exception to the above would be if the winery sold out of the vintage you were expecting prior to the purchase order. This is still something that should be discussed at the time of the P.O. and certainly prior to shipment. If you have not tasted the new vintage, they should send you samples immediately. Vintage variation for estate grown, smaller vineyards is the norm, rather than the exception. This does not mean it will be inferior of course; it may even be better. It gives you the opportunity to determine if you feel it meets the right price point, consumer tastes and your requirements. If it does not, but is still marketable, then you can reduce the order. Conversely, it may be even better and you want to increase the order in anticipation of higher sales.

FDA—Food and Drug Administration

Your winery will have to register with the FDA (Food and Drug Administration) www.fda.gov in the country of origin of the wine. This is a relatively new—post 9/11—requirement covered under the Bioterrorism Act of 2002. In the event of a threat to the food or beverage supply, the FDA has access to your winery's contact information to advise them of the threat, trace the source or eliminate them in the event of a trace.

They can easily register on the FDA website, under the section titled Registration of Food Facilities. The US FDA considers all alcoholic beverages under the "food" umbrella. The link for this section is http://www.cfsan.fda.gov/~furls/ovffreg.html. At that time the winery will assign an agent in the U.S. This can be anyone with a U.S. address, but I certainly advise having your winery assign you as their agent of record, since you then have access to their information, their registered number and notification of prior entry submissions. As their agent, there is nothing to do at the time of registration except review the email the FDA will send you to confirm your agent of record status. Carefully check your company's name and address as they will now be used on all prior notifications and any notices issued by the FDA.

Prior notice is required for all shipments entering the U.S. The FDA site is not as user-friendly as, e.g., the TTB site, but there is a lot of good information once you recognize where to look for it. In the case of prior notice regulations, there are helpful background information, FAQs and tutorial sections under http://www.cfsan.fda.gov/

~pn/pnoview.html Prior notice for all shipments is required no more than 5 days before arrival, but in the case of air shipments (samples) no less than 4 hours and for water shipments (containers) the minimum time is 8 hours. My advice on this is to leave it to the customs broker to incorporate this prior notice notification into their routine. It is something they do as a matter of course and the cost is nominal. You could drive yourself crazy trying to track the timelines on these shipments and there are far more important uses of your time ahead!

Primary American Source (Appointment Letter)

Although Federal guidelines do not specify exclusivity on any products you import, each state has a different set of guidelines (as stated in the state license overview in Chapter I). I used the words "wildly disparate" to characterize their differences, and I don't believe this was hyperbole on my part. All fifty states behave as if they are fifty different countries, due in great part to the stringent lobbying on the part of distributors in the years following prohibition. How successful they were, and remain, is evident in the resulting laws.

One requirement that will come up time and again is a requirement that you prove you are the Primary American Source of this wine (authorized by the winery) also called an Appointment Letter. Suffice it to say that you must obtain this at the very beginning or you may find yourself shut out of the very states in which you wish to sell wine. It is a simple letter stating simple intentions, and can be withdrawn by the winery at any time. I stress the latter frequently with new clients. It is not a time sensitive or legally binding document. It merely states the intention of the winery at that particular moment. If you are intent on keeping the particular brand, you will no doubt hope that it will continue in perpetuity—and it may—but the winery can sleep at night knowing that they can change their minds at any time (subject to any other legal agreement you may have). These are two examples of Appointment Letters, one an example of limiting both brands (see Figure 5.2) and region and the other for U.S. exclusivity for all wines produced by the supplier (see Figure 5.3).

In the first example, Jane Smith Wines may have already appointed a U.S. importer for their primary brand, or have a representative importer appointed for the remaining states. Either one can be changed at any time to limit or expand brands or coverage.

COLA Guidelines and General Information about Labels

Commitments made, wines chosen and now it is time for the process of label application to obtain approval from TTB to import these wines, known as COLA (Certificate of Label Approval).

There are many services that provide compliance and you may choose to hand all matters regarding COLAs and state brand registration and licensing to a service. This is a perfectly viable option, particularly if you do not immediately have the time and personnel resources. It is time-sensitive and each state has its own requirements, which can appear daunting at first, and this is understandable. But in covering COLA issues here, I have provided you with the option to do this part yourself, or at least food for thought for the future.

Most, if not all commercial wine label printers around the world, will have access to, or be intimately familiar with, U.S. label regulations. There are specific facets to this which must be adhered to without deviation, but if the printer follows these guidelines they will prepare a label graphic that should be submission-ready for you. If a winery's printer professes to have no knowledge of these mandatory requirements, or prepares something that is completely wrong, I would not hesitate to suggest to the winery that they find a printer, perhaps through referral, who is more familiar with the U.S. labeling process. In the long run, it will save you and the winery countless hours of frustration, and no doubt save the winery the expense of reprinting when they discover that the printed label was still incorrect. That is not to say that the experienced printer will still not make mistakes; omissions and misconceptions happen all the time, but once you learn what the basics are it is really very easy to review label proposals from your suppliers for compliance. It will save you time, headache and expense.

One Mile Winery

Letter of Appointment as Importer of
One Mile Winery into the USA

June 2, 2011

Jane Candide
Mayflower Wine Imports
2000 California Street
San Francisco, CA 94109

Dear Ms. Candide:

We are pleased to confirm your appointment as the importer for the following brands produced by One Mile Winery exported to the United States of America, commencing 1st August 211:

Lone Dog Paddock
Wombat Hills
Brett's Estate

This appointment is effective for the following U.S. states:

Washington
Oregon
California
Colorado
Arizona

Should you have any questions regarding this appointment, please do not hesitate to contact the undersigned.

Yours sincerely,

John Emile
One Mile Winery
25 Still Water Road
Canterbury
New Zealand

Figure 5.2   Letter of Appointment as Importer

One Mile Winery

Letter of Appointment as Sole Importer of
One Mile Winery into the USA

June 2, 2011

Jane Candide
Mayflower Wine Imports
2000 California Street
San Francisco, CA 94109

Dear Ms. Candide:

We are pleased to confirm your appointment as the sole importer for all wines produced by Jane Smith Wines exported to the United States of America, commencing 1st August 2011.

Should you have any questions regarding this appointment, please do not hesitate to contact the undersigned.

Yours sincerely,

John Emile
One Mile Winery
25 Still Water Road
Canterbury
New Zealand

Figure 5.3   Letter of Appointment as Sole Importer

For purposes of this exercise, I will assume you are applying for label approval online. To me, as stated in a previous chapter, it is the only viable way to go in this technological age. It is faster and easier to submit and the turnaround time is far less than paper submissions, so why would you still use snail mail? Some do, but I imagine it is because they have been doing it this way for many years and see no reason to change. You may as well start yours with the most current methods and systems!

The basics for the mandatory information, directly from TTB, are these. Italics are mine.

Brand Label *which can be a front or back label depending upon where the manda-tory information is in compliance:*

1. Brand Name
2. Class or Type Designation *red table wine, e.g. or specific varietal, e.g. Zinfandel*
3. Appellation *if applicable*
4. Alcohol Content

Any Label *can be front, back or side:*

1. Bottler's Name and Address
2. Net Contents *750ml, e.g.*
3. Sulfite Declaration *specifically "Contains Sulfites"*
4. Health Warning Statement *as set out below:*

GOVERNMENT WARNING: (1) According to the Surgeon General, women should not drink alcoholic beverages during pregnancy because of the risk of birth defects. (2) Consumption of alcoholic beverages impairs your ability to drive a car or operate machinery, and may cause health problems.

---

5. Importer Details *Imported by… and location—phone & website optional*

Brand Name, Class/Type, Bottler's Name and Address, Net Contents, Sulfite Statement and Appellation:

- At least 2 mm for containers larger than 187 ml;
- At least 1 mm for containers 187 ml or less

Alcohol content:

- At least 1 mm but not larger than 3 mm for containers of less than 5 L

Health Warning Statement:

- Not smaller than 3 mm for containers larger than 3 L with a maximum of 12 characters per inch
- Not smaller than 2 mm for containers over 237 ml to 3 L with a maximum of 25 characters per inch
- Not smaller than 1 mm for containers of 237 ml or less with a maximum of 40 characters per inch

---

There are minimum font sizes for the mandatory information and, dry as this may sound, becoming familiar with these requirements will also enable you to review and approve the printer's proofs like a pro. This information on font sizes is directly from TTB.

The label graphics should be submitted to you in separate jpeg attachments, one each for the back and front, for each label (see Figure 5.4). There should be no surrounding or extraneous information, such as printer's marks, color notations or approval sign offs on design. Each label must be as it will look when printed and affixed to the bottle. Each attachment must be no more than 450kb.

Before we go any further, I will stress what I feel is one of the most important aspects of this particular issue: under no circumstances should you allow the winery to print the label before it is approved, unless it is an exact duplicate of a previously approved label and the only thing to change is your unique importer details. Even the experienced printer and your careful eye may miss a key element that will be the cause of the label rejection. There are other challenges with submitting online, but you should be able to check your attachments before submission and within a short time it becomes second nature. According to TTB:

Top Ten Submitter Corrections for COLAs Online

- The images that were submitted are illegible
- Images(s) were distorted during upload
- Dimensions provided generated a skewed or distorted image on the printable COLA
- Labels must be saved and uploaded as separate image files
- Files are uploaded in wrong area
- Problems with the Government Warning (Health Warning Statement) *they are very strict about the exact wording, punctuation, bold of the actual words Government Warning, but not the text itself*
- Terms are placed in incorrect fields…i.e. "zinfandel" in the fanciful name field *example of fanciful name might be Block 28 Reserve*
- Appellation of origin is missing from application
- You must designate a "brand (Front)" label
- Brand name on application does not match labels

These are examples of reasons for COLAs online to return the application with a status of "Needs Correction." This notice is made immediately to the submitter and receives priority attention upon resubmission. If all changes are not made when resubmitted, the COLA will be rejected.

Once rejected, the wine will not be allowed to enter the country, until a new submission is made from the beginning, with the correct information. This submission must comply with the label on the bottle in the event of a customs inspection, or individual state registrations. This is one reason, among the others stated above, why it makes sense to submit online. The average turnaround time (as of this writing) is 4 days, compared to up to a month through the mail. Notification of either "needs correction" or "approved" will be made to you via email.

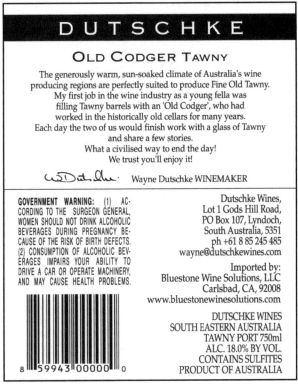

Figure 5.4   Brand Label Example

Trade Sample Waiver

In the event you are bringing in wines for evaluation, either because you are assessing their potential as a new supplier, or a current winery is submitting a new wine or style to you for inclusion in your portfolio, and there is no label approval, you may apply for a waiver, which will allow the samples to be cleared through customs without the necessity of a COLA. TTB does make it very easy for you to submit the waiver. The section on their website is under International Trade and can be accessed through this link: http://www.ttb.gov/itd/importing_samples.shtml. There is a template you can download, which can be seen in Figure 5.5.

This requirement has been in effect since post 9/11, but does not appear to be precipitated by the September 11 terrorist attack. According to TTB, they recognized a need to allow for exemptions of COLAs under certain circumstances, such as for sample evaluation or for a trade show. Despite being part of their requirements for years, I rarely had to provide a waiver until 2010, when it now seems more customary. Many sample shipments still require no action on my part (after the initial setup with the carrier, as outlined in Chapter I) and show up at my door, with full customs clearance.

TTB's International Trade Division seems to be a small department and its inhabitants are very friendly and accommodating—a kinder, gentler form of government at work. They will turn your request around within 24 hours if you submit the form via fax, even sooner if you call and beg. Since the winery should notify you via email when a shipment has been organized, including the airway bill attachment, you will have all you need to make this waiver request within plenty of time, or even if you are caught unawares.

Sample Bottle Requirements

This would be a good place to mention that in addition to the paperwork the winery must complete at their end to consign the samples to you—an airway bill that lists your contact details, the contents of the case(s), your license numbers, continuous

[LETTERHEAD]

[DATE]

Director, International Trade Division
Alcohol and Tobacco Tax and Trade Bureau
1310 G St. NW, Suite 400W
Washington, DC 20220
Fax: (202) 435-7020

To Director, ITD:

We request a waiver from the Certificate of Label Approval (COLA) requirements for a shipment of [**TOTAL# OF BOTTLES/QUANTITY OF PRODUCT**] of [**PRODUCT NAME/TYPE**] that will be used as samples for [**PURPOSE/TRADE SHOW OR EVENT**].

Our permit number is [**IMPORTERS PERMIT #**]. The shipment, which will be imported from [**COUNTRY OF ORIGIN**], consists of:

[##] bottles of [**PRODUCT NAME—LIST INDIVIDUALLY**]
[##] bottles of [**PRODUCT NAME—LIST INDIVIDUALLY**]
[##] bottles of [**PRODUCT NAME—LIST INDIVIDUALLY**]

We are aware of the various requirements that apply to imported alcohol beverages. All applicable taxes and duties will be paid on the imported products. Any Country of Origin markings will be indicated in English. Each individual container shall bear a label stating "*Sample Only—Not for Sale*" or similar phrase. Likewise, each individual container will bear a label with the government health warning statement mandated by law. If wine, the product will also contain a "Contains Sulfites" label.

We also attest that the products indicated in this letter will be in compliance with the above requirements prior to the product arriving at the U.S. port of entry, and understand that the approval of this waiver is dependent on compliance with these obligations.

If the waiver is granted, please fax a copy to the attention of [**CONTACT**] at [**FAX NUMBER**].

Should you have any questions, please contact us at [**PHONE NUMBER**].

Regards,

[**SIGNATURE**]
[**NAME AND TITLE OF AUTHORIZED COMPANY REP.**]

Figure 5.5   Trade Sample Waiver

bond number (if you have one) and detailed contents of the shipment—the winery must also label each and every bottle, per the waiver letter, with the following:

1. Sample Only—Not for Sale
2. Contains Sulfites
3. Mandatory Health Warning

Please note that "individual container" in the TTB letter refers to each bottle. If customs chooses to inspect a shipment and these statements are not on the bottles, they will either destroy the goods or return them to the sender—your choice, but your charge too.

My Story

The COLA process is much easier than it used to be, before printers had templates for the U.S. label requirements. But it's not always the mandatory information that presents a problem. Pay attention to statements that can be construed as promoting the consumption of alcohol, even slightly. I once had to remove the phrase *In Vino Veritas* that had been artfully incorporated into the label design, because the translation, *In Wine is Truth*, was deemed to encourage drinking. Another time, the word "lively" had to be removed from the description, because it was a still wine and "lively" connoted a sparkling wine. A beloved family crest can provide an almost insurmountable obstacle, as in this story:

Several years ago, at the beginning of my import journey, I represented a brand whose label proudly bore the family crest, a running fox, beneath which was a Latin inscription in a decorative banner. I submitted my carefully scrutinized COLA, duly affixed to a paper form and submitted via mail. A few days later, the COLA was returned to me, without approval and with the words "translate inscription" scrawled across the bottom. I called the winery and discovered the crest had been in the family for approximately 500 years and roughly translated into *Trust, But Beware*. I duly returned the COLA with the translation and a few more days passed. The mail arrived, I opened the envelope, withdrew the long-awaited form and, to my dismay, there was still no approval. Instead, on the bottom of the form the scrawl, "beware of whom?"

I became increasingly more concerned about time frames for labeling and container bookings, and frustrated with the faceless person at ATF (the former TTB) who kept delaying the process. I returned the COLA, along with a cover letter that outlined in some detail the long and illustrious origins of the family crest, with the explanation, "it has been at least 500 years since this inscription was devised by a long ago ancestor. No one remembers 'whom' anymore."

The label was approved.

6

CONTAINERS

Whether you are the corporate executive retiree with a golden parachute looking for an investment or the self-professed wine geek who has scraped together the funds to start the business of your dreams, there is value in learning about ways in which you can maximize your investment. Therefore, just as I have already approached each subject matter, I will address containers from a budgetary and common sense perspective. Presumably, whether you are retiree or wine geek, the idea is to turn a profit from your wine business!

All You Need to Know and More

Sizes and Weights

All cargo shipments coming into a U.S. port must also move overland and therefore come under road laws governed by weight restriction established by both federal and local government agencies. There are two sizes for containers, referred to as 20 foot (see Figure 6.1) and 40 foot (not feet). Whilst it appears you can cram more into a 40 foot

Figure 6.1   A 20 Foot Cargo Container

container, this is not actually the case. A 20 foot container weight is limited to 39,500 lbs and a 40 foot container to 44,500 lbs. Although there are state variations that allow you to exceed the weight limits, with the use of special equipment to distribute chassis weight more equitably on roads and bridges, it hardly seems worth the effort, cost and risk. The consequences of exceeding the legal limit are fines, rejection of load, and potential damage, and having to offload the contents into other transportation.

In addition, Long Beach has its own restrictions, which are currently:

- 20' (general purpose) in excess of 44,000 cargo weight lbs
- 20' (reefer) in excess of 41,500 cargo weight lbs
- 40' (general purpose) in excess of 44,500 cargo weight lbs
- 40' (reefer) in excess of 41,500 cargo weight lbs
- 45' in excess of 41,500 cargo weight lbs

Personally, I have never shipped in anything other than a 20 foot container. I can always have two containers on the water at the same time if I need to, and generally it allows for flexibility and staggering of invoice payments. Depending upon whether your wines are palletized (on pallets) or stuffed (loaded without pallets), the capacity of a 20 foot container averages 700 to 1100 cases, based on 9 liter cases (12 × 750ml bottles). Particularly in your new brands' introduction—your (metaphorical) throw-it-against-the-wall-and-see-what-sticks, find-the-right-distribution-channels stage, it would behoove you to plan your initial order conservatively, to fit within a 20 foot container.

Pallets

A pallet, also known as a skid, is a flat, wooden structure used to confine the cases in a (usually) shrink wrapped, stacked configuration, with access underneath for a forklift to raise and move the load around with stability. Typically, the average U.S. pallet is deemed to hold 56 cases. In other parts of the world the pallet load is considered to be anywhere between 50 and 64 cases, so this is also a fact to keep in mind when discussing pallets with suppliers. You may both be talking about different amounts when you refer to an order as "five pallets."

When palletizing your order for an ocean freight container, the actual quantity per pallet may depend upon load distribution and may not adhere to a generally accepted number of cases or layers, but in discussion with people in the U.S. and other countries, keep in mind that each individual has a particular number in mind when referring to a pallet, or pallet order.

U.S. Customs and Border Protection, a department of Homeland Security, enacted regulations in 2004, which were enforced in its final form in 2006, to reduce the incidence of transported plant pests into the U.S. As a result of this ruling, all pallets (which come under the heading of Wood Packing Materials or WPM) must be treated and stamped with a mark certifying that the heat treatment or fumigation has been undertaken according to proscribed guidelines. More information can be found on their website www.cbp.gov. It has been in place long enough now that all freight forwarders, agents, ports and shipping companies will be familiar with the requirements, but I am a firm believer in acquiring the knowledge you need to oversee, monitor, explain, fix, modify, assist, supervise or whatever the situation calls for in your own business. This is just one of those checklist items that is easy to confirm at the outset and disastrous if it is discovered to have been overlooked at arrival.

Reefer vs. Dry vs. Blanket vs. ...

I feel I am metaphorically about to wade into shark infested waters as I embark on this subject, but it is a really critical aspect of not just container shipments, but your overall business and I cannot, in good conscience, ignore it. I am also mindful that, despite any advice or recommendations I might make, this is your business and you have to make decisions with which you feel most comfortable. I will do the best I can to arm you with knowledge and from there you can either choose to follow the most conservative precautions, settle on a hybrid of the choices or take the most cost-effective route and run the risk of temperature damage to the wine. In the latter example, I am not saying you *will* incur wine spoilage, but that the possibility exists.

Reefers are refrigerated containers that control the temperature for the contents of the container, via a generator, for the duration of the voyage. It adds considerable cost to ocean freight, but guarantees that the goods will arrive in optimum condition. That said, there is a difference between a reefer and a "working" reefer, which actually means that the generator is turned on. A "non-working" reefer is still an improvement over a dry container, because it is insulated, but you should understand the difference and what you are paying for. In opting for a reefer, it will negate its benefits if you do not also concern yourself with the conditions during consolidation at port of origin, the temperature of your warehouse upon arrival and the arrangement for reefer trucks during overland transport.

Insulated or thermal containers provide insulation on all sides of the box, but no refrigeration unit.

Thermal blankets can be requested for use from your shipping company to provide insulation for the wine at an affordable cost.

Dry containers are not temperature controlled. They are metal boxes in which the wine is either palletized or stuffed, and temperatures can fluctuate wildly during the ocean voyage.

In the case of a reefer, the guarantee of temperature integrity is inherent in the arrangement, but in the event you wish to confirm the temperature, or for peace of mind, it would be considered prudent to invest in a temperature recorder for either the first or periodic voyages. It is a sealed unit that records the temperature at intervals throughout the trip and prints it on a paper strip (see Figure 6.2), also sealed within the unit. The unit is embedded in the shipment and returned to you upon unloading

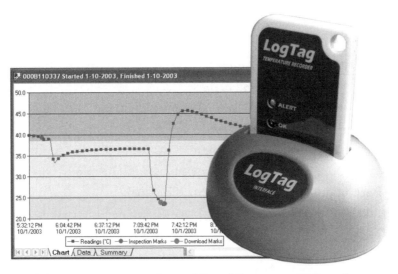

Figure 6.2   Temperature Recorder and Log (Courtesy of Microdaq.com, Ltd)

by the warehouse. Since the container is sealed at port of loading and remains sealed until it arrives at the warehouse (except in the event of a customs inspection) there can be no tampering with the wine and the temperature recorder en route.

Additionally, you can give stowage instructions to the shipper that stipulates below deck storage, but there is no guarantee that this is always done, nor that it ensures optimum conditions. If you know the ship starts at the port from which your product is loading, you have much more assurance that the container will be below decks because this is where they are going to start loading an empty ship. It could conceivably stop at a couple more ports and continue to take on containers, which will now occupy above-deck space.

If you are weighing options, based on budget, price of wine, type of wine, origin (Europe vs. Southern Hemisphere), which coast the wine will enter and where it will go from there, also factor in time of year. You may consider working reefers in the hottest months and insulated containers or thermal blankets during other times of the year.

Irrespective of any decision, insurance is really affordable—at this writing, around twenty two cents to twenty eight cents per case, in temperature-controlled containers, with a deductible of $500 and a limit of $10,000,000, as one example. Insurance, at a slightly higher cost, can also be obtained for insulated or standard containers with insulated blankets.

CIF vs. FOB

Although you will find that the most common form of payment arrangement is FOB (Free on Board), it still pays to be familiar with the term CIF (Cost, Insurance and Freight) in the event it either works for you at the outset, is offered to you by the supplier as an alternative, and to generally understand the difference as a matter of education.

CIF can be an advantage in the beginning, because in this scenario the exporter (the winery) arranges and pays for the vessel, and insures the freight during the voyage. The winery, or their representative agent, also arranges all shipping details, including selection of the vessel, consolidation and packing of the goods and monitoring of the shipment through their own resources, which could include direct contact with the steamship company or a freight forwarder.

Legal and financial responsibility passes to you, the importer, "at the rail," meaning when it clears the rail during unloading as it heads for the destination dock. This allows you to minimize both your initial financial outlay and having to arrange for a container at the early stage when you are unfamiliar with the process, but it comes with its drawbacks. Freight and insurance will ultimately become your responsibility. It is just delayed. Relying on someone else to arrange your shipment means you are not able to monitor it firsthand, do not receive direct notification of any delays or problems and usually end up paying a surcharge for the arrangement. Additionally, the exporter may not find the most competitive shipping company for you. It is all basically out of your hands.

FOB means that title for the goods passes to you at the "ship's rail" at the overseas port. In both situations you are responsible for all duty, taxes, customs clearance and overlandfreight at destination, and in this case you are also responsible for ocean freight andinsurance. It allows you to choose your own shipping company, develop your own relationship with a freight forwarder or consolidator, make your own bookings to suit your time constraints or planned arrivals and be informed of any delays or problems en route. You would normally be able to negotiate your own more competitive shipping rates.

Your Own Container (FCL)

Using the premise that you have sufficient selections to bring in your own full container, consider the mix of wine, for the initial container at least, on the basis of price points, styles, introductory focus or the brand identity you are establishing, and time of year.

Seasonal changes, and new wine placements, take place in spring and fall. There is overlap of course—people still drink red wines in summer and white wines in winter from personal preference or food pairing—but it should be a factor in your planning, as you can well imagine.

Additionally, the *real* selling season, for an importer, is September and October. It is the best time to introduce new brands (as long as you have laid the foundation first) and will be the time of year you are likely to sell the most wine—with the exception of unexpectedly high ratings anywhere in the year, but that's for another section. Distributors are buying from you at that time to sell to retailers, who will sell to consumers in the holiday season. So, keep this in mind as you go about hunting and gathering your wines to introduce them to the U.S. market.

Arranging your own container is a time-saving and cost-effective alternative, under almost all circumstances over a LCL (less than container load). Therefore, although a 20 foot container may comfortably hold 1,000 cases, if you have at least 500 cases, I am of the opinion that it is still better to book a container under your own license, than to deal with an outside consolidation. Although rates may vary slightly from shipper to shipper, freight charges *within each company* are the same for any container you book yourself, no matter how much wine you load. It is the duty and taxes that vary, and that's dependent upon the actual number. It is therefore to your advantage to have as much as you can reasonably put in a container, *if you need it*, to decrease the per case freight charge. For example, (using a figure solely for purpose of this illustration and not to indicate an exact freight rate):

500 cases = $2,300 or $4.60 per case

1,000 cases = $2,300 or $2.30 per case

Clearly you are realizing savings with the 1,000 case example over the 500 case example, but the 500 case example is still less financial outlay, time in transit and aggravation than you will encounter with an LCL arranged through an outside consolidation. You may wonder how that could be. Five hundred cases is still 500 cases. Is it really that different? Yes, I can assure you it is. Avoid it, unless absolutely necessary, or unless your markups or your financial structure can withstand this erosion of margin.

Pallets vs. Stuffing

There is an argument to be made for each, and sometimes a time and place. In the case of palletizing the wine, the number of cases will be considerably less, but the wine is organized, often into a particular winery, brand or varietal that makes it easier to assemble and count at the outset and at the other end. There is also less time spent at the warehouse end, when unloading the product is charged by the hour.

With a stuffed container, there is the ability to load considerably more product, thereby ensuring that wine you need will make it onto that particular container, and also reduce the per case freight cost. But whereas you saved money with the palletized unloading, you will spend more on unloading case by case at the warehouse. It also has to be loaded into the container in such a way that it does not shift in transit and break.

Consolidation Through Shipping Co. (LCL)

In the case of an LCL, you will be relying on a consolidator—either through a freight forwarder or with the shipping line itself—to put your wine in with any freight destined for almost any location. You don't know where it is loaded, how long it will take to get here, what route it takes (often through China) and how long it will wait in port while they arrange for devanning of all the different products. It is often a three to five week delay, over which you will have no control. Can you afford that kind of time? Remember, the clock is ticking on your investment and the invoice due date. And the longer it takes, the greater the likelihood of missed opportunities, damage and loss.

For this privilege it will cost up to three times as much as the FCL you arranged for yourself with the same weight and number of items. The 500 case example now looks like this:

500 cases = $2,300 or $4.60 per case FCL

500 cases = $6,000 or $12.00 per case LCL

FCL vs. LCL Summary

Clearly, the more cases you can put into the container the more economical it becomes, but being in control of your own container is to your advantage under most circumstances, even when the load is much less.

Exceptions, when the overall consequences or benefits outweigh the expense of a LCL:

- If you need, e.g. 75–200 cases of wine to supply an order or distributor, because you will lose forward business and have no need of a container for some time. This isn't a large amount, you may realize very little or even no profit, but the good will is worth it.

- A premium wine is in continual demand and, as it commands a very good price, your margin erosion by the additional cost is sustainable. You have either run out or it is only available in small quantities, and it is going to ensure continuity for you with a customer or in the market in general.

- A wine, also in demand or need, (but not necessarily of a particular price point) missed a container because of unforeseeable circumstances—bottle and label delays, mix-up at port, e.g.—and, perhaps because it is mid-summer or just before Christmas, you will not need another container for a number of weeks.

- There is a special event—wine dinner, trade tasting, consumer tasting, etc.—that you promised this wine for and for which publicity has already been generated and there is no FCL container leaving fast enough.

The point is to try to avoid these contingencies as best you can. They will happen—they have happened to me—but prior planning is always advisable, especially in this business.

Controlled Consolidation (a FCL hybrid)

The other alternative, if you find yourself short of product but do not need an entire container, is to try to coordinate with competitors (other importers) who may find themselves in the same position of needing to bring in a couple of pallets or a few hundred cases. A joint consolidation benefits everyone, either under one import license or with each importer taking responsibility for their own charges, billed separately under each individual license. The latter is slightly more expensive, but ensures that you are not paying for someone else, expecting them to reimburse you, if you do not feel comfortable doing so. This effectively allows each winery to put together a FCL by making arrangements for one container, which each importer has agreed to share, to be offloaded at one destination. Each importer pays their proportionate share of the freight, duty, customs clearance and all charges related to the container. If you can find compatible individuals, it can be a worthwhile collaboration, and save each party the LCL surcharges, whilst maintaining control over your own shipment.

If you decide to have another importer clear a container for you through their customs agent (which means you reimburse them rather than the other way around), you will need to give the importer a letter authorizing them to clear for you. For an example, see Figure 6.3.

I have done this, to good result, on several occasions. However, I would advise knowing something about the importer beforehand, either through developing your own relationship with them, or through referral from your warehouse or a trade organization. I suggest you also maintain open communication so that you each know when the container is due to leave and have the goods there in plenty of time, or conversely that you understand if there are to be any delays, which may impact your sales.

Freight Forwarder

You have the option of contacting the shipping company directly, and I would certainly recommend that you do so to understand charges and to make rate comparisons between companies. However, a freight forwarder can be a very worthwhile addition to your resources. With their specialized expertise, they are able to negotiate rates,

Mayflower Wine Imports

June 2, 2011

Super Duper Wine Importers

To Who It May Concern:

Please be advised that Super Duper Wine Importers is authorized to utilize label approvals issued by the Alcohol Tobacco Tax Bureau to Mayflower Wine Imports on the following shipment:

    (list shipping company and vessel name)

Sincerely,

Jane Candide
Mayflower Wine Imports

Figure 6.3   Authorization Letter

determine shipping line schedules, book ships, coordinate shipments for you from multiple suppliers and keep you informed during the consolidation and pre-boarding stages. A good freight forwarder is an arm to your business. You provide them with your purchase order, which apprises them of the exact goods to expect for the shipment. They will be proactive in contacting you if they know you want certain wine quickly and they manage to find an earlier booking date, can notify you if a winery's goods will be late, which could delay the entire voyage, or if they are delivered short, not as indicated on your purchase order or damaged. They are the contact point for the suppliers at the country of origin, which makes it easier for you, a continent away.

An alternative is to negotiate rates with a member co-operative, such as WSSA, which can save you some money on freight rates and do the coordination for you. They charge a membership fee, but it is affordable. Whether they save you money over other companies, and provide the services you require, is up to you to decide.

Customs Broker

This is an essential resource, and a function you cannot perform yourself. Choose a company wisely, because you must depend upon them to clear your shipments expeditiously and accurately and—once again—save you time and money in the process.

Typically, customs brokers manage all documentation related to your shipment, including label approvals, provided by you, and B/L (Bill of Lading), provided by the freight forwarder or shipping company. They track the vessel, pay duty to customs in a timely manner, can arrange for cargo pickup and delivery and, at your discretion, arrange for an "express" clearance, while the vessel is still at sea, to minimize the time your cargo spends on the dock before pickup.

Should your container be chosen for a physical customs inspection (rare, but not unheard of, especially with a new importer), the customs broker will also manage and expedite the container removal and pickup, in an effort to avoid demurrage charges—fees accruing per day in excess of the "free" time allowed for cargo, currently 7 days.

My Story

There are times when insurance comes in handy for more than temperature variance.

The first container I ever received, and perhaps because of that very reason, was targeted for a customs inspection. It was a "stuffed" container and Customs managed, in the process, to break most of the contents of twenty-two cases of my father's best wine, The Cowra Estate Reserve Chardonnay. The remainder of the twenty-two cases was unsalable, because of stained and ruined labels. I imagine, although was never told, that it occurred when the doors were opened and cases that had shifted during the voyage came tumbling out. But whatever the cause, there was no compensation and no recourse. The wine was finally released, along with a number of soggy cartons filled with shattered glass.

Although it has not happened to me, I have heard of containers going overboard at sea, and shipping collisions resulting in significant damage. Insurance is there in the event of the unexpected, catastrophic event.

7

THE NEXT STEPS

You will discover that the wine industry cannot be approached like most other businesses in the corporate world. Although you must create a budget which includes a pricing model for each wine and accounts for markup and margin, there are many variables that become apparent as you start trading. Responding to the demands of the individual distributors, and the industry itself, in a positive and flexible manner, is a necessity to survival and to be seen as a savvy player. To sustain a viable business model, you must throw out preconceived notions and rigid corporate paradigms and be prepared to adapt quickly to the changing environment.

First Container Budgeting

Earlier, I suggested that the first container comprise sufficient wine to sustain your markets for approximately three months. This is often, understandably, a difficult figure to accurately calculate, especially if the wines are brand new to the market, but if you don't make the effort it is more probable that a miscalculation will start eating up your margins. Even if brands were previously established in the U.S., there is no guarantee that they will remain in demand, that sales were not already declining or that the market has not changed since the brand was with someone else, because of a difficult economy, or the varietal or country is over-saturated. Considerations for this introductory time period would be:

- **Pricing**

  If the wine is priced at the higher end of the market, it is likely to start out slowly. This is before market demand has developed and when the distributor may be reluctant to be the vanguard of the brand's sales. They must also consider their own budgets in committing to a brand that may not provide them with the cash flow or pull-through they envisioned. Because of the higher pricing they will have more money tied up in these wines than they would in others.

  If the wine is priced competitively, or even below its peers, it could conceivably begin selling more rapidly. This is no guarantee, but the probability that your customers will buy with less deliberation, and in volume, is greater than for a higher priced wine. The investment on their part is smaller, the risk is reduced, and potential for a faster rate of sales turnover, (therefore payment) is more appealing.

- **Ratings**

  Usually, when first introduced, the brand has no U.S. ratings on which to base demand. This makes introduction slower, and requires more investment in time and money waiting for distributor decisions. This must be part of your budgeting exercise, along with travel to meet with distributors, if necessary, or to work the market later on. It means you must be the driving force behind the wines sales, rather than the ratings either pushing sales or providing a positive impetus, at least in this initial phase.

I don't happen to agree with importers who submit samples to a renowned publication to await a rating before they commit to being the winery's importer. Not only is this disrespectful to the winery, forcing them to wait months for your decision and perhaps foregoing an introduction that year in the market, but what happened to relying on one's palate? I am not so naïve as to believe that ratings from the right publications aren't only helpful, but have become the bellwether for sales. However, if we all

You paid three goats for this? Robertus Parkerus only rated it LXXIV.

Figure 7.1   © **David Pike**

made decisions on wine purchases based solely on the perspective of another palate, then we are dangerously narrowing the flavor profile for an entire market, thereby ignoring and marginalizing the much more important factors of region, terroir, wine-maker's signature, vintage variables, etc.

- **New brand demand**

   This may be created through pre-selling (discussed later) or through your own relationships with distributors. It may be the next hot region, still on the upswing, or the opportunity to capitalize on the buzz created in the brand's home country. It could hit just the right note with the distributors you have contacted and to which you have made proposals. But generally, this is a difficult area to gauge and should be approached with caution.

- **Old brand demand**

  If you are fortunate enough to take on a consistently high volume, highly rated, icon brand or household name that has left its current importer, then you will be in a much better position to throw out some of the cautions in the first stages. But as a new, unproven importer, this is unlikely to happen. This type of brand can virtually write its own ticket and will likely have its pick of solid, seasoned veterans.

  A more likely scenario is a brand owner who is unhappy with the sales performance of his or her importer, is losing ground in the U.S. and wants to try someone who they feel will (after proving yourself financially viable) be able to regain the focus that their previous importer has lost. This is still a great opportunity (assuming all positive aspects are aligned) and you can start with a ready-made base of sales and good distributors on which to build the brand back up or to new heights. My counsel to you regarding this situation: last year's sales do not necessarily presage the future, nor are the current list of distributors likely to all stay in place. Brands wax and wane with distributors all the time and this could be their opportunity to bow out of representing this particular one.

- **QPR (Quality Price Ratio)**

  The happy convergence of label, price, quality, perception, style and taste may mean a blast off in sales right from the start, in which case you have done your homework well, but the starting line is usually farther away than you might think, as summarized below.

- **Timing**

  Consider the time it takes for the ship to leave port and make its way over here—anywhere from two weeks to a month, (depending upon the point of origin) with perhaps delays at either port, as well as overland transport to take into consideration. A container trucker to bring it to the warehouse, unload and inventory will take an extra two to three days, if they are able to pick it up immediately.

  Now, if you have not done any pre-selling, *with order commitments*, you will organize a ground shipment, via UPS, DHL, FedEx or other carrier, of wines from the warehouse (if it is not in driving distance) to your office and start the process of contacting distributors to determine their interest. I advise starting with at least one to two cases of each wine. There may also be publications to submit to, and some of these require two bottles of each submission.

Some pre-determination should have been done at this point, so that you have at least identified potential distributors, but this may be only a short way down the decision track. In general, it can take several months from expressed interest to an order and this is one of the most important considerations of your budgetary concerns.

- **Seasonal Timing**

  If you have already laid the necessary foundation—obtained label approval, researched the market, turned targeted potential distributors into solid distributors and pre-sold wine, the optimum months of the year to land a **new** brand, and minimize the time the wine will spend in storage, is early September to October. A launch at this time gets the wine to the retailer for the holiday selling period. Remember, in the pipeline the winery and importer are at the beginning and the consumer is at the end. The wholesaler and retailer must make their choices and bring wine in well prior to the holiday kickoff.

  The first quarter (January to March) is also a favorable launch time for a new brand. At the beginning of the year, distributors will be looking at their holiday sales and how well their brands performed over that holiday time frame. If the brands in their book performed poorly when sales expectations are at their highest, this may be a time to jettison a brand, or pull back on commitment, and leaves the door open to new, potentially more exciting, income generating brands to come in and make their mark.

  Naturally, if everything you have done results in a convergence of functions that determines a container shipping or arriving at another time, then you probably don't want to wait, but the months to try and avoid would be July and August, when heat is of paramount concern and wholesalers are laying low, away for school holidays or waiting for the fall season to begin.

- **Incentives**

  Incentives, in this case provided by the winery, can include:

  o free goods—usually cases of the current release in the container
  o special bottles such as magnums or jeroboams
  o winery marketing paraphernalia
  o money
  o contests for trips or prizes

Not all states allow incentives to distributors, sales people or retailers and we will discuss that further later, but some do and this is an opportunity to jumpstart a brand.

If a winery is able to offer incentives that can be passed on to the wholesaler, this may also present an opportunity to partner with your distributor or provide ongoing support to periodic promotional efforts by their sales staff.

It generally takes a larger winery to offer incentives beyond free goods and is not considered an essential part of doing business, but a roll out with skillfully integrated incentives can create the excitement, and sense of professionalism, to put the brand introduction into a different category in the wholesaler's minds. It is an element in the decisions you make regarding budgeting for the first containers.

Pricing the Wine

This is such a subjective area and I want to make it clear from the outset that I am providing guidelines only. Your markups and margins are entirely up to you and should not be dictated by anyone else, but my guidelines have worked for me throughout my many years as an importer and they can provide a springboard from which you may create your own.

In addition to the actual costs and percentage markups, these are other pricing considerations, which may or may not come into play for your situation:

- maintain a competitive edge in a specific state or the country.
- fit a perception of the wine
- allow for incentive programming
- remain on a relative par with the pricing in the country of origin.

I am constantly asked by wineries to calculate their retail for them in the U.S. There appears to be nothing definitive on the internet, through trade resources or in the marketplace to fully apprise them of the intricacies of U.S. markups and expenses throughout the three tier system that exists in the wine industry here. They want to know where their wine will sit, after they have set their FOB price. They want to know what importers, distributors and retailers are making. They want to know if a point or two in discount will make their wine a better price, or make not much difference at all. The system here is so foreign to the way the rest of the world works that they just want to get a better handle on it any way they can, and one of those ways is to get a feel for where the markups are and what to expect at the other end of the pricing spectrum.

You may also be wondering, which is understandable. As with most other aspects of this world, I received a myriad of false, misleading, incomplete and mystifying information when I first embarked on my importer path. There is some justification for this, in that there are fifty states, hundreds of importers, thousands of wholesalers and tens of thousands of retailers—all with their own unique markups and ways of doing business. But you have to be able to start somewhere. And for that purpose I have included my own tables that calculate the price from the winery to the consumer in a generic type of way that allows you to have a fair idea of where the wine will end up (see Table 7.1).

Caveat: this can vary even more from what I've stated above for the following circumstances:

- Consciously setting small margins for the sake of high volume turnover or DI (whole container purchases) on specific wines
- Marking up high end wines (expensive) less than lower priced, higher volume wines, which are marked up at a normal percentage
- State and local taxes
- Trucking costs
- Government intervention in control states such as, e.g., Ohio, Pennsylvania and Utah (there are currently 18)
- Small wholesalers with higher overhead
- Large wholesalers working on smaller margins
- Large retail chains with narrower margins
- Small, boutique wine stores with higher margins
- Meeting a target retail price
- Building in specific programming (incentive) dollars

Table 7.1   Pricing Tables for New Zealand, Australia and Europe

1	2	3	4	5	6	7	8
NZD .75 Bottle	12x750ml Case	USD Case	Container Clearance	Importer Markup/ FOB	Wholesale Case	Retail Case	Retail Bottle
3.50	42.00	31.50	43.50	58.73	85.15	123.47	10.29
3.75	45.00	33.75	45.75	61.76	89.56	129.86	10.82
4.50	54.00	40.50	52.50	70.88	102.77	149.01	12.42
4.75	57.00	42.75	54.75	73.91	107.17	155.40	12.95
6.50	78.00	58.50	70.50	95.18	138.00	200.11	16.68
6.67	80.04	60.03	72.03	97.24	141.00	204.45	17.04
7.00	84.00	63.00	75.00	101.25	146.81	212.88	17.74
8.00	96.00	72.00	84.00	113.40	164.43	238.42	19.87
9.00	108.00	81.00	93.00	125.55	182.05	263.97	22.00
10.00	120.00	90.00	102.00	137.70	199.67	289.51	24.13
AUD .65 Bottle	12x750ml Case	USD Case	Container Clearance	Importer Markup/ FOB	Wholesale Case	Retail Case	Retail Bottle
3.50	42.00	27.30	39.30	53.06	76.93	111.55	9.30
3.75	45.00	29.25	41.25	55.69	80.75	117.08	9.76
4.50	54.00	35.10	47.10	63.59	92.20	133.69	11.14
4.75	57.00	37.05	49.05	66.22	96.02	139.22	11.60
6.50	78.00	50.70	62.70	84.65	122.74	177.97	14.83
6.67	80.04	52.03	64.03	86.44	125.33	181.73	15.14
7.00	84.00	54.60	66.60	89.91	130.37	189.04	15.75
8.00	96.00	62.40	74.40	100.44	145.64	211.18	17.60
9.00	108.00	70.20	82.20	110.97	160.91	233.31	19.44
10.00	120.00	78.00	90.00	121.50	176.18	255.45	21.29

AUD .90 Bottle	12x750ml Case	USD Case	Container Clearance	Importer Markup/ FOB	Wholesale Case	Retail Case	Retail Bottle
3.50	42.00	37.80	49.80	67.23	97.48	141.35	11.78
3.75	45.00	40.50	52.50	70.88	102.77	149.01	12.42
4.50	54.00	48.60	60.60	81.81	118.62	172.01	14.33
4.75	57.00	51.30	63.30	85.46	123.91	179.67	14.97
6.50	78.00	70.20	82.20	110.97	160.91	233.31	19.44
6.67	80.04	72.04	84.04	113.45	164.50	238.53	19.88
7.00	84.00	75.60	87.60	118.26	171.48	248.64	20.72
8.00	96.00	86.40	98.40	132.84	192.62	279.30	23.27
9.00	108.00	97.20	109.20	147.42	213.76	309.95	25.83
10.00	120.00	108.00	120.00	162.00	234.90	340.61	28.38

Euro 1.2 Bottle	12x750ml Case	USD Case	Container Clearance	Importer Markup/ FOB	Wholesale Case	Retail Case	Retail Bottle
3.50	42.00	50.40	62.40	84.24	122.15	177.11	14.76
3.75	45.00	54.00	66.00	89.10	129.20	187.33	15.61
4.50	54.00	64.80	76.80	103.68	150.34	217.99	18.17
4.75	57.00	68.40	80.40	108.54	157.38	228.21	19.02
6.50	78.00	93.60	105.60	142.56	206.71	299.73	24.98
6.67	80.04	96.05	108.05	145.86	211.50	306.68	25.56
7.00	84.00	100.80	112.80	152.28	220.81	320.17	26.68
8.00	96.00	115.20	127.20	171.72	248.99	361.04	30.09
9.00	108.00	129.60	141.60	191.16	277.18	401.91	33.49
10.00	120.00	144.00	156.00	210.60	305.37	442.79	36.90

I used New Zealand dollars, Australian dollars, and Euros for the purpose of having three different tables. They can obviously apply to any other currency, such as Chilean or Argentine Peso or South African Rand. The table functions are the same; only the exchange rate changes.

I also included two tables for the Australian dollar to illustrate the changes that have occurred in the past couple of years. As you can see, a fluctuation in rates makes a huge difference in retail price. The fluctuation is far greater than my experience with an average year, based on global economic changes, making it much more difficult to both preserve your margin and not overly inflate the price.

In 2009, Australia varied from approximately .65 to .91—an astonishing extreme.

In 2009, New Zealand varied from approximately .51 to .74.

In 2009, the Euro varied from approximately 1.27 to 1.5.

Again, I used very generic markups in each area for ease of arriving at a figure quickly under any circumstance. This is not for the purpose of stipulating a wholesale figure to the distributor, nor dictating a retail that this wine must sit at on the shelves. *This is for you to set your own markup, which you can control, and have a fair idea of where it will lead*. It is broad and simple, but does the job without all the manipulations and calculations you could spend countless hours on, time better spent in sourcing, marketing, selling and running your business.

Columns 1 & 2

Using the original FOB from the winery, which will include getting the boxed, palletized wine to the port of departure, this is the bottle price for a 750ml bottle and the same price for 12 750ml bottles in a case (a total of 9 liters). At this stage it is in the currency of the originating country, assuming they are not quoting in US dollars.

Column 3

In each template I have used the currency indicated and multiplied the original currency by the indicated exchange rate to arrive at the USD, e.g., $42.00 × .60 = $27.30.

Column 4

I have added $12.00 USD to account for ocean freight, taxes, duty, associated container charges, overland freight and delivery to the warehouse. It is an arbitrary figure for this exercise, but you will find it is not over stating the costs from Australia and New Zealand, and many importers use this figure. You may choose a baseline landed cost that is specific to your region and use that instead. I would plus or minus it to allow for your own origin, destination and related costs and consider whether you add your markup before or after this inclusion. Gathering this information on specific clearances at the beginning, utilizing the billings from the customs broker, will help establish a reasonable cost and preclude surprises. Be particularly aware of whether you have a preponderance of sparkling wines, fortified or >14% alcohol. All of these can increase the duty considerably. From that point, establish one figure for subsequent shipments. Checking invoices periodically will determine if you remain on track, but using a different figure for every single shipment and every single brand is time consuming and not worth, in my opinion, the additional expense for the return.

Column 5

This assumes a markup of 35% for the importer. Again, you may configure it in another way, and in fact some importers use 30% and make a good living on large volume, some use a little more to allow for incentives. You are starting out with little volume and high overhead and will find this margin is eaten up quickly. However, I would caution you to be careful about getting greedy. The wine is worth or perceived to be worth something definable to the individual making the purchase. In addition to this rather nebulous rationale, there is plenty of opportunity for the distributor, retailer or consumer to use the internet to research its cost in its country of origin. Exchange rate notwithstanding, there is certain to be pushback if your end point—the retail—is too high.

You may take a stance, as an example, that the higher priced wines produce a higher dollar profit and therefore charge a lower percentage for those and 35% for the rest of the portfolio. You may decide to aim for a specific retail for the lower priced wines and cut the margin to reach that all important figure. It is up to you and I won't belabor it further. In your circumstance, consider what you have invested in the wine and what you intend to invest in travel, marketing, discounts for volume and free goods.

Column 6

Wholesaler and retailer markups enter a very grey area on any importer's spreadsheet. You can predetermine your own markup and this is your prerogative. You cannot dictate someone else's, except in rare situations, which we can get into later. I have used an arbitrary figure of 45% for the distributor markup. You will drive yourself mad if you start looking at every state's taxes, likely freight charges and other expenses that go to make up what is known as 'laid in costs.' A distributor may only mark up 33%, but by the time you add in the laid in costs, you have arrived at a point that is 45% from the wine they purchased from you.

Column 7 and 8

This also allows for a 45% markup. The same conditions apply for the retailer; he has laid in costs of his own and the markup might actually only be 25%, but at smaller, fine wine stores in high rent areas the markup could be 60%, *after* the laid in costs. I use 45% in both wholesale and retail columns to smooth out the differences a little. In current economic conditions it may be considered too low or too high. taking into consideration rising costs on one hand, and competition in a declining economy on the other, but it will get you to within sight of the actual retail. Over the years, markups have crept higher overall, perhaps because of the cost of fuel or salaries for salespeople. There are several states in which this would still be too low based on freight and state and local taxes, but usually not by more than $1–$2 a bottle at the retail end.

If you are particularly concerned with a magic retail number—< $10 or <$20, e.g.,—or achieving realistic glass pours, you may wish to hone your numbers further, speak to the winery about a bit of leeway, see what the distributor in a particular state has to say.

Most stores still price their wines with a .99 remainder—$7.99, $19.99, etc. The spreadsheets reflect the raw numbers reached by the calculations, but a retailer will normally take it to the next available .99. In the first sheet $8.80 becomes $8.99, $9.22 would most likely become $9.99, rather than the closer $8.99, because the margin is higher and as long as the wine is under $10 there is not a great deal of difference between $8.99 and $9.99, but it could still go either way. If they price it at the upper end it also enables them to offer a case discount or other promotional opportunity.

There are additional exceptions to these calculations. In Ohio, e.g., you can actually figure out quite accurately how the wine will sit at retail, because the State of Ohio sets its pricing and those who do business there must follow. In many states, being at $24.99 or $26.99 makes little difference to the ability to sell the wine. In Ohio, it is far better to price at $19.99 and $29.99 than somewhere in between. Their matrix looks like this:

$174.00 Wholesale FOB

$6.00 laid in costs (tax, freight)

$180.00 total

$360.00 case/retail by doubling the laid in wholesale

$29.99 bottle/retail

Or, if you look at Costco: at this time, their markup in the fine wine bins is 14%. They also expect, as well they should based on the volume and exposure they offer, that the distributor's price is the leanest it can be. This could result in a 10% discount from the distributor, based on a customary across the board pallet discount to their customers, or it can mean a price they arrive at to give them the most competitive advantage with this buyer. Clearly, it changes the retail dramatically. It will take a $21.99 wine down to $16.99 in most states and in the Ohio scenario it will mean the difference between $29.99 and $16.99!

What is readily apparent from the spreadsheets is that even a small change in exchange rate creates quite a different pricing scenario. Once you reach the Euro rate, the difference is marked and takes it from one pricing level to a completely different one. This must all be taken into consideration when setting your own prices. Build sufficient room in the price to allow, as much as possible, for the following factors:

- exchange rate fluctuations
- promotions—incentives, programming, contests, rewards
- sample usage—sales people, publications, spoilage
- overhead—whatever your own situation dictates, including travel and personnel

In addition, consider where you want the wine to "sit" as a price point on the shelf, or how well it might fit a glass pour in a restaurant.

Summary

These stories are told to illustrate the advantage of relying on your palate, your intuition, your research and your own circumstances in making decisions. It is something to weigh in your own career, whether or not you think you already have the best wines or insufficient gravitas, whether sales of an established brand were blockbuster or lackluster. These may influence your decision in a way that prevents you from seeing a clear picture. The new wine could turn out to be better than the best wine you currently have, or a dismal failure. Previous sales offer some indication of the immediate future, but are no barometer for the long term success of the brand.

My Story

I can give you two very good examples of wine selection that did *not* rely on two of the criteria that many new and seasoned importers use to determine a brand's value: ratings and history. In both cases, I relied on my own palate and intuition, something that is all too lacking in our industry these days. There is too much reliance on numbers as a criteria and a guaranteed history of sales on which to base future sales. I am not saying that either is not beneficial—clearly they are. But to build one's own portfolio on those criteria alone is to miss out on golden opportunities.

A few years ago, a competitor approached me to see if I was interested in taking on a brand he was giving up. This is a friend of mine and I knew he had the best of intentions. I had lost a couple of strong brands in the implosion of the greedy brand owner's business I alluded to earlier and this importer had a conflict. He represented two brands from the same area and one, a stronger and more reliable seller at the time, was applying some pressure to focus on their brand.

I looked at the brand. It had history—a great 'story' of family-owned vineyards in a renowned area and some interesting wines. The family was financially secure and was poised to increase volume. The wines themselves were not particularly strong, the ratings were mediocre at best, but they had potential. The young, energetic winemaker talked enthusiastically of his plans for the brand and assured me that the wines were only going to get better—more fruit-forward, more redolent of the character and style of the area. He also talked of what he wanted to do with some of the older plantings on the vigneron's land.

Quite frankly, if I had already possessed my own stable of stars I might not have been so ready to take on this brand, but in seeing the holes in my own portfolio and the potential of this brand, I decided it was a worthwhile opportunity. It turned out to be the best decision I ever made.

The quality did go from strength to strength, and although the old distributors had fallen away and I could not rely on them for a distribution base, sales increased and I added more selections to the range. The older plantings turned out to be arguably the oldest Shiraz vines in the world and although the yield from these vines was miniscule, it added cachet to the brand.

In two short vintages, one of the wines was rated higher than any wine *of its price point ever* in *Wine Spectator*. There was a feeding frenzy for this vintage and the other varietals and blends were drawn along with it. Sales skyrocketed and exposure for the portfolio was greatly increased. It has twice made the Top 100 Wines of the Year in *Wine Spectator*.

(continued)

My Story (Continued)

In the next story, the winemaker, a good friend of mine, formed his own brand with partners and produced one, small production, unusual cuvee, to launch in the States. He said I could have 200 six packs in the first year. I loved the wine, the label, the unusual blend, the price point and, just as importantly to me, the opportunity to work with these fine people. It was also a modest beginning and did not require a huge financial outlay from me.

I launched the brand without any ratings or reviews, and attracted some early interest. In a few months, the wine gained a couple of respectable ratings in two publications, but in today's market if it doesn't break the 90 point barrier it does not contribute to the wine's success. I continued to sell the wine based solely on the interest of the customers, my enthusiasm in presenting it and the story behind 'the little brand that could.' I asked for more allocation and ended up selling 1200 six packs that first year—easily three-quarters of their production—all without resounding national reviews. I also credit others with thinking outside the box in making their buying decisions and contributing to the success of this wine's national sales.

And finally, a story of when I didn't just ignore my gut instinct, I failed to even check in with it. In the first two examples, all went happily right, because it was a reasonable risk, based on the evidence of my palate, coupled with attractive pricing. In those days, at least, before the economy went to hell in a hand basket, you could rely on finding markets for solid, well priced wines. I came across an individual who was well connected to Hollywood, a lovely man with an equally engaging wife, both film directors and producers. Their story was unique and intriguing and I felt sure I could rely on the couple's connections to sell the wine, at least in California. In addition, they had retained a respected vineyard consultant to plant their beautiful property and a recognized, if pricey, winemaker to make the wines. The downside? The wines were from esoteric varietals and expensive and, quite frankly, I wasn't that crazy about them. I overrode red flags in my zeal to represent a brand that appeared to be courted by others, something I felt would sell on reputation and connections alone, and my ego got in the way.

Needless to say, the wines were not a success. I believe if they had been priced much more realistically, they could have stood a chance. There were LA restaurants that clearly wanted to make that connection for the prestigious brand owners, but balked every time at the price. In the end, this was a valuable lesson about not allowing emotion to override practicality.

8

IT'S ON THE WATER— MAXIMIZE YOUR TIME

If your terms with the winery start at B/L, then the clock is ticking as soon as that ship leaves the dock in the port of origin. It is to your advantage to begin making good use of your time while waiting for the shipment and there are many tasks ahead of you, both in terms of organization and sales.

Winery Marketing Materials

At this stage, we will operate on the premise that the wines are brand new and you have no U.S. ratings. As I have stated before, I don't believe this is a detriment to your sales at all. Most people do not wait for a *Wine Advocate* rating before they commit to a wine. The release timing for publications these days seems to be counterintuitive to this approach anyway. For example, the Australian issue, originally slated for an October release in time for holiday buying, was last released in February. Ratings are a boon, there is no doubt, and quite possibly an essential tool in most U.S. markets, but remember in the beginning you selected the wines for your portfolio based on criteria *other* than a U.S. rating. Now you must do the groundwork to ensure their successful release without a rating net.

Most winery owners will point proudly to the trophy they were awarded at the local wine show, the five stars they garnered in an obscure publication, accolades they received from the home town wine stores. And of course they should be proud. These are barometers of the wines desirability and worth on a national level. They mean absolutely nothing to the U.S. industry professional or consumer.

There are always exceptions to every rule. If the gold medal is from a show that has international recognition, the rating is in a publication such as Decanter, Great Britain's most significant wine magazine and widely available in the U.S., James Halliday's Wine Companion or Michael Cooper's Buyer's Guide, or the recommendation from Master of Wine and renowned writer, Jancis Robinson, then the rules are slightly different. Sadly, they don't ultimately replace the U.S. ratings, but they are a providential boost to the wine in the early days, a reasonable precursor of how well it will do when it does appear in a U.S. publication and an immediate marketing tool.

In the meantime, what does the winery have? Brochures? Printed material on the winery? Tasting notes? Lists of medals, awards and favorable reviews? All of these can be utilized in the quest for sales.

Brochures and background materials can speak of the professionalism of the winery, the history—or perhaps just 'story'—behind the vineyard operation, the credentials of the winemaker, the open faces of the family. By themselves, these aspects will not sell the wine. Together with the perfect storm of packaging, style, price and rapport with you, it will begin to build a foundation for the distributor and a desire to get behind the brand.

Tasting notes are essential to your operation. Ideally a few full-color copies will come to you in a press kit, complete with bottle shot and good technical information, which will be followed with a jpeg or PDF document for ease of printing and transmitting. But, I've also had them emailed to me in garbled run-on, unformatted plain text and I've had them dictated to me from the top of a tractor in a foggy pasture early in the morning. If they are not already in a tasting note/tech sheet format, you must put together something you can send to your potential customers, or use in a tasting for reference.

Winemakers are as individual as people in any profession and they tend to compose notes in individual ways, sometimes as bare technical data and sometimes as a fluffy PR piece that would be interesting to a consumer at cellar door, but virtually useless to someone in the field. Technical data, tasting notes and viticulture and vinification should ideally be kept to one sheet. Whatever else you learn about the vineyard, through observation, education and additional notes can be stored for your own tastings and presentations.

I find the following details to be helpful, for which I have included one type of example for each. This is an example only. There are many other ways that the more subjective areas can be characterized and described and much of the information would be lumped together in sections:

1. Synopsis of conditions for that vintage, including anything that made it particularly difficult or particularly favorable.

   The climate is characterized by hot summer days and relatively cool nights with diurnal ranges of up to 26 degrees Celsius. The 2002 season was an exceptional vintage, long and warm with cool nights, which is reflected in the wine. The summer/autumn rainfall was low.

2. When grapes were picked and how.

   Grapes were harvested by hand. Each clone of fruit was harvested separately and kept separate at all stages of vinification. The fruit was destemmed, with some batches having a percentage of whole clusters retained.

3. Yield.

   The vineyard is trellised on a Geneva double curtain and spur pruned to 10 shoots per metre. It is extensively thinned to 6 tonnes per hectare.

4. Varietal, including percentages of blended grapes, no matter how small—the purpose being to identify what is in the wine, not complying with a legal requirement.

   Cabernet Sauvignon 72%, Merlot 23% Petit Verdot 5%

5. Where grown (estate, sourced, steep slope, soil, etc.)

Soils are free-draining river gravels.

6. Fermentation process.

The must then underwent 3–5 days of pre-ferment maceration after which it was warmed to 17 degrees and inoculated for fermentation. Most batches were pressed off at dryness while some were left on skins for 7–8 days.

7. Aging, including type of oak if oak aged

14 months in seasoned French oak.

8. Other details of interest, such as whether it was fined and filtered, whether the grapes were organically or biodynamically grown, etc.

Sourced from 90 year old bush grown vines in the northeast of the valley.

All fruit was organically grown on the estate and certified by Certified Organic Farmers.

9. Description of wine characteristics such as color, weight, flavors, finish—this is a very subjective area that becomes a bow to the winemaker's own style, which can be short and succinct or flowery hyperbole.

Color—Intense garnet

Aroma—A very attractive Cabernet which doffs its cap to the great wines of Bordeaux. Earthy and complex, it oozes ripe blackberries and black cherry fruit. Developed cigar box character and vanillin oak mingle pleasantly with nuances of cloves and star anise.

Palate—A stylish palate that offers loads of ripe fruit, but avoids jamminess. It has terrific flavor persistence, complexity, fine elegant texture and oak integration. A wonderful example of cool climate Cabernet at its best.

10. Technical data, such as that which relates to a particular wine

Sulphur dioxide at bottling—Total (ppm)	42
pH	3.40
Acid (g/L)	6.80
C6 Sugars (g/L)	0
Alcohol (%)	13.9

11. If appropriate, i.e., of a higher standard, a SUMMARY of medals, awards and trophies

Gold Medal—Cowra Wine Show

Decanter—Top 100 Wines of 2008

Silver Medal—Royal Melbourne Wine Show

Five Stars—James Halliday

12. food pairing suggestions, which are at the discretion of the winemaker—not essential by any means, but often an interesting—and unusual!—guide

Try this with aged beef and a reduced red wine sauce. However we have been known to drink it with garfish, salads and paella and makes for a sensational celebration regardless of a meal!

This is a lengthy list, but as you can see, some aspects can be handled in a word or number. Ultimately, the more comprehensive it can be, the better prepared you are to discuss the wines in an informed and knowledgeable fashion. I also include a bottle shot of label graphic. A tasting note/tech sheet can be in many different styles, but none of that is important (beyond being neat and clear) as long as it includes much or all of the essential information (see Figure 8.1). You can find other examples in the "trade" section of many winery or importer websites.

Figure 8.1   Example of a Technical Sheet

Setting up a Website

Whether you are a webmaster or have only used your computer skills to navigate your way around the internet, a website is an essential tool for an importer. Budgetary constraints—or not—will dictate the scope of your site, but if you have the time, inclination and a limited budget, it is extremely easy to put together a credible and useful site utilizing the inexpensive templates of companies such as Go Daddy at www.godaddy.com or Network Solutions at www.networksolutions.com. They can look customized, informative and appealing, with very little expense.

The work you put into it initially will be offset by the following benefits:

1. Credibility. A website says you have some stability and shows clients and customers the wines you carry.

2. A mission statement that clearly states your objectives and philosophy, which gives assurances to your clients and encourages prospective wineries to consider your representation.

3. Trade tools for your distributors and their sales people. This is a lifesaver when sales people are looking for assistance in their sales endeavors, and provides information for their own marketing materials. It often saves them from calling you to send or email the information, or gives them last minute material to download and print for an event.

4. News and updated reviews and ratings can give distributors the edge in selling and alert them to new vintages or exciting new brand arrivals, or when items are sold out or in limited supply.

Although the site should be attractive and welcoming, my suggestion is not to become too ambitious with graphics, Flash, large file sizes or audio on your website. You want a site that is easy and quick to load, doesn't require too many maneuvers to navigate away from scenes and audio intros, and each area or page can be accessed with a simple click of a mouse.

Bookkeeping, Invoicing, Forms and Inventory Management

Setting up your general ledger and chart of accounts for tracking financial activity should be undertaken in the early stages of your business establishment, once you have decided what type of legal entity you are going to be. It can, and often should, be handled by an outside service, depending upon your level of expertise and that of office employees, if any. The Small Business Administration www.sba.org is a wonderful resource for small businesses, and the experienced retired professionals at SCORE www.score.org can offer advice and direction from their real world experience and qualifications. The definition on their site is:

> *Counselors to America's Small Business is a nonprofit association dedicated to educating entrepreneurs and the formation, growth and success of small business nationwide. SCORE is a resource partner with the U.S. Small Business Administration (SBA).*

In addition to mentoring, advice and training, they offer inexpensive workshops on a regular basis on financial statements, setting up a small business, QuickBooks and many other subjects.

Purchase orders, invoices, statements, accounts receivable, inventory management, sales history, invoice ageing—all very important tools once established—can easily be linked to the financial side through a program like QuickBooks Premier: Manufacturing and Wholesale Edition, from Intuit. It is a comprehensive program that covers all aspects of conducting business for an importer and distributor. It is not designed purely for this field, in fact it is a generic program for a myriad of businesses, but it will ably fill all your requirements. There are programs more suited to winery operations, where, in addition to distribution of their product they also have to keep track of vineyard operations, harvest, production, etc., and perhaps other proprietary systems that I may not be familiar with, but this is the definitive tool for all your needs, in my view and a relatively inexpensive program.

Set up can be a steep learning curve and I urge you to begin as soon as possible. The earlier you start capturing information, the less catch up you have to do later on by inputting items that have already been processed and stored elsewhere. It will soon become an invaluable and straightforward tool for access to the types of reports you need to run your business and manage your customers and vendors.

Purchase order quantities to the vineyard can now be used to set up inventory. At this stage it will be inventory in transit, which will then easily convert to inventory received, upon arrival. Tracking inventory in QuickBooks is optional, in my opinion. It depends upon several issues and can be the one aspect that is cumbersome to track consistently. It will require diligent attention to recording every movement of a case or bottle and mistakes may take a while to unravel. If you have multiple locations, will be storing all product yourself, or have a desire for this level of organization and order, then this may work well for you. It will allow you to know immediately when a product is low, or insufficient to supply a particular order. On the other hand, commercial warehousing companies offer real time product information on line these days and data such as item inventory, open and shipped orders can be accessed daily or as often as you like.

At whatever stage you are setting up your books, you will want to include a customized template for the forms you will be using and there is very little in this arena that could be as important as the invoice—the means by which you will bill and collect monies owed. A company invoice should have preprinted boxes or line items for the following information:

- Company name and contact details
- Date
- Purchase order number (assigned by your customer, the distributor)
- Invoice number (establish a working system to track easily—could be dated, e.g., 09-0001, numbered, e.g., 0001 or by state, e.g., CA-0001—or anything else, as long as it is something that makes sense to you)
- Ship to
- Bill to
- Terms
- FOB point
- Due Date

- Item
- Description
- Quantity
- Rate (cost per case)
- Total per item quantity
- Total owed on invoice

Optionally, it can include:

- A preprinted message to your customer thanking them for the order or specific directive
- A preprinted statement as to how past due bills will be handled, i.e., interest or penalty
- Sufficient room for messages that apply only to that invoice, e.g., "short 4 cases of '07 cabernet sauvignon—will ship with next order."

Aside from the one I have provided, several examples of invoices can be found in QuickBooks and modified to cover the above items and any others you may need.

Warehouse & Customs Broker Notification and Arrangements

Warehouse Notification

With all the warehouse review, selection and licensing in place, you will have met and spoken with the warehouse personnel sufficiently at this stage to establish the start of another important relationship. These are the people who will handle all your goods in-house and arrange for their disbursement around the country. Treating them with courtesy and consideration from the outset will make life a great deal easier when you run into problems, incorrect inventory and mistakes. They will go above and beyond for you if they feel you respect what they do.

Notifying them of an impending shipment arrival is not only courteous, it saves you and them considerable time in scheduling and potential delays in receiving the goods. Individual entities can tell you of their own requirements, but at the least you should send them a list of each item, including brand, varietal/blend, size of individual container and number per box.

For example:

Cassowary 2008 Cabernet/Merlot 12/750ml	20 cases
Billy Bob 2009 Botrytis Semillon 6/375ml	10 cases

And so on. This ensures that the warehouse easily identifies the item and counts and segregates appropriately. It also helps to avoid mistakes, such as assuming that the entire pallet is one wine, simply because the outside cases all look the same. Giving the warehouse a heads up also allows them to plan its arrival and put the delivery in a queue.

Overland Container Transport

This is also the time to consider what trucking company you will use to transport the container from port to warehouse. It has to be a trucking company that specializes in this type of transport, rather than small truckloads or local pickup and deliveries. Warehouses often either have their own logistical arm, or can recommend a carrier. Customs brokers can do the same. As with everything else, do your due diligence to compare costs and references. Give them a chance with a couple of containers to see if they are communicative, deliver on time and follow up diligently. If you see a pattern of disinterest or chronic delays, move on quickly to someone else.

Customs Clearance

At this stage, you have the necessary COLAs, invoices, shipping docs and bills of lading to submit electronically to your customs broker while the container is on the water and they can begin the clearing process. The easiest way to effect this is with *express clearance*. It allows a pre-clearance of goods before arrival through the normal U.S. Customs channels, and decreased potential waiting time at dock. If the customs broker encounters any problems with documents or the information you have provided, there is presumably plenty of time to rectify the issue before docking.

By contracting for your own FCL, this is the stage where you have the most control over the process through clearance and transit to warehouse. Through express clearance, booking a trucking company and alerting the warehouse ahead of time, you have streamlined the process, cutting days off the schedule, and shaved weeks off the time it would take with an LCL container.

Pre-Selling

This is an optional, but potentially important early task, if you have the necessary wines and connections. The winery may elect to airfreight wine ahead of the container for you to use in interesting potential distributors and jump starting the order process. Air freight is a fairly expensive proposition, however, and may not be feasible, or the winery may be reluctant to continue to eat into their margin. In later containers, new release wines can be put in the container along with your order and save the winery the expense of an air shipment. You will be paying for the freight on the samples in the container, as opposed to the winery paying for the air freight, but the cost is negligible and you will most likely receive far more in the monetary value of samples with your ocean freight than you would have via air.

It is important to put these wines to good use. If you have identified, or worked with, a viable distributor who expresses interest, knows the pricing and has some idea of the style and type of wine, then this is most likely an excellent use of samples. If you are simply contacting random distributors from the phone book or without thorough vetting, they may be wasted. Most wholesalers don't have the time or inclination to tell an importer to send them product they have no intention of representing, but the idly curious may do so. And even worse, the less scrupulous companies may do so, simply to drink free wine.

We'll get into the distributor search process more in the later section of the book, which will apply both in pre-selling and finding long-term distribution. It's all the same as far as you are concerned. You are not looking for a one time sale; you're looking for a working relationship.

Submitting to Publications

Depending upon the number of samples you receive ahead of time, if any, this is an excellent time to submit to national publications. Most publications will require two samples, and recently some of them have agreed to just one bottle if under screw cap. You should call and check on the requirements. You should also call and request to be put on email notifications of these major publications:

Wine Spectator

Wine Enthusiast

Wine & Spirits

They will notify you of the tasting deadlines for each country or specialty editions: reds, whites, Pinots of the Northwest, e.g., and will also send you forms to download and print to submit with the samples. Each publication's requirements will vary as to whether they want tasting notes, suggested retail pricing, production or number of cases imported, or if an extensive history is helpful, along with viticultural practices and winemaker's notes. The forms will provide the information they require.

If you have limited samples, my suggestion is to submit to *Wine Spectator* first. I say this without bias, only that it is the most widely read, visible consumer wine publication if you are choosing only one publication for review at this time. It is also a review that retailers will give the nod to for an estimation of quality and worthy of attributing to a shelf talker, the ubiquitous cards that front the bottle in a retail wine store.

Wine Enthusiast is accorded noteworthy status in some circles and others find it too lenient in its scores. *Wine & Spirits* would possibly be the least weighted of the three publications in general, I would say, although it is also widely available in stores and, as far as I am concerned, is a credible opportunity for great scores (if applicable) that makes a nice quote and looks good on shelf talkers.

You will undoubtedly find many and varied opinions regarding the significance of each publication's rating and the reviewer, "oh, she only likes cool climate wines" or "he's a Bordeaux fanatic," but you can find value in submitting to these, as a start, and to build up name recognition. It is, after all, free, with the exception of the cost of the wine and shipping.

There are many other publications to which to submit, most notably The *Wine Advocate* (see Figure 8.2). To many wine savvy collectors it has enjoyed iconic status that is unequaled in the wine world and they will buy only on its recommendation. There is an entire, very active internationally read bulletin board on the web started and run by Mark Squires, one of The *Wine Advocate*'s reviewers. The publication itself is a scholarly looking periodical that accepts no advertising and is only available via subscription. It has only so many pages to its issue and therefore not all wines will make it into the publication. It has also had the reputation of only reviewing notable or established portfolios, so the opportunity to review your new wines in your new portfolio might best be reserved as a next step, maybe not the first step.

Robert Parker used to be the final arbiter of reviews of all countries, but recently, after many years, has turned over regions to others—very fine, educated and experienced wine experts. This has done three things: 1) opened up the tastings to more wines and a broader base of each country or region, 2) broadened the range of reviewer palates and 3) given the devotees a wait and see attitude about the future of its iconic status and whether, without Robert Parker's personal endorsement of each and every wine, the rating has the same impact and prestige. To some extent in the short term, it has inevitably diluted the value of the rating.

In terms of submissions, you may send one bottle of each wine directly to The *Wine Advocate*'s offices, along with whatever information you feel would best serve the wine, or you may request a face-to-face tasting so that you have a chance to discuss the wines, vineyard, region and stories with the reviewer in person. This necessitates traveling to the reviewer's location, but can be well worthwhile at the right time. Initially, I would suggest making judicious use of your samples and consider where they will

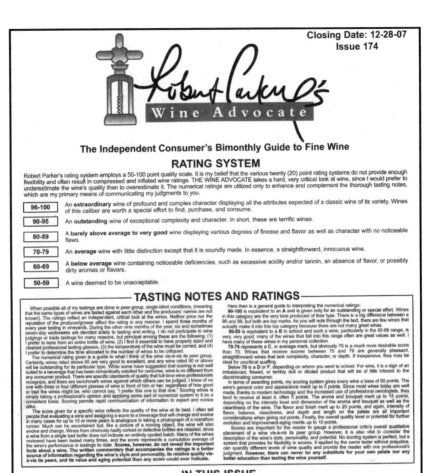

Figure 8.2   *Wine Advocate*

have the most potential, and immediate impact. Unless, of course, you have taken on an iconic brand with a history of high *Wine Advocate* ratings, and a likelihood of more high ratings, given the wine's consistently strong quality. I would not bother sending generic, inexpensive wines that may have value and purpose for you, but are not likely to be the types of wines that will make it into those limited page issues.

There are several other media channels for submissions, depending upon your country's origin, notably Burghound (for Burgundy) and Stephen Tanzer's International Wine Cellar. Both of these are esteemed online review outlets and a favorable review and rating in one of these will be well respected by the trade.

In the case of most publications, expect to wait at least six months for a review to appear. This is why it is helpful to be able to shorten your wait by submitting before the wine has reached the U.S. shore.

In the case of *Wine Spectator* and *Wine Advocate*, an online subscription, in addition to, or instead of, a magazine subscription, is advisable. This will allow you to receive advance notification of issues and you can easily check a review and rating. From *Wine Spectator* you will receive advance notice of issues and "insider" reviews, and it is advisable to periodically search for ratings for your wines in the event they have listed a "web only" review. This is not as helpful as having it in the print publication, because of the lack of consumer exposure, but if it is a high rating it is just as valuable to you as a shelf talker and PR tool. Make sure to track your package to verify it is received. If you are waiting for a review and have not seen anything within six months, I suggest calling to check. They will not give you much in the way of specific information, but can certainly advise you as to the physical status of your shipment, such as it has been reviewed and expected to be in an upcoming issue, or you will learn if it has somehow been misplaced. This is rare, but has happened to me. They will not give you a rating over the phone.

In the event of a high rating, you will be aware of the status of your wine without enquiring, because *Wine Spectator* will call you to request a label to include with the review (free of charge) and *Wine Enthusiast* and *Wine & Spirits* will alert you via email to the rating and whether you wish to submit a label (for an advertising fee) as an accompaniment to your review.

Some people are of the opinion that a good rating in *Wine Enthusiast* and *Wine &
Spirits* is dependent upon this advertising supplement, but I have rarely ever exercised
this option and still received some very high reviews. They notify you of the rating
prior to their solicitation for a label fee. Others will say that *Wine Spectator* gives favor
to the big advertisers in their publication, but I have also had some very high ratings in
this magazine and never advertised. I think the personal palate bias that is inescapable
in any taster's review of a wine has more to do with the rating variable than anything
else. Certainly a wine is either well made or deficient, true to its varietal, its heritage
and expectations of the vintage, but after that there has to be, even in some indefin-
able, unconscious way, a tendency to rate higher or lower because the wine fits, or does
not, the style the reviewer enjoys most. So be it. It's an imperfect system, but it is so
heavily relied upon that we must, for the time being, incorporate it into our marketing
plans and rejoice when we receive an exalted rating.

Conversely, when the rating is poor in one publication, or these days below 90, we
can elect not to use it in our PR efforts, or pick out a choice phrase or two to quote. It
will usually be forgotten and perhaps another publication will be more positive. It
becomes a game at times, but occasionally we're firing on all cylinders in all publications and the consensus among our potential customers is overwhelmingly favorable. In
that case, we're on the way towards building a highly sought-after brand.

Summary

The point of this time between P.O. and arrival is to take advantage of it to approach
tasks in a cost-effective, efficient and well organized way and keep building that solid
foundation from which you construct a successful wine business. Don't cut corners and
don't wing it during this time. There is too much to do and too many areas in which
you can run afoul of authorities, or create unnecessary backtracking and delays for
yourself. You may think of this period as the last opportunity to take a break before
you really have to get down to work, but it is really the perfect time to get this out of
the way before turning your attention to the real business of selling.

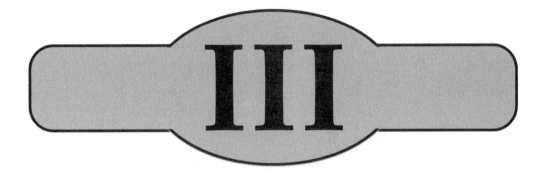

9

DISTRIBUTION— THE FIRST STAGES

Whether you are in the first stages of looking for a distributor or the latter stages, the point is to find the finest candidate to represent your wine at the next level (that second tier on the three tier system), with the greatest chance for long term success. It is not something to plunge into lightly, desperately or with a laissez-faire attitude. As with most things in life, there are no short cuts. You either go for immediate gratification: a quick sale that could be the only one you get, or a well researched approach that sets the stage for an enduring, mutually beneficial relationship.

Narrowing the Search for the Right Distributors

Now, I'm not suggesting that, despite all your efforts, each and every distributor choice is right forever. Some are right for where you are at that particular time, or some are right only as long as they remain the type of company they were when you found them. Some get too big, some struggle to pay the bills, management changes, focus realigns. These are the inevitable evolutionary journeys businesses take. But if you don't at least do your homework at the beginning, you can not only be doomed to failure, but at best you will spend more time playing catch-up, making allowances for their shortcomings and giving them second, third and fourth chances, while the months tick by. So, what should you look for?

- A company with the same general business philosophy as yours.
- A financially sound business.
- Terms that are reasonable—i.e., 30-60 days and they stick to it (preferably 30 days, but there are exceptions we will get into later).
- One that covers the geographical area you are looking for—whether that is three adjoining states or only one county in one state.
- Management that communicates well and is accessible.
- A company that has a plan to invest in your brand(s) and is willing to take a position across the board, instead of cherry-picking.
- Not necessarily a company that will take *all* your brands, if you have taken on more than three or four, but one that is willing to look at representing a healthy segment of your portfolio.
- A company that fits what you represent—e.g. small, organically farmed, bio-dynamic, estate grown, or obscure French chateaux—and has the skill and expertise to represent the wines appropriately.
- Focused management and sales people.
- A portfolio that may include some of the country or region you represent, but is not saturated.
- A company not so large that you, presumably the small, new importer, doesn't get lost amid the demands and quotas forced upon them by the big brands.

How do you find these paragons of virtue, these business soul mates? If you are coming from some other sector of the wine industry, you should definitely take advantage of the connections, relationships and acquaintances you have made and mine them for information and assistance. These particular individuals or companies may not be what you seek, but like six degrees of separation may know someone who knows someone who is. This may start the chain of referrals to an obscure distributor or someone who may just be looking for what you represent. Very often, as in a job search, you call your acquaintance Jill, who happens not to have an opening. She refers you to Joe at ABC Wine Distribution and when you call Joe, you mention Jill's name and this immediately opens the door to a conversation, which may not find you a job, but takes you to Bob…and so it goes.

Having prior experience working for an importer, distributor or retailer gives you specialized knowledge and some advantage in the search. It also shows you who you would *not* want to be in partnership with.

- **As a retail** employee, did one wholesale company stand out as having a series of lazy sales people who didn't last long, rarely came by and when they did, begged you for a sale because they needed to meet a quota? Did the salesperson seem ill-prepared or lacking in knowledge?

- **As a distributor** sales rep yourself, your inside knowledge of the company you worked for may have made you aware of how they sloughed off their importer supplier, or gave too many excuses as to why they hadn't sold through a vintage, when in reality the wine was collecting dust in the warehouse. Did the company discourage giving sales reps samples, or were stingy with allowances, making it difficult for the rep to do an effective job?

- **As an importer**'s employee, you knew distributors first hand and while there may be some type of non-compete in place to preclude you doing business with this importer's customers, the experience you had with these companies demonstrate what to look for in partnering with your own distributor.

For the new importer, armed with the tools and guidelines from this book, but who may not have been in the field before, the starting search is much like it will be further down the line. Some of the methods I myself have employed are these:

Google wineries you respect, whose wines you enjoy, are of high quality, may be from a similar region (thereby ensuring a distributor's familiarity with this region) or which may simply have been on your radar for some time as having grown quickly, because you see more and more of them on the shelves. Many of them will list distributors in different states. Print out this list or copy down the ones you wish to start with.

Start looking for trends among the distributor names. Is there crossover? This may indicate a discerning wholesaler, or it may indicate a full portfolio, but it's a point of reference.

Figure 9.1   © David Pike

Discard, for now, the behemoth wholesale houses. I do not mean to disparage them—and don't we all wish for their degree of success—just as I would not denigrate *Two Buck Chuck* or *Yellow Tail*. Who among us would not want the income produced from their volume? However, they are much less likely to be receptive to a new, unseasoned importer and you may well spend valuable time spinning your wheels waiting for callbacks, responses to samples shipped for evaluation, etc. They also have their mistresses, and they are legion—the brands to whom they owe their size and their success and will always come first.

Now look with a discriminating eye at the distributors' websites from your list.

- How professional, updated and friendly is the website?
- What other brands do they represent (Google to check them out as well)?
- How big is the portfolio?

- What other importers' portfolios do they represent?
- How well does it fit your own style, brands, regions?
- What is their mission statement and how well does it reflect yours?

Another approach is to contact fine wine stores, well known retailers or retailers you have researched that carry wines of the type/style/price point/region that gives you confidence. Ask them which distributor *they* like dealing with. I've done this on many occasions when a retailer has emailed me looking for one of my wines and I haven't had distribution in their state. I will respond that I would love to supply them with the particular wine, but unfortunately it is not available in their state and do they have a recommendation? In almost all cases, the person has responded with at least one suggestion, and sometimes several, including reasons for their recommendations.

These are all guides at first, but give you far more information than if you were to randomly take a name from a phone book or look up companies in an industry reference book. Or just wonder how on earth you begin.

The next step is to call one of these targeted companies and find out who makes decisions regarding new wine purchases, if the website has not indicated a clear contact. Unless you're engaged in the "Jill gave me your name" process, this is very much cold calling at this stage and can be daunting, frustrating and unfulfilling. But if you speak with someone, or get their voice mail, try to personalize it. Show them you've sought them out for a reason. If applicable, tell them that such-and-such retail store recommended them. Let them know you really like the way their website is set up, their mission statement, or the quality of the wines in their portfolio. Do they carry wines of your region? If so, let them know why yours would be a good fit. If not, this is an opportunity to see if they might like to fill a void. Let them see a glimpse of your personality, your expertise in the area, a reason that they might want to initiate a new relationship. Don't keep them on the phone forever, or take up their whole voice mail memory; refine your pitch so that it is friendly, informational, engaging and succinct. This is a sales pitch, to a degree, and, usually, you only have one chance to make a good first impression.

If you are not able to reach the purchaser/principal when you call, my suggestion is to call back at least once. Speaking with someone is far easier if they are not required to return your call. Many will, and they do so with pride, irrespective of their response or particular wine needs. They know that what you are doing is difficult and put themselves in your shoes. I respect that immensely. I think it's also indicative of the quality of the individual. However, people are also out of the country, very busy, working with a deadline, not given the message, or sick. So if you left a voice mail message, persevere a bit and see where it goes. Be systematic in your line of attack. Don't call too soon, or let too much time elapse.

I rely heavily on the Tasks component of Microsoft Outlook to record my calls, emails and general activity, especially as it relates to sales efforts. You would be surprised at how quickly time goes by, or how easily you can forget whether it was this or that company you called and the result. I have kept this for years, including a folder labeled *Inactive Potentials* for those I have contacted in the past and it led nowhere, or had a negative experience with the company (e.g. sent them copious samples and no one responded to numerous follow up calls). You may find you can resurrect one or more of these because circumstances have changed, or sufficient time elapsed. In any event, it's helpful to have the records as a reference point.

Following the Distribution Trail

At the point you elicit an expression of interest, this will most likely be in the form of a request for an emailed FOB price list, or a snail mailed press kit. These days, it is almost always an email. Be prepared to submit a professional, well-organized and informative attachment. Do not bombard the recipient's email box with huge files or multiple attachments. If not included on your FOB, send one or two additional attachments to show a label or particularly impressive press from credible sources. "*Wine of the Year!*" "*Highly Recommended,*" "*94 points...Editor's Choice*" type of thing. But try, if possible, to include pertinent details on your FOB and avoid the additional attachments.

Refer the potential customer to your website for more information. Show them how informational and helpful this site will be for them as your new distributor. Be brief in the body of the email, and personable. Tell them you look forward to hearing from them.

And then wait. Until several days have elapsed and then you may email them with a polite "Just checking to make sure my FOB came through on your email" or "You may not have had a chance to look at my FOB, but wondering if you have any questions." Many times, the recipient will tell you they had meant to, and glad you reminded them, or he or she intended to find the time to go over the list with the sales manager and to email them again on Friday. Other times, it is not on their radar or they are putting out unexpected fires. This is not the time to be annoyingly persistent. This will signal to the potential customer that you will be even more annoyingly persistent when they become your actual distribution partner.

There is no realistic short cut through this process, unless you happen to have a brand that has already demonstrated it is eminently desirable, or has achieved national recognition for a spectacular rating in a major publication. Then they'll cold call *you*.

Some time has passed, weeks, months, years…it all starts to run together after a while, and finally the distributor requests samples. Hallelujah! Now we're making progress. Not so fast. Yes, this is a good sign, a very good sign. As I've pointed out, most distributors, and certainly any reputable, honorable ones, will not request samples if they do not intend to give serious consideration to your portfolio. However, it is another stage of the journey and the destination is not yet in sight.

Consider which items you will send in response to the request. Unless they have specified, after reviewing your list, exactly which wines they wish to preview, make a one case (12 bottle) selection based on what will be most representative of your portfolio. You may only have 8 wines at this stage, so send them all 8. They all need homes. But if you have 40 wines spread over 8 brands, consider your choices carefully. Don't make the mistake of sending all top-end, to impress them. They want to see a cross-section of each brand, something indicative of the style and quality of the brand overall. They will want answers to the same criteria questions you posed to yourself at the outset, regarding QPR, packaging, etc. Don't send all reds, just because you think they will be weightier and more serious, unless the distributor specifically makes the request. Send a balance of reds and whites, again to show the versatility of your portfolio.

If you have more of an idea of their needs from conversation, this will influence your sample selection. In terms of South America, they may be more interested in

Chile than Argentina, e.g., certain price points, restaurant wines, cooler climate, and so on. Pay attention, respond accordingly and they will appreciate it.

More waiting is bound to ensue. They say they must find the time for a sales meeting to gather the team together in a democratic process. As I've been told on several occasions, "they are the ones who must go out and sell the wines; therefore I need them on board from the outset." That's not how behemoth distributors operate, of course, but then you're trying hard to find a more compatible, friendlier match and one in which you will presumably receive some attention after the initial sale.

They may have more wines in the office to taste through than they at first envisioned and want to do them all justice. There can be any number of reasons why this will again become a somewhat protracted process. Which is why you always want to start the distributor search as early as possible, and pre-selling while the container is on the water is one way to do that. Make sure you have a system of checking and following up at each stage. It is the only way you are going to ensure that it doesn't get away from you and turn into months instead of weeks.

The value of holding inventory in a recognizable warehouse will become apparent as you are about to receive your first order from this customer and they ask where it can be picked up. The relief at knowing they don't have to make special arrangements and incur additional expense is almost palpable over the phone. It is somewhere they go frequently and can add this to their order, or their trucking company can incorporate it into their regular routine.

What They are Looking For—
Are You on the Same Page

There is no magical answer to this question. It always goes back to what your expectations are, and what they are willing to deliver. It can vary from individual to individual and change with circumstances, but whatever it is, the key to a harmonious relationship is clearly communicated objectives and aspirations. Don't be desperate. This is too important. Don't hope—like entering a marriage—that you can "change" that individual in the future. Whatever they are now, is what they are likely to manifest towards you as you proceed.

On occasion, you will find a distributor who is only interested in "cherry picking" your line-up, i.e. taking only the very best item of a brand or only one brand from your portfolio, because that's the one with the eye-catching ratings. This should not only be discouraged, but avoided, unless it is a wine in good supply and suits your program. It is understandable that you would want to secure distribution with a live body now that you have one, but remember this is a long term proposition. Is the distributor who ordered the one 95 rated wine in your portfolio going to drop you the following year when the rating for that one wine drops?

The wholesaler you choose, who in turn chooses you, should be making a reasonable effort to invest in your wines across the board. It demonstrates fair play and a willingness to look at a long term plan. This does not necessarily mean they should order a comparable amount of each wine, but a good faith effort is required. They may be surprised at the result and continue to purchase more and more of the other wines, especially when the highly rated one has been allocated and quickly sold out. During the recession, some additional flexibility may be needed on your part to establish business and weather a challenging economy, but in general this is good advice to follow.

Does this distributor rely heavily on restaurant placements? Is this a good thing, because your wines are esoteric, require hand-selling and tend to be far better when paired with food? Or do they have supermarket or chain store relationships, which better suits your lower priced, daily quaffing wines that need to be sold in volume to make your margins more attractive? Their focus and their experience are important components on the decision making path.

Vetting the Distributor

The evidence of their interest really only becomes clear when they indicate a desire to place an order. Until that point, they may like the wines, be only marginally interested, not have room now but could have in future, or they are just looking at annual projections to see if they can incorporate your wines into their budget. Before this order, but after an expression of substantial interest, ask them if they would fill out a credit report and provide references. These references should include a couple of their vendors, but more importantly, their other winery customers. Of course they are going to give you their best customers, but the information you glean from this winery's answers will allow you to determine whether it is a reasonable risk.

- How long have they been supplying the distributor?
- How frequent are the orders?
- What is the size of the orders?
- What terms do they have with this winery?
- How well do they adhere to these terms?
- Are there any other issues they have with the distributor that could be helpful to know?

You would be surprised at what people will tell you.

Don't make it so onerous that you deter them from completing it at all, but sufficiently thorough to establish your professionalism. Include the following items (see Figure 9.2), but refine it further to suit your needs:

Include a statement regarding your terms, and interest penalty, if any, on unpaid balances. The industry, as a whole, is very much about handshake business and contracts between importer and distributor are rare, but this does not mean you should neglect good business practices in evaluating a credit risk.

If a wholesaler is brand new, has no previous credit history or references, I suggest you ask for an LC from the company, or at least make a determination, based on some information, such as banking references and/or prior business history, to extend a manageable line of credit for the first order and limit your financial exposure. You could also ask for a deposit with the balance strictly in 30 days. All of these options will depend upon the circumstances you are faced with and to what degree you can logically feel comfortable with the arrangement. Do not fall prey to the idea that no one else will want your wines and you had better take this opportunity—sort of like marrying someone because you think no one else will have you, only to endure an inevitably messy and expensive divorce.

```
CREDIT APPLICATION

Date:

Business name:                              License:
Type of business:
Trade name (if different):
Address:                                    City:
State:                                      Zip:
Telephone:                                  Owner/President:[name]

How long in business:                       Credit rating:

Trade references (names and addresses): (2 vendor, 3 winery)


1.

2.

3.

4.

5.


Bank references (include account numbers & addresses):

The undersigned authorizes an inquiry as to the credit information of the business. I certify
the above information to be true.

_____

Owner/President
```

Figure 9.2   Credit Application

Partner with your Distributor

The early preparation ensures your distributor is everything you want them to be—or at least as close as you can get—and protecting yourself. But once you have made the decision and the stage is set for distribution with this company, then make sure you keep your brands at the forefront of their thinking. Be a proactive partner by letting them know:

- how you would like to launch the brand(s)
- what you are willing or able to do

- what wines are available or what is available among your brands in general
- if there is an allocation of limited production wines.

Discuss early expectations and give them some extra time to introduce wines that may be unknown, at least to them, and solicit their suggestions and objectives. In short, let them know that this is a combined effort. You do expect them to put effort into selling the wines once they have brought them in, but they are not alone in this effort. You are there to support them every step of the way.

Franchise States

The appointment of a wholesaler in a particular state becomes especially critical when applied to a "franchise" state. This definition, for purposes of the wine industry, refers to the inexplicable and over-reaching protection afforded the wholesalers in certain states. It has nothing to do with the concept of franchise as most of us know of it. It does not mean the appointment of a licensed entity to sell recognized goods and services in a cookie cutter format, such as McDonalds or Starbucks. It defines the relationship between supplier (you) and the wholesaler in that particular state as being all on the wholesaler's side. Although laws vary in each franchise state, essentially it does not permit you to change distributors, even if you want to, even if the wholesaler has not paid its bills or ordered sufficiently from you to make doing business with them worthwhile.

Originally, the repeal of Prohibition back in 1935 led to laws being enacted for the protection of each state, depending upon the strength and will of its legislature and the lobbying efforts of its liquor distributors. At one time, this may have afforded the tiny wholesaler protection from the large distributor, but today all it seems to do is afford the unscrupulous wholesaler protection from you, the supplier.

It is important to know which states are franchise states at the time you go into business, and this may change and be modified from time to time, depending upon the challenges that are taking place from the local to the Supreme Court level. If in doubt, check with the appropriate licensing board at the time you consider your foray into that state. There should be no doubt about the status of the law regarding your ability to withdraw your product in the event that the wholesaler does not perform adequately or appropriately on your behalf.

It is an important matter to discuss with the potential distributor of that franchise state before entering into business with them. What are their policies regarding termination of a brand? Of course, what they state to you now may change as time elapses and relationships metamorphose into something less positive than the optimistic, friendly days of the inception. But their stated intentions may raise a red flag or gut reaction from you, or go a long way towards assuaging your concerns. They may have been in business for many years and encountered sufficient termination situations to handle them all with fitting resolution. After all, if I were to put it in a more cynical light, how many brands can a wholesaler hold hostage before the wine world (a most intimate place at times) gets wind of it and steers clear.

In most instances, the supplier can terminate the relationship "with cause," a criteria that also differs fromstate to state, but usually encompasses issues of gross under-performance or non-payment. A contract between you and the wholesaler, spelling out your rights and termination intentions will not protect you if it negates the franchise laws of that state, so although I would not discourage a contract, it might be more advisable to specify and document reasonable performance levels and the results. We go into every relationship with the hope of a long and wildly successful ride—or should—but this does not mean we should enter into it with our eyes closed.

Control States

This term refers to those states in which the state has the monopoly over the sale of alcohol, again as a result of the repeal of Prohibition. As of this writing, there are eighteen control states and one county in Maryland. Utah and Pennsylvania, e.g., are the sole purchasers of alcohol and operatestate run stores. In fact, Utah has one individual who decides the wine choices of an entire state. Pennsylvania makes these decisions through a board. Alternatively, some states may license retailers, or only certain counties in a particular state have elected to control sales. The important point to take away from this section is that control states exist and each one is approached from a different perspective than the 32 states that are equally regulated, but provide less monopolization of the sale of alcohol.

The Utah Department of Alcoholic Beverage Control states:

> *The purpose of control is to make liquor available to those adults who choose to drink responsibly—but not to promote the sale of liquor. By keeping liquor out of the private marketplace, no economic incentives are created to maximize sales, open more liquor stores or sell to underage persons. Instead, all policy incentives to promote moderation and to enforce existing liquor laws is (sic) enhanced.*

Unlike franchise states, there is no monopoly of a single brand by an independent wholesaler, but the degree to which the state adheres to the control model dictates to whom you can sell. In some states, including Utah, Wyoming and Mississippi, it is almost essential to appoint a broker who understands the presentation times and has a relationship with the State's purchaser(s). The states in which you elect to utilize a broker does not necessarily indicate to what extent alcohol sales are "controlled" by the state. In Pennsylvania, an example of a pure control store model, a wholesaler may sell to restaurants, and most wholesalers have experience making presentations directly to the Board. In many states, you may approach and sell to a distributor in the same manner you would to a distributor in a non-control state.

State websites are often an invaluable resource, although there is no standard across the web and some are clearly more helpful than others. Always call the state board to determine their exact requirements, even if it is a well documented site. This advice is offered in your quest for distribution in any state. It can be a lengthy process to obtain a license and far better to have all paperwork completed when the office receives your submission. In the case of control states, it is easy to determine which those are, as indicated on the TTB site.

Territory Assignments and Restrictions

Certain states, such as Ohio, Tennessee and Georgia (using only a few examples) require territory designations from you to the distributor (see Figure 9.3). Are you going to allow them access to the entire state or only one segment? Are they capable of covering the entire state?

When you see the confusing array of counties, none of which you recognize, the temptation is great to just let them have the whole state. In the case of franchise states, this may well be a mistake and certainly not a decision to be taken lightly. Wholesalers may tell you that they "plan on expanding" or "will be putting a salesperson in that area soon" and would like you to designate the entire state in the brand registration or state license application. Find out when this is likely to happen and what steps they have taken to set this in motion and weigh the answers.

In Ohio, for example, it is quite common to have several distributors in different quadrants of the state. There is even a place on Ohio's territory designation form to select a *partial* county. Fragmenting sales areas is not likely to incur an objection from your prospective wholesaler, unless they really do cover the entire state through a cohesive network of delivery sites and personnel.

It is in your best interests to determine what area the wholesaler is legitimately able to service and be specific in your territory designation. In the case of Georgia, it can mitigate the damage in the event of a poorly performing wholesaler if you have only assigned limited territories in the original designation.

Brokers

Whether to use brokers can be a controversial issue in many states. A sore subject for some, a necessity for others. First of all, it should be understood that most brokers charge a 10% commission for their services, to be paid after the invoice funds are remitted to you, the importer. Occasionally, they charge a higher percentage or a retainer, but I'd really want to know why and what they intend to do with it and it had better be worth it. It adds yet another layer to your pricing, making it a *four* tier system, instead of the already burdensome three, or cuts 10% from your margin. So,

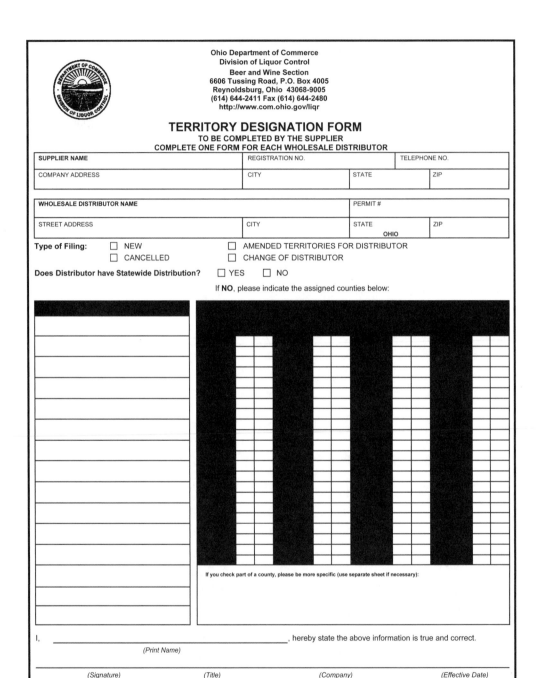

Figure 9.3   Ohio Territory Designation Form

irrespective of what they charge, be aware of **why** you need them, **where** you need them, **who** they should be and **what** they can do.

For these purposes, I'm talking about regional or state brokers, rather than local brokers who support your efforts as a distributor in your own state, but we'll get into that later.

- **Why**—because you can't be everywhere and do everything, because you may be a small, under capitalized start-up, who cannot expend funds in putting sales managers on in various regions, or any sales personnel at all—which is not unusual. A broker can be your independent sales person in that region or state and be well worth their commission. It is up to you (in non-control states, e.g.) to decide whether you can afford the additional tier in your pricing model, or whether you should absorb the difference.

- **Where**—in control states they can be invaluable, and actually a necessity. They know the players, understand what they may be looking for, what they are not looking for, when a particular country's wines are scheduled to come up on the State's calendar, how to monitor sales in specialty stores, manage reorders and generally perform functions that you are unable to do yourself. In highly competitive non-control states, it can mean the difference in securing a great distributor or no distributor at all.

- **Who**—a broker is only as good as their sales. If they don't sell, neither of you make money. Taking on wines they put no effort into makes no sense, yet does happen. A broker should have a proven track record, have a reasonable, but not enormous, portfolio of their own and be a full-time, energetic proponent of your wines. Someone with extensive experience will have the ear of a distributor in any state in which they operate—perhaps even a strong, warm relationship—and will endeavor to present your wines, follow up, monitor and market successfully. This is not to say a new broker cannot do well, but connections and prior experience does have a bearing on the success of their approach and the ability to secure distribution.

- **What**—the right broker can actually save you money, despite their commission, by limiting the quantity of samples going out to prospective customers, lessening the number of visits you need to make to the market, and working with the distributor's sales people to keep your brands at the forefront of their attention.

Initially, they can vet distributors for you in areas with which you are unfamiliar, get the attention of those who may not be willing to respond to you—in their mind, "yet another new importer." Most distributors would very much like to deal with only so many suppliers, or portfolios, much like a retailer who would rather contain the number of distributors they deal with and have to see every week. For a wholesaler, this can mean that they would rather transact business with a known quantity, in the form of a broker, rather than take on the unknown quantity, in the form of you.

The right broker will also be honest with you about the assessment of your wines by the various distributors or retailers (as opposed to the way these same entities invariably share less transparently with you), have an ear to the ground for which wines are likely to be in demand, and be poised to recommend a switch if they see a negative trend in the current wholesale house.

Summary

It absolutely comes down to avoiding the short cuts, whether you are dealing with distributors, franchise states, control states or brokers. The consequences can be anything from a costly inconvenience to a long, time-wasting, money-draining delay. In the case of a franchise state: a catastrophic mistake that requires an expensive buy-out or a requisite two year absence from the state. Brokers don't replace the need to do your own homework, evaluate the prospective customer yourself and establish your own relationships, but they can, under the right circumstances, be an invaluable arm to your business and allow you to focus your attention on more pressing tasks or regions. Just don't forget chemistry. It will enhance your life or make it a living hell.

My Story

Most of my early stories in the search for meaningful distribution originate from inexperience and naïveté. For example, the number of times I continued to send samples to one particular prospect who kept promising to look at them, or could he see some of the other wines, or now that that vintage has changed could he see that, and call him back, call him back, call him back…all to no avail. It was a classic carrot in front of the horse. If I just kept trotting along, keeping the promise of sales in sight and continued to respond with whatever he needed, I would have distribution. I should have stopped at the second set of samples and 2-3 months, not four or five sets and 12 months, but I didn't know any better and I was desperate enough to ignore the warning signs. I later learned that he did this frequently, inexplicably just to have wine for free.

Probably the worst experience I have ever had was with an experienced broker in the South who appeared to offer me a lucrative opportunity for several of my brands. The problem? He was foul-mouthed, rude, sexist and irrational. He seemed to like me and wanted to place the brands, so I persevered with gritted teeth, constantly justifying his behavior with the thought that he was in his late sixties and had honed his skills in the old school liquor distributor days. It really didn't mean anything, I told myself, although I needed a stress relieving power walk every time I got off the phone with him. Suffice it to say, the brands were never placed, he abusively blamed me for the failure and I wasted a great deal of time once again ignoring my instincts. Fortunately for everyone else, he is no longer in the business. He recently burned his last bridge.

On the other hand, I have enjoyed a long and fruitful relationship with another broker, in the Midwest, without whom I would not have achieved the same degree of success, or even the number of distribution partners.

10

DISTRIBUTION—
THE NEXT STAGE

I am sure it has become readily apparent to you that the appointment of a distributor does not end your wine sale participation there. It requires a vigilant, ongoing and organized strategy to support your customer and manage your assets. Much as you would water and fertilize your plants to support their viability and encourage their growth, your wines require continued attention and nurturing to thrive and grow. There are many wonderful distributors in the country staffed by people who work hard for their suppliers, but in this age of consolidation there is also a burgeoning crop of wholesalers with massive books filled with thousands of wines. There is no way—however magnificent and desirable your wines may be—they will receive the full attention they deserve without your help.

Incentives—Wine Launch

The first question often asked of you by a prospective customer is: what incentives can you offer to launch the product? This is the question asked **where it is legal.** They are all important points when it comes down to it, but this is one of those critical ones, because you do not want to run afoul of the statutory regulations of a particular state, which may prohibit the use of incentives. In some states, this can be construed as giving a customer unfair advantage over another. Be aware, through your own preparatory calls to the state board, or simply by asking the distributor, whether this state allows incentives of any kind. With legality established, the next question you must ask yourself is whether you can afford it.

- Have you built a bit of fat in your margin?
- Have you received an incentive allowance from your winery?
- Has the winery given you sufficient free goods to make *those* cases the incentive, or to be able to support your own incentive program?
- Can you "afford" it, because you've budgeted for marketing in the first year, knowing your initial profit loss will be recouped in the second year?
- Is the prospect of volume worth making a big incentive push now?
- Will the distributor share the launch incentive cost with you?
- **What is the distributor prepared to do to partner with you in introducing the brand and starting off on the best foot?**

Notice the bold print on that last question. This is because, among critical points, this becomes über-critical. For the greatest likelihood of success, the wholesaler must become invested in the success of the brand. In fairness, they may not always have the budget to commit towards this incentive at the time they take on your brand, however enthusiastic and committed they may be. But, as in all business relationships, the most committed parties have a vested interest in the outcome. There are a number of examples to illustrate this in the general business arena: commission structures, profit sharing, or simply employees who know that they participate democratically in decisions. These are all incentives for people to work harder towards a common goal. In the case of the distributor, if they share equally in your incentive program, the more likely they are to encourage and monitor their sales staff.

Distributors will sometimes commit personnel and marketing resources to the effort, either in place of or in addition to a monetary contribution, such as making your brand or portfolio a priority for all sales staff for the first month. This gives you

The merlot is 100% merlot; the pinot noir is 100% pinot noir, and the chardonnay is 100% Swiss chard.

Figure 10.1 © David Pike

an advantage in your launch, while the product is fresh to the market and the salespeople, and it also gives the distributor an early perspective on how well the brand is likely to perform.

The downside to the latter is that the brand may not initially perform well, which may be more indicative of the effort put forth than it is a forecast of the brand's future performance. It is therefore incumbent on you to work on its behalf either behind the scenes or in concert with the distributor.

Initial incentives should be short-term and designed to generate immediate results. There is nothing less likely to incentivize over the life of the brand, or vintage, as a program that is taken for granted as a static component of the price. My suggestion, to those who are in a moderate budget category, is to offer incentives on the first order of perhaps free goods or a modest contest. Therefore, the term of the launch incentives could be limited to either:

- The first order
- The first month
- The current quarter
- When a certain dollar sales volume is reached
- When a designated number of accounts are established

The incentive can be modest or lavish, depending upon your budget. It can be one case of free goods on a pallet (or equivalent discount) or a contest for a trip to Tuscany. Whatever the incentive, it must be logical, meaningful and easily quantifiable. By logical, I mean to you. The launch of a product cannot bankrupt you nor have you praying no one reaches the target, because of your potential financial outlay. If you have the necessary capital to fund a trip to Tuscany, or have put together a program with the winery, this is an exciting way to get started. But if you cannot afford it, it makes no sense.

In terms of *meaningful* and *quantifiable*, there is also nothing worse than a program than either cannot be understood, and will therefore be ignored, or has no discernible way to monitor its results.

Additionally, the incentive program must be tailored to the circumstances: state, region, distributor's resources, desirability of your brand, ease of selling or contemporary expectations. For example, if your program is to offer $5 for every case sold, this may be a thoroughly appropriate incentive for an inexpensive wine that is likely to be case stacked in stores and generate volume. On the other hand, you may offer $5 a case for a wine that is a hand-sell, high priced, unknown and difficult to sell. Or, in this particular wholesale house, they are accustomed to incentives of $10 a case. I am not suggesting you should do the same; I am making it clear that your incentives should count for something and be customized to the situation. If you see that $10 a case is the only way to get the salespeople's attention, but you cannot afford it, *do not do it*. Find another way to promote and support your brand.

It is quite possible to establish and grow your brand on its attributes, along with your judicious management and fostering of relationships within the ranks of the distributor's salespeople. When you receive extra samples from the winery, use that opportunity to pass them along in the form of an incentive.

Incentives—Ongoing

To me, they are different—launch and ongoing, that is. The initial stages are to start buzz for an unknown brand, unknown at least to the distributor you have just appointed. The timing is certainly optimistic and hopeful. Later, you may be just as hopeful, but it's time to stimulate sales. Or sales have languished, the brand is getting lost amid new offerings or big brand quotas, or you are ready for a vintage change and you want to make room.

As indicated previously, there are states in which incentives or programming, as it is known, is illegal and in the ones where it is legal, some inducements that work better than others. I would be guided, primarily, by your contact at the distributor—whether it is the hands-on owner, sales manager or the salesperson with whom you have established a close connection and can rely on his or her input. They really do know what works and what doesn't and how easily it can be managed, given their sales team or their territory.

The programming you put in place after the launch should be at least for a quarter (three months), in my opinion. It can even run all year for a very big contest, but a quarter should keep interest high and attention focused, whilst also maintaining a sufficient period for you to realize a significant sales bump. For more immediate impact, with high expectations and perhaps tied in with wine dinners and tastings, a month or even a week can be appropriate. This is most often utilized when a winemaker or company principal is in town.

Incentives can additionally be divided into two categories:

- Salesperson
- On-premise (restaurant) and off-premise (retailer)

In other words, what you initiate may benefit the salesperson directly in the form of cash, prizes or trips, or indirectly in terms of free goods to the retailer or a by-the-glass program (wines poured by the glass, rather than sold by the bottle) pricing for the restaurant. Both benefit the salesperson, but operate quite differently.

The salesperson programming can also be sub-divided into two categories:

- On-premise sales
- Off-premise sales

This is another one of those important distinctions, because if you decide to set up a program for volume, e.g., the on-premise salesperson cannot compete with it. The off-premise salesperson (if the distributor sets their staffing or territories up this way) may be able to sell one retail account fifteen cases of a product that the on-premise salesperson will need fifteen accounts (or twenty if split cases are allowed) to accomplish the same thing. The ongoing sales benefit and exposure of the glass pour at a restaurant may far outweigh the one-time sale to the retail account, but it cannot be quantified in the initial programming period.

Suggestions for programming incentives follow.

Launch or Pre-Sell

- 3% sample allowance deducted from invoice or included in free goods across brands.
- Large format (1.5L or 3L) bottles as percentage of order or "prizes" for performance.
- $5 for each new wine placement on-premise
- $5 for each case in a minimum 3 case stack off-premise
- $20 for by-the-glass placements (with minimum time frame or case purchase)

Be guided by the distributor and the circumstance. Be aware that you may be setting a precedent for future orders that you may not wish, or be able, to fulfill. Do not fall into the trap of being expected to include standard free goods or sample allowance deduction on each shipment or invoice. This will become absorbed into the price and taken for granted, instead of being used as liberal tasting samples as should be the intent.

Ongoing—Off-Premise

- "One case on ten" i.e., one case free for every ten cases sold—one quarter time period.
- "One case on 13" i.e., one case free for every thirteen cases purchased. The logic to this is that fourteen cases is a "layer" on a pallet. If you take the fifty-six pallet premise, it is divided into four layers of fourteen cases each. Very often a distributor may say, "I'll take a layer of xxx wine."—as part of an order.
- $15 per each (min.) 3 case stack—one quarter.
- $200 gift certificate for highest volume sales over the designated sales period, by brand or portfolio, depending upon how many wines—one quarter.
- Contest for specified elements of a trip to the country or region of origin for the brand in question. This may be airfare (and winery provides accommodation at their winery) with the winner on their own the rest of the trip. It may be an organized, accompanied, all expenses paid trip. Just spell it out, so there are no surprises. Recommended contest period for something of this nature could be whatever your budget dictates, but twelve months would be a reasonable timeframe. Since this is an extended program, make sure the sales or brand manager is keeping everyone abreast of progress and it stays at the forefront of their minds.

Ongoing—On-Premise

- $20 for glass pour placement—3 case minimum
- $10 for wine list placement
- Same as above trip contest, but with requirements that are tailored to on-premise parameters, such as number of wine or glass pour placements or hotel or chain placements.

Restaurant placements have some inherent pitfalls in understanding what the glass pour or by-the-glass program entails, which is why you should indicate a minimum order or time period. Preferably, the restaurant will put the wine on their printed list and not on a chalk board which is erased when they run out of the six bottles they brought in as a favor to the rep. It is imperative that you understand how your programming will work. It would be an extremely apathetic or unprofessional wholesale principal (brand manager, owner, sales manager or other similar liaison) who would not advise you as to the incentive that is likely to have the best outcome for you in their market, or period of the year.

You can see the impact a program can have when the wholesaler matches your incentive, so that instead of $5 a case, it becomes $10. Instead of a $200 gift certificate, it can become $400. Not only is the distributor more invested, but the sales person is obviously more motivated to sell your wine.

Whether you have a program in place or not, it's always good business to offer discounts on larger volume, such as for pallet orders of the same wine.

Sample Allowance and Handling

Wines will not get sold without sampling; this is a simple truth. Except in the case of highly allocated, tiny production, expensive wines rated 100 in *Wine Advocate*, which may be pre-sold to special accounts on the basis of their rarefied desirability. In the case of just about everything else, the customer tastes the wines and makes their decision accordingly. Your decision becomes, again, one of not bankrupting yourself through allowing the indiscriminate use of samples, with no accountability.

Most distributors will find the convention of sharing equally in the cost of samples to be acceptable and customary. Samples are handled through a statement called a "bill-back," which should be sent monthly or quarterly to you from the distributor.

Paperwork, especially at small wholesale houses, is not at the top of the priority list. Wine sales and the supervision of wine sales personnel is their focus. Therefore, some find that the preparation of bill-back statements gets pushed back until the end of the year. I find this understandable, but not acceptable. Whether bill-backs are compiled from memory, from little pieces of paper from the salesperson or from a master list, the longer it takes to organize it into a billable format the greater likelihood of error. Despite the fact that the distributor is willing to share this cost equally with you, there can be a tendency to allow sample usage to get away from them. There is also less opportunity for you to incorporate it into your budget or put the brakes on over-sampling, as evidenced by the sales generated from the sample usage.

Conversely, if you inhibit salespeople they will be less likely to promote your wines. If they can't sample they can't sell. If there is a restricting limit placed on samples, they may take them out for a certain period of time and then stop. After all, the wholesale house will either discourage the use of samples, or require the salesperson to be responsible for their own samples if the supplier is not splitting the cost at all.

And finally, I do not recommend that you allow the distributor to simply deduct a sample allowance percentage from every invoice, because "we are too busy to do the paperwork." I have done this in the past, and found the sample allowance the wholesaler set probably equaled the volume of samples they used, based on sales. *But, also based on sales, they did not share in the cost to any discernible degree, despite their assurances that this would be the case.* I believe there is also a tendency to incorporate it into their pricing for additional margin points, just as they might do if you were to run an incentive program indefinitely.

The other customary practice with samples—so much so as to be an industry norm—is for the distributor to charge 100% bill-back on the following:

- spoiled product (generally corked wine)
- when the supplier (you or the winery representative) work the market
- trade shows.

There seems to have developed an unwritten code around the use of trade show and supplier visit samples, presumably because they are not dispensed at the company's discretion and out of their control. I accept this and reimburse distributors who ask for it in this manner.

Without sounding too suspicious, because paranoia certainly should not be the basis for your relationship, monitor the sample usage and require accountability if you feel it is too high. Perhaps a salesperson has been working on an account, or series of accounts, for some time and they are expected to come to fruition in the following sales period, which is perfectly reasonable. Or perhaps the company principal is not aware of their own bill-backs, which are generated by an accounts receivable department, and may find, through your follow-up, that there are a preponderance of samples going to one individual, disproportionate to their sales. If so, this will most likely not be the only indication of this salesperson's lack of demonstrable results.

I also suggest making comparisons with your other distributors' sample usage around the country through their bill-backs to you. It is not a scientific method, but is often a helpful tool in zeroing in on sample usage that appears to be an aberration and can be brought to the attention of the distributor. It may also help you evaluate their effectiveness.

On the other side of the coin, there are actually some wholesalers who do not bill back at all for sample usage. I'm not sure if this is largesse on their part or a lack of desire to generate more paperwork. Whatever the reason, I don't look a gift horse in the mouth and am grateful.

Purchase Orders

The purchase order from the distributor should indicate everything they are expecting from you in relation to the following:

- Brand
- Vintage
- Number of cases
- Volume of cases, e.g., 12/case or 6/case
- Size of bottles, e.g., 750ml, 1.5L, etc.
- Any samples included with shipment (with prior agreement)
- Price for each item
- Terms (as already determined between the two of you)
- Trucker

Optionally, it can include:

- P.O. number
- Pick up point
- Notes from distributor, such as "will pick-up remainder of xxx next month." Or "60 day terms on first invoice, as agreed."

A P.O. number is not an essential item, but is included if the customer keeps track of their orders that way. If you receive a P.O. without a number, you can assign your own identifier such as today's date or the name of the purchaser on your invoice, if desired. The warehouse's numbering system and your own invoice number are more important.

To clarify, the pick up point, per se, is not optional. But one can reasonably assume that you have established where you warehouse long before this. The pick up point may be on your customer's P.O. because it differs on a one-time basis—perhaps your office or a prior importer's warehouse, or just because the customer wishes to make sure it is clear.

Notes, if they are included at all, are simply ways in which distributors make sure you are both on the same page with housekeeping issues related to orders.

The very first thing you do when you receive a P.O. is to check to see that all items are correctly identified, for the correct price, and in stock. If the distributor has indicated 2009 vintage and you are still on 2008, or conversely, they indicate 2006 and you have sold out and have 2007, you must let them know immediately. It may not be important, but it could be critical. Restaurant wine lists, special orders by customers, distributor expectations or ratings could all affect how they will receive this news. Don't assume it is okay. Don't expect them to accept a vintage they did not order.

If you are completely out of stock on a wine, *let them know.* Don't fill the order, with the exception of wine x, and the first they learn of it is when they unload the goods at their warehouse. Call and explain you unexpectedly sold out and will expect another shipment on such-and-such a date. Or tell them that you sold out of the '07 a while ago (maybe it's been a some time since this wholesaler has placed an order), but you will be happy to fill it with the next vintage. Get their okay. You will learn what they really want and they will appreciate the heads up.

If a price is incorrect, *let them know*. It may be an incentive program that has expired, or it may be a simple transposition of figures on their part, but they cannot be surprised by your invoice.

If they exceed their allocation and you cannot fulfill the order—such a happy occurrence!—make sure you let them know. All distributors will attempt to put in for extra in the hope the order will be filled. Your inclination may be to wonder if they ever read your allocation spreadsheets or emails, or whatever means you use to communicate, but it's a natural tendency on their part. I've done it myself when I've been given an allocation on a wine in high demand and I've used up my allocation from the winery and occasionally it has worked. Circumstances may have changed since the allocations were made and perhaps someone else has been late on payment too many times or cherry picked too often, or just haven't picked up their allocation. Perhaps you *can* fill this particular order, but make sure they know that you know they have exceeded their allocation and that you will not (most likely) be able to do more in the future.

Other P.O. items to review would naturally be terms, to make sure this is what has been agreed upon, and any sample allowance, incentive goods or discounts they may have included.

Pick Up and Delivery

All distribution orders are arranged by the distributor through their own trucking options, either a contracted company or, if they are large enough, their in-house trucks. The cost of shipping is incurred by them, not the importer. Your invoice is FOB point of origin—i.e. the warehouse. From that moment forward the wine is in possession of the distributor and becomes their responsibility. Distributors are well aware of this, of course, and will make arrangements that best suit their needs, their pocketbook and the timing of the trucker schedules.

Pickup can often take a couple of weeks to a small distributor if a trucker is trying to take a complete load back to the customer or their originating state, or only goes to California every two weeks on a Wednesday. If they miss that date, it may be another two weeks. In terms of budgeting, be aware that when a distributor puts in a P.O. for net 30, it may take two months or more to get paid, because of the pickup schedule, not their tardy remittance.

If it is a first time pickup for this distributor, make sure they are aware of your warehouse's requirements—such as 48 hours minimum notice, fax number or who to ask for.

As soon as you have determined that all aspects of the P.O. are correct, submit the release order to your warehouse. Then make sure you receive a confirmation, or make that confirmation yourself online or by a phone call. The worst thing you can do in this situation is to assume the warehouse has your order and the trucker misses his window of opportunity in scheduling an appointment, which needlessly delays your order. It's not only the delay of this one order; it starts to put you behind on subsequent orders. It can even rescind an order placed by a retailer or restaurant for a particular event or customer, because the product did not arrive on time. The other part of the confirmation is to be sure the warehouse also has the correct vintages and product count. As you can see, this is an integral aspect all the way down the line, for plausible reasons.

Invoicing

An invoice from you should mirror all the necessary items from the P.O (see Figure 10.2). from your customer and the release order to the warehouse. It should also now include an invoice number, of your own designation. There are no rules about invoice numbers. It is whatever makes it easier for you to readily identify and quantify in your office. Examples of system choices could be:

- 000001, 00002, 00003 (numbering from your first order in sequence)
- SC-00001, SC-0002, SC-0003 or TX-0001, TX-0001, TX-0003 (numbering by state—these indicate South Carolina and Texas orders)
- 09-0001, 09-0002, 09-0003 (numbering from the beginning of each calendar year)

These are just suggestions to illustrate the point. You may think of many other permutations that better suit your style or need.

The invoice should also include:

- Bill to and Ship to (since these may differ)
- FOB point (this is the location of your warehouse)
- Ship Date
- Due Date

You may also wish to include one or more of the following statements:

- Interest will be charged at the rate of xxx for accounts past due
- Returned checks will incur a charge of $xx

These last two statements are entirely optional, but may protect you in the event that the account proceeds to collection. I would not, however, institute any actual interest charges while invoices are past due, but the distributor remains in good standing. This will not go over very well with your distributor partner and is not customary.

QuickBooks has a number of examples of product invoices (as opposed to service invoices) and there are others available to download online. You also have the opportunity to design or redesign your own using their template options.

Invoicing should be done as soon as the wine has shipped—i.e., the trucker has picked it up. You should receive a shipment advice from the warehouse and once again, through an established system in your office, make sure you have checked pick up details against order details. It will become second nature after a while.

If you do notice a discrepancy, and it happens more often than any of us would like, determine the cause. It can be any one of many: boxes left sitting on the dock, miscounted inventory that resulted in depletion of an item or it simply could not be found. Your first choice would be to have them call you before the trucker leaves, but this is not always possible, so now you are left with explaining the discrepancy to the distributor. Do not avoid telling them, or assume that it isn't necessary because they'll find out soon enough anyway. They may have been counting on this item to fill an order, or end up paying more for what is now a LTL. They will not necessarily be pleased, but will be far more understanding because you took the initiative to pick up

Mayflower Wine Imports

2000 California Street
San Francisco, CA 94109

Date	Invoice #
7/26/2009	IND-0016

Bill To

Ship To

P.O. Number	Terms	Rep		Due Date	Ship	Via	F.O.B.
				7/26/2009	7/26/2009		

Quantity	Item Code	Description	Price Each	Amount

Total	$0.00

Interest may be charged at 1.5% per month for accounts past due.	Phone #	Fax #	Web Site
Returned checks will incur a charge of $25.	(760) 729-4900	(760) 730 7465	www.mayflowerwineimports.com

Figure 10.2 Example of a Wholesale Invoice

the phone and inform them. It is also the opportunity to determine how this will be remedied—arranging for another pickup, substituting product, etc.

The invoice should be prepared that day, as the next stage in your system, and either emailed from QuickBooks (or other accounting program) or snail mailed to the attention of the distributor's accounts payable (most prefer email these days). If terms are 30 to 45 days, you may think you have plenty of time, but two things are at odds with that: time goes much faster than you think and it can easily be put aside and forgotten, and the sooner you put up your hand for payment, the sooner you enter the wholesaler's queue.

Collecting

The wholesaler knows very well when the invoice is due, but may only have limited funds, an unexpected expenditure or a disappointing sales month. In that case, the supplier whose invoice reaches them first goes into the system first and presumably is paid on an aging basis. Hopefully there is an accounts payable person or department, which removes both you and the company principal, or executive, from having to deal with financial matters, and this person can be contacted to pursue a past due invoice.

As soon as the invoice is due, send a statement (see Figure 10.3). This is an innocuous announcement that simply reminds the customer that it is due. If it has already been sent, it doesn't offend and if, by chance, they have forgotten or have not received your original invoice, this alerts them before too much more time elapses.

Presumably, you have done the necessary reference checking prior to the relationship, to ensure that the distributor is credit worthy and reliable, but circumstances change, as we have all seen during the recession, and now the invoice becomes quite past due. Stay in touch with the appropriate party via phone. Give them the chance to offer explanations, proffer a new (exact) date and generally bring the account current whilst retaining your good will. They have agreed to terms, to which you are expecting them to abide, but if their customers are stretching their terms or someone cancelled a large order, they may find themselves in unexpectedly difficult circumstances. There are still dependable, financially viable wholesalers in the business, but financial challenges have become increasingly more common during these times, despite the best of intentions.

Statement

	Date
	8/12/2009

To:

Amount Due	Amount Enc.
$2,871.50	

Date	Transaction	Amount	Balance
07/07/2009	INV #OH-0002. Due 07/22/2009. Orig. Amount $11.50.	11.50	11.50
07/10/2009	INV #OH-0003. Due 08/09/2009. Orig. Amount $2,860.00.	2,860.00	2,871.50

CURRENT	1-30 DAYS PAST DUE	31-60 DAYS PAST DUE	61-90 DAYS PAST DUE	OVER 90 DAYS PAST DUE	Amount Due
0.00	2,871.50	0.00	0.00	0.00	$2,871.50

Figure 10.3 Past Due Statement to Distributor

The more desirable your product and the easier it is to sell (i.e., a 'cash cow' for them) the more likely you will be paid. It is also incentive, at some stage defined by your own finances and commonsense, to tell them that no further orders can be filled until invoices are all paid.

There comes a point, of course, when you are acting as their bank with no end in sight and people are avoiding you and this becomes unacceptable. This is when you realize there is no longer a relationship and cutting your losses with this individual is the only prudent course of action. This is when you issue a final notice and a deadline for collection agency activity. It is an action of last resort, but it does happen and you must be prepared to recover monies due you. This is when you retroactively apply interest to the entire bill!

I have only found this to be necessary three times in all the years I have been importing and distributing. Each time, if I am being honest, it was because I either abdicated my responsibility in background checking to someone else, or I exercised recklessness in the early days of distributor appointments. The odds that it will happen to you are considerably less, because you will presumably be better prepared!

Summary

The theme throughout your wine importing career should be preparation, communication and organization. Evaluate potential customers carefully and thoroughly, communicate with them consistently, even when you would rather avoid an uncomfortable situation, and keep all paperwork. You never know when you will need it.

My Story

I have been very fortunate to have encountered distributors who most often became friends rather than distant business associates. I have stayed in their homes, attended barbecues, gone on shopping trips and mountain hikes and been included in family events. I even assisted with the planting of a vineyard—a hobby of the wholesaler—a completely enjoyable day, where a group of us started out diligently planting root stocks in evenly spaced, straight rows and after lunch, where wonderful food and much wine was consumed, continued those same rows in erratically placed, meandering furrows that easily identified what came before and after imbibing.

Over the course of my many years as an importer, very few instances resulted in conflict or a breakdown in civil interaction. Most often, wholesalers are just like their suppliers (us)—reasonable, hard working, honest people who struggle and stress and want to do their best for their customers. Some are incredibly successful and others are experiencing financial difficulties, but all are looking at your wines and you as an opportunity to increase their profits or bring their finances into the black. The fact that they become friends should not deter you from protecting your business, but it makes it a lot easier to work together for a common goal.

11

TIPS FOR DISTRIBUTION SUCCESS

Some of these are going to appear obvious, and others will come as a complete surprise. After all, you sold the wine to the distributor, you have provided samples, initiated a launch, given them a competitive price. What else is left to do other than to tell them, "go forth and deplete inventory?" A lot!

These days, distributors are overloaded with product, internal and external demands and maintaining a competitive edge. They *expect* you to help them sell your product. Yes, the wine that took you so long to bring in and find the right distribution for, and which you have just happily sent off on its way to its new home. That wine.

Communication

You've seen considerable mention of this before in the book, but I'm saying it again in a different way, for a different reason. I'm talking about the right communication at this particular time in the process. For example, you don't want to communicate so often with the distributor that they are tearing their hair out and regretting the moment they ever said "yes" to your wine. Believe me, this does happen. You don't want to communicate with force, pressure or inappropriate requests. And you don't want to leave them to their own devices and only communicate when you need something. But you do want to communicate.

Travel Budgeting

This is a reference to time as well as money. Many people feel they must rush all over the country meeting potential customers before any one of them has committed to wine. And if you have the money, well, that fits your budget. However, it really isn't necessary and can bankrupt you in no time. It will certainly be one of those items that can potentially erode your margin.

Appointing distributors can easily, with the appropriate preparedness, be done via phone, fax and email. If the potential business is enormous—volume, coverage area, etc.—meeting with the company and making a presentation prior to appointment is well worthwhile. They may get the sales team or upper management together and your presence will make all the difference in a life-changing decision for you. It may also be advisable when the distributor feels this step is crucial to the process and it is a company you want to be partnered with. In other instances, you could combine it with a trip to a neighboring state, or coincide with meeting two or three potential distributors. But in most initial transactions, it is not critical. They would prefer to get the product launched with their sales people, and utilize your assistance at a later date.

Budgeting for travel is essential during the ongoing relationship, and for the most part, this should be *at the distributor's convenience*. Suppliers are well aware of the sales bump that takes place during a market visit and are usually clamoring for time and attention. It can become overwhelming to the sales force and burn them out when all they find themselves doing each day is entertaining a steady stream of suppliers. Therefore, most distributors have a carefully orchestrated calendar of visit schedules and if you call far enough in advance (thereby working it into your annual travel budget as well) you may have your pick of dates and salespeople. If you leave it till the last minute, prepare to be disappointed.

Generally, depending upon the wholesaler's size, market coverage, population density, number of wines from your portfolio and several other factors, you may want to visit a market anywhere from once a year to once a quarter. Once a year would be considered essential and this may be determined by their annual trade show or by your own needs. If at all possible, spring and early autumn would be the optimum times. By spring, I mean from end of January to end of May, very much depending upon the region and time slot availability. It's not necessarily that helpful (or pleasant) to go to Minneapolis in January, but Florida or the ski resort mountains of Colorado may be perfect. In that January to May time frame, it is the optimum time to introduce new brands for the year, or new varietals for summer, and generally kick off the year. In early autumn, it should be central to your sales budget to have wines positioned in both the sales people's minds and in the stores and restaurants for the holidays.

The 101 basics of market visit protocol once you are on the ground will be covered in a later section.

Staff Training—In-House

Start with sales staff if you want them to remember your wine and perhaps take it under their wings and nurture its growth in your market. This can be accomplished by working with each individual salesperson over the course of the year, but bigger and faster impact commonly requires scheduling a presentation for a Friday morning sales meeting. This is the traditional team meeting held once a week or once a month, depending upon the company, and whilst part of it is devoted to their own business and housekeeping matters—quotas, reports, problems, etc.—a portion of the time is typically allocated to suppliers who wish to come in and ply their wares.

- First of all, please make it interesting and keep them awake. These poor people have frequently been subjected to boring presentations with the same tired product, or overly technical discourses delivered in a monotone. This is their time you are taking up. They could be putting it to better use and furthermore will do so as soon as you release them, if you haven't made it motivating, intriguing, fun and/or potentially financially attractive.

- Secondly, stick to the time limit. This could be five minutes or thirty, but there *will* be a time limit. There could be presentations before and after yours, or they've already spent part of the morning on their own agenda. It is only courteous to adhere to this stipulation and will endear you to the sales team if you do.

- Bring wine for them to taste. Not so much that they develop palate fatigue (remember there could be others before you) but sufficient in number and diversity to reflect your portfolio. These could be wines already in their book, or could be new vintages, or wines under consideration by management. Tasting through the wines while you describe something of the vineyard, background, style and pricing allows the information to marry with the product. Very often, this may be the first opportunity they have to taste the wines and this is the occasion you may find your champion—the one who falls in love with it and whose mental wheels are turning over as to where they can place it and how they can sell it.

- Give the sales team key words to use with each wine or the brand in general— phrases that distinguish it from other wines, or makes it easier to remember. Keep it simple. Don't overload them with technical information or complicated descriptions. It is not to suggest anyone is mentally challenged, but consider you are one of many portfolios in their book and they cannot possibly absorb it all at one meeting. It could be something about the wine or grapes: an unusual, but pleasant simile for the aromatics, age of the vines, yield, about the vineyard: volcanic gravel, source of another brand's success, unique trellising, or about the vignerons themselves: third generation, same winemaker as…, previously made… Whatever it is, try to make it a point of difference and not the usual descriptions they have heard a thousand times before. Keep the technology and elaborate backgrounds for the handout material or direct them to the website.

- Give them more reason to take out your wines. Make the week you are there, or the week following your presentation, a time of monetary incentives for most sold, most placements or $xx a case program. This is not essential by any means and I have often conducted sales seminars without it, but it is an opportunity for a tangible value-added piece of your presentation if it fits your budget. A non-tangible way would be to develop a rapport with all or some of the team, so that they feel they are aiding the relative success of someone they like and respect. You would be surprised at how often a supplier can be lacking in personality or arrogant or insensitive.

- Leave them with an invitation to call you if they need more information or have questions. They should each have your business card.

Staff Training—On-Premise

Initially, it may seem like such a coup to get your wine into the most prestigious restaurant in town…until you look at the list. It is twenty-three pages, and that's just the reds. Unless you have a wine on a restaurant wine list by the glass, or the list is very small, you can expect your wine to languish along with possibly hundreds of others. In many states and with many distributors, broken case sales (as in partial case orders) are common, and in these instances the restaurant only has to have three to six bottles of a wine they like to put it on the list. Perhaps they wish to qualify for *Wine Spectator*'s Award of Excellence, or they simply want a list of a wide range of wines to complement their food.

At any rate, the sommelier may have loved your wine when it was presented, but the servers will generally have no clue as to its qualities and will have no reason to recommend it, and the lack of name recognition will discourage most people from ordering it. This becomes especially true if it is expensive or an esoteric grape. It is an additional chore for you, one you might rather avoid and put your time to continuing your sales journey, but it can really help move your wine if you can give the servers a reason to recommend it. Preferably you will have more than one wine on the list, to make it worth your while and theirs to conduct the training.

Restaurant staff trainings are usually done just prior to dinner service, when they have their meeting to review the evening's specials. This means they do not have to be called in on their day off or at a time for which they will receive no remuneration. I believe they actually enjoy this exercise. They benefit from a free drink, or at least a substantial taste, before starting their shift and most servers in fine dining restaurants want to learn more about their wines and feel comfortable making recommendations.

Key words are again important in this setting, but not the same words as for distributor sales trainings. In this instance, they want to be able to satisfy a guest's food pairing or predisposition towards a certain style of wine. The server also wants to be able to up-sell, if possible, since their tip will be reflected in the overall check size. It may be that your wine is more expensive than some, or it could be less expensive, but by satisfying the guest's palate they will order a second bottle for the table.

Some examples of words that are useful to the guest could be "dry," "complex with blackberry fruit," "full-bodied," "earthy," "rich with fine grained tannins," or ways in

*The bouquet is reminiscent of rubber nose —
but then, it always is...*

Figure 11.1   © David Pike

which to compare them to wines with which they are familiar if it applies, such as "Rhone style," "Burgundian" or the opposite of Burgundy, such as a Pinot that is very cherry, fruit-forward and young. Obviously, they will want to present the wines in the most flattering way possible. Steer them away from saying "light" and substitute "soft" if that applies. "Sweet" may in fact refer to the fruit, rather than the residual sugar and can be misleading. "Rounded," "mouth-filling" or "ripe" could be a more appealing way to describe the wine.

Once again, your personality and presentation of material will resonate with this group. If they like you they will be more apt to remember you and recommend your wines.

Ongoing, Consistent Pricing

You may wonder how this element comes under the heading of a distribution success tip. It is one of those items that can be overlooked until it is too late and already creating headaches for you and your customers. Developing a well thought out pricing strategy from the outset, one that enables you to absorb exchange rate fluctuations for a time and allows for the vagaries of doing business is essential.

Once you establish the FOB pricing from which the distributor has chosen, ordered and placed your wines, you cannot come back too soon and say the pricing is wrong, did not take certain costs into consideration, the exchange rate has gone haywire or the winery has increased their price to you and you must pass this along. You also cannot surprise them with a price increase—no matter how much time has elapsed since the last one—by including it on their invoice or giving them no notice. They are trying to manage their own sales and keep items on wine lists.

My advice is to keep the price consistent for at least one vintage. There are many occasions where I did not increase a price over three or four vintages, if a winery did not increase to me and the exchange rate did not change. I touted that fact to my customers as proof of the reasonableness of my pricing and I encourage you to do the same. Of course I have had to institute increases in the normal course of business, but on occasion I have even decreased, especially if the exchange rate moved substantially in my favor or the vineyard owners decided to reevaluate their pricing structure. Even in the event of a rapid and unanticipated rise in foreign currency, try a manageable increase over time. It may not keep pace with your shrinking margin, but it is far better to maintain business at a reduced profit margin than lose the business altogether.

Whatever your decision on price increases, try to mitigate the impact by giving as much notice as you can and offering to preserve the current pricing for orders placed by such-and-such a date, even if they have not been picked up by the price increase date. Or hold pricing on larger orders, if you can. Anything to increase orders (which will reduce your carrying costs) and let your distribution partner know you are trying to work with them.

Relationships Outside the Wholesaler

We have touched on the value-added components to your wine sales and one of the value-added items is you! By developing sales and relationships beyond the distributor's workforce and efforts, you have made yourself a more valuable supplier in their eyes.

True, this is not something you should feel compelled to do, nor is it expected. But if you know the sommelier at the upscale resort in town, or have connections with a chain, or feel like developing connections with a chain, this can not only endear you to the distributor, it can secure one for you during an otherwise fruitless search.

Perhaps you eat frequently at a chain in your hometown that is likely to have a varied wine list, such as P.F. Chang's, Ruth's Chris or Roy's. Chains of any ethnicity or certain price tier will usually buy on a corporate level for a core list, but regionally they also often have latitude to supplement for local tastes and cultivating that buyer could mean a stepping stone for the distributor in another state. Be aware of whether they limit to a particular region or exclude certain countries.

It is not only worth your while on behalf of your distributor relationship, but who knows what other business this could establish for you nationwide.

Working the Market on Your Time

This can be a delicate area and should be handled with the full cooperation of your distributor. If you start charging around town like a bull in a china shop without regard for pricing or product availability in inventory, you will most likely annoy your distributor and could make it difficult for the sales team if you are going to their accounts without their knowledge.

Working the market alone could come about because there are no more slots left at the time you wish to go into their area, or you have an extra day after your regularly scheduled visit. It could be something you plan on the way to another market, or on either side of a trade show when no one is available to work with you. It could be your own home base and you have specific accounts where you have developed relationships.

Set the stage with them beforehand by establishing a balance between what you wish to do and what they would like you do to and most importantly, let them know you are roaming loose in their territory! Take their price book with you so you quote correctly, learn what products are in their inventory and don't try to take orders for anything they cannot fulfill. Instead of just the 'A' accounts which appeal to you the most, go to accounts they may need assistance with or find difficult to get into and you'll be a help instead of a hindrance. If there are incentives available, make sure you don't step on any toes, and that it is legal in the particular state.

Done appropriately, with transparency, they will appreciate your efforts and the resulting sales.

Placement Reports

This one is for you. It refers to the account placements made by the distributor and is specific as to which wine and vintage is placed at what account in their region. It can be a difficult report to obtain from the wholesaler, especially on a regular basis. It takes time they may not wish to devote to something that has no discernible value for them to prepare and provide it to you. Occasionally, wholesalers are reluctant to divulge what they consider proprietary information they fear may be passed along to their replacement in the future. However, many have computer programs that readily allow them to produce these reports and have no problem supplying the information (see Figure 11.2). It can be useful to tie your incentive programs to the quantifiable placements, and in the case of restaurant glass pour programs is essential. Knowing where your wines are placed in the market also equips you with knowledge you can use to assist with targeting accounts and stimulating sales. These are the priority objectives to obtaining placement reports, rather than as a means to entice a prospective new distributor.

The reluctance distributors have about handing you the specifics of all their placements can be well founded, but this should not be their first concern. If they are performing well to reasonable expectations, and honoring their financial commitments, there should be no reason for you to consider taking your brands elsewhere and nor

Superior Wine Distribution
Sales by Item Detail
January through September 2006

Type	Date	Num	Memo	Name	Qty
Service					
Brumby SGM 2002					
Invoice	9/15/2006	1578	Wholesale Case Price - Brumby Canyon Jillaroo Red SG...	Wine Styles	1
Total Brumby SGM 2002					
Cigale GSM 2004					
Invoice	3/21/2006	1325	Cigale Barossa Valley Grenache Shiraz Mataro 2004	Vino Venue	1
Invoice	3/29/2006	1328	Wholesale Case Price - Cigale Barossa Valley Grenach...	Oola	1
Invoice	4/13/2006	1361	Cigale Barossa Valley Grenache Shiraz Mataro 2004	Vino Venue	1
Invoice	8/28/2006	1541	Cigale Barossa Valley Grenache Shiraz Mataro 2004	Wine Club Santa Clara	2
Invoice	8/31/2006	1552	Cigale Barossa Valley Grenache Shiraz Mataro 2004	Wine Club San Francisco	5
Invoice	9/8/2006	1560	Cigale Barossa Valley Grenache Shiraz Mataro 2004	Wine Club Santa Clara	1
Total Cigale GSM 2004					
FE Botr Chenin					
Invoice	2/14/2006	1088	Wholesale Case Price - Forrest Estate Marlborough Botr...	Oakville Grocery Palo Alto	1
Invoice	7/21/2006	1488	Wholesale Case Price - Forrest Estate Marlborough Botr...	Home	1
Invoice	8/30/2006	1546	Wholesale Case Price - Forrest Estate Marlborough Botr...	Mollie Stones Greenbrae	1
Total FE Botr Chenin					
FE Botrytis Riesling					
Invoice	2/14/2006	1088	Wholesale Case Price - Forrest Estate Marlborough Botr...	Oakville Grocery Palo Alto	1
Invoice	3/17/2006	1244	Wholesale Case Price - Forrest Estate Marlborough Botr...	Swirl on Castro	0.5
Invoice	5/25/2006	1414	Wholesale Case Price - Forrest Estate Marlborough Botr...	750ml Wine Bar	1
Total FE Botrytis Riesling					
Forrest Estate Gewurztraminer 2					
Invoice	1/4/2006	1033	Wholesale Case Price: New Zealand Marlborough Gewu...	Dosa	2
Invoice	1/12/2006	1036	Wholesale Case Price: New Zealand Marlborough Gewu...	Oakville Grocery San Fran...	1
Invoice	1/20/2006	1048	Wholesale Case Price: New Zealand Marlborough Gewu...	Dosa	1
Invoice	1/26/2006	1068	Wholesale Case Price: New Zealand Marlborough Gewu...	Dosa	2
Invoice	3/27/2006	1290	Wholesale Case Price: New Zealand Marlborough Gewu...	Blackwell's	2
Invoice	4/13/2006	1356	Wholesale Case Price: New Zealand Marlborough Gewu...	Dosa	1
Invoice	5/25/2006	1414	Wholesale Case Price: New Zealand Marlborough Gewu...	750ml Wine Bar	1
Invoice	6/23/2006	1439	Wholesale Case Price: New Zealand Marlborough Gewu...	Dosa	2
Invoice	7/7/2006	1451	Wholesale Case Price: New Zealand Marlborough Gewu...	Dosa	1
Invoice	7/28/2006	1499	Wholesale Case Price: New Zealand Marlborough Gewu...	Dosa	2
Invoice	8/22/2006	1531	Wholesale Case Price: New Zealand Marlborough Gewu...	Dosa	3
Total Forrest Estate Gewurztraminer 2					
Forrest Estate Riesling 2004					
Invoice	2/14/2006	1088	Wholesale Case Price - New Zealand Marlborough Riesl...	Oakville Grocery Palo Alto	1
Invoice	3/15/2006	1240	Wholesale Case Price - New Zealand Marlborough Riesl...	Home	2
Invoice	3/29/2006	1331	Wholesale Case Price - New Zealand Marlborough Riesl...	Swirl on Castro	2
Invoice	4/6/2006	1346	Wholesale Case Price - New Zealand Marlborough Riesl...	Oakville Grocery Palo Alto	1
Invoice	6/5/2006	1422	Wholesale Case Price - New Zealand Marlborough Riesl...	Swirl on Castro	2
Invoice	7/7/2006	1452	Wholesale Case Price - New Zealand Marlborough Riesl...	Swirl on Castro	1
Invoice	7/21/2006	1488	Wholesale Case Price - New Zealand Marlborough Riesl...	Home	1
Invoice	7/24/2006	1491	Wholesale Case Price - New Zealand Marlborough Riesl...	Swirl on Castro	1
Invoice	8/7/2006	1516	Wholesale Case Price - New Zealand Marlborough Riesl...	Swirl on Castro	1
Invoice	9/11/2006	1563	Wholesale Case Price - New Zealand Marlborough Riesl...	Home	1
Invoice	9/15/2006	1578	Wholesale Case Price - New Zealand Marlborough Riesl...	Wine Styles	1
Total Forrest Estate Riesling 2004					
Forrest Estate Sauvignon Blanc					
Invoice	1/12/2006	1036	Wholesale Case Price - New Zealand Marlborough Sauv...	Oakville Grocery San Fran...	1
Invoice	3/27/2006	1290	Wholesale Case Price - New Zealand Marlborough Sauv...	Blackwell's	1
Total Forrest Estate Sauvignon Blanc					
Forrest SB 2005					
Invoice	1/26/2006	1064	Wholesale Case Price - Forrest Estate Marlborough Sau...	Eos Restaurant and Wine ...	2
Invoice	2/14/2006	1088	Wholesale Case Price - Forrest Estate Marlborough Sau...	Oakville Grocery Palo Alto	1
Invoice	2/14/2006	1090	Wholesale Case Price - Forrest Estate Marlborough Sau...	Woodlands Market	1
Invoice	4/27/2006	1375	Wholesale Case Price - Forrest Estate Marlborough Sau...	The Jug Shop	1
Invoice	5/25/2006	1414	Wholesale Case Price - Forrest Estate Marlborough Sau...	750ml Wine Bar	1
Invoice	6/15/2006	1429	Wholesale Case Price - Forrest Estate Marlborough Sau...	Woodlands Market	1
Invoice	6/17/2006	1432	Wholesale Case Price - Forrest Estate Marlborough Sau...	WINE Bar & Shop	2
Invoice	7/17/2006	1460	Wholesale Case Price - Forrest Estate Marlborough Sau...	Mollie Stones Greenbrae	1
Invoice	7/17/2006	1470	Wholesale Case Price - Forrest Estate Marlborough Sau...	K&L San Carlos	1
Invoice	7/17/2006	1475	Wholesale Case Price - Forrest Estate Marlborough Sau...	K&L San Carlos	2
Invoice	7/17/2006	1476	Wholesale Case Price - Forrest Estate Marlborough Sau...	K&L San Carlos	2
Invoice	7/19/2006	1478	Wholesale Case Price - Forrest Estate Marlborough Sau...	Blackwell's	2
Invoice	7/20/2006	1477	Wholesale Case Price - Forrest Estate Marlborough Sau...	East Side West	2
Invoice	8/30/2006	1546	Wholesale Case Price - Forrest Estate Marlborough Sau...	Mollie Stones Greenbrae	1
Invoice	8/30/2006	1548	Wholesale Case Price - Forrest Estate Marlborough Sau...	K&L San Francisco	1
Invoice	8/30/2006	1549	Wholesale Case Price - Forrest Estate Marlborough Sau...	K&L San Francisco	1
Invoice	8/30/2006	1550	Wholesale Case Price - Forrest Estate Marlborough Sau...	K&L San Francisco	1

Page 1

Figure 11.2   Placement Report

should you. On the other hand, if they are not doing all those things, then you should move on, and the placements can come in handy.

Depletion Reports

Incentive programs should be tied to depletions, translated to mean depletion of their inventory by means of sales. Otherwise, there is no "incentive" for the distributor to produce records to back up the program. The programming you put in place should hold them accountable, to the extent that programming money is not paid until a depletion report shows the cases sold that month or quarter. This is a basic and good reason for depletion reports, but there is more.

It's really in your best interests to see how well the distributor is performing with your brands overall. It allows you to see the pace of sales, determine an order point, see where they may require some assistance to move a wine faster and anticipate your own container compositions. Hopefully, this information indicates progress. In some instances, what the depletions show you are that your wines are moving at glacial speed and at this rate you will be three vintages ahead before they are ready for the next order. If this is the case, another order is unlikely anyway. But if you can catch this trend soon enough you can possibly reverse it. Start by calling the wholesaler to see if it is a problem that may be addressed. If the issue lies with how your wines fit in their market, or lack of interest from their sales team, better to know when to move on than to languish for additional months in ignorant bliss.

Summary

Keys to making your wines a winning combination for you and your distributor can be summed up by one word—communication. If you keep in touch with them, they know it is a true partnership and they will work harder to make it work for you. Listen and learn from them, tailor your programs, presentations and sales efforts to their individual personalities and styles.

My Story

In the beginning, I ran around all over my own market in Atlanta selling up a storm for my new distributor. It was a heady time; the wines sold extraordinarily well, I made inroads into country clubs and restaurants that became new accounts for the distributor and it seemed my portfolio was going from strength to strength. These were the halcyon days of ignorant bliss.

Eventually, I moved my business to Colorado and all those fabulous sales ground to a halt. Apparently, I was virtually the only one out there selling my wines. After all, why should they expend valuable sales force when I was doing so well for them? In those early days of my occupation, I did not know the importance of fostering relationships, holding the distributor accountable and all the points I raised for you above, and will elaborate further into the book. It was certainly a hard lesson.

I recall one of the first Friday sales meeting presentations I made to a large New Jersey distributor. I was confronted by a sea of blank faced, bored liquor guys to whom I was just one more in a long line of presentations. Beforehand, one of them had pulled me aside and offered me a free bottle of a new liqueur if I kept my pitch to less than ten minutes. That was the extent of their interest. I'm not saying that anything would have worked with these guys in the old days. Liquor was still king then and wine the also-ran to these guys, but knowing my audience, and more experience, might have allowed me to tailor my presentation to the circumstances, possibly getting in on the ground floor of a burgeoning wine groundswell.

But there's a much more positive story to illustrate this section too. In California, now many years into my wine career, I made a presentation to Costco, where I made a connection with the buyer that resulted in placements at a time when Costco was developing its fine wine program, still somewhat under the radar for most distributors and importers. The prevailing feeling was that it was not worth the loss of local retailers or potential fallout when they discovered that a discount chain was undercutting them.

That relationship has resulted in many years of successful placements and furthermore, secured distribution in other states, through the ability to offer them Costco business within their states. This is one of those chain relationships that bring the "value-added" component to your distribution relationship.

12

MARKETING

There are many things you can do as part of your overall marketing plan that require little or no financial outlay. There are others that are more costly, but an essential part of doing business in the wine world and ultimately recouped. The trick is to find a way to get the most bang for your buck.

Website Trade Support

Setting up a website is a great vehicle to enable people to find you, to establish the philosophy and mission statement of your company, provide details of the principals and contact details. But don't expect the wine world to come flocking to your door. For one thing, it takes quite a long time for your website ranking to rise above the chaff of millions of websites out there, even with SEO (Search Engine Optimization) and unless you have happened upon a prominent brand that inspires people to seek you out, they won't even be looking.

In the beginning, a website is handy to refer prospective distributors to for credibility more than anything else, an imprint that imparts a sense of permanence. When you actually have brands in your portfolio, it becomes much more of the tools of your trade—and theirs. The trade tools the distributor's sales people are looking for are:

- Tasting notes—latest vintage
- Tasting notes—previous vintages (if they still have them in stock)
- Ratings
- Shelf talkers
- Labels
- Biographical information on the vineyards
- News and Reviews

Tasting notes can easily be downloaded for sales staff to take out on calls, to familiarize themselves with the wines and to leave with the customer, if required. They can bring far more interest to their own presentations and increase their knowledge base. Having previous vintages satisfies the needs of those who are still working on a prior release or interested in the difference between vintages.

Ratings will benefit the salesperson's efforts if they can mention the consistent pedigree of a particular wine or that the one they are showing a prospect, "rated 92 in *Wine Spectator*."

Shelf talkers are not essential on your site (essential in many other ways), but can quite easily be prepared using Publisher or Adobe, will look professional and are very helpful to the salesperson. Once printed on glossy white card stock, e.g., which is my preference, they will look as if they were commercially printed. Any sales rep who needs to replenish his/her supply, or replace one of the shelf talkers in a store that mysteriously disappeared after a visit by the competition, can easily download and print them at the office. Set them up four or six to a page to print and cut out without waste, both for yourself and any downloading by distributors. They should not be so large as to obscure or appear to be referring to the next "facing" on the shelf (someone else's bottle), and not so small that you cannot fit essential information or they will be overlooked.

Labels are used for the distributor's own marketing efforts and for promotions in restaurants (see Figure 12.1). They will often ask you for a set of labels and it is so much easier for you, less time consuming and costs nothing to direct them to the website.

Biographical and historical information gives them a story to work with, something—as has been mentioned before—that differentiates your product from every other brand or wine. This point of difference is what the salesperson is always looking for and becomes an important element, up there with communication and relationships.

News and reviews updates the brand with current elements, including personal winemaker awards, magazine articles, changes at the winery, achieving organic status, interviews—anything noteworthy to add to the presentation for the salesperson, or to enhance the image for the distributor.

Figure 12.1   Te Kota Wine Label

It's easy to make the website fresh by announcing new ratings, recognition or news about brands, winemakers and other noteworthy additions to the front page. It not only educates the salesperson, but alerts the distributor, or prospective distributor, to information they might not previously have known.

Some importers add a tab to identify which wholesalers represent the portfolio in each state and this can be helpful, but not vital. It can become outdated or fail to indicate whether they represent a particular brand or wine the consumer or retailer may be looking for. I consider this an optional choice and one that will not measurably affect your sales efforts one way or another. Receiving the odd email or phone call is not burdensome, in my view, and if you are besieged with calls or emails then I'm sure you will be happy to add the information.

Wine Dinners

In terms of marketing, this takes the subject down to its lowest common denominator—what does it cost and how does it benefit your wines. As with everything else, it has to make sense. Donating dozens of bottles and flying in for a wine dinner without measurable financial gain is just throwing money away. The restaurant will appreciate the exposure and additional revenue they receive, the distributor will think you naïve and you will realize that you just wasted valuable resources.

Wine dinners should only ever be agreed to if you have determined one or more of the following:

1. The cost of wine to you is negligible, nil or reasonable and shared equally with restaurant and/or distributor.
2. There is a tie-in with either a local retailer or the restaurant has its own adjoining wine bar/retail outlet.
3. Wine(s) will go on the restaurant wine list or are already there.

There is never any reason to conduct a wine dinner when you are expected to foot the wine bill in its entirety, there is no exposure for either restaurant or wholesaler and there is no plan for follow through. As much as the evening's guests will enjoy the wine and food pairings, the opportunity to learn about the nuances of flavors and your scintillating banter, they will forget the name and what it looks and tastes like as soon as they don their coats and walk out the door. It's just a law of nature. They don't mean to, but once the magic of the evening wears off, they are back to their lives and the wine is relegated to a pleasant experience. Unless they can find it at their local retailer, who has supplied flyers for the dinner with the enticement of 10% off for participants, or who attends the dinner himself. Often, if it is a special event or wines of some note, they will bring their customers to the evening.

At the very least, the wines have to be available in the area. There is absolutely no point in making the effort to do a wine dinner when the wines are not likely to be available for a couple of months, because there is no return on your investment. Unless—the usual caveat—it is an iconic, high demand brand where consumers are waiting with bated breath for the next vintage and this is a privileged insider's preview. Under that circumstance, they will be very familiar with the brand and feel a connection with the wines that will provide a further impetus to purchase them when available.

Determine how many different wines are desired and how much wine volume is anticipated, how many people are expected and the number of courses. If you don't have a dessert wine, a Cabernet or Merlot may take its place with chocolate or cheese, but often the chef or restaurant owner would prefer to have a true dessert wine to expand their choices and finish the meal with flair. In those cases, I have agreed to the inclusion of something such as a botrytis wine, Port, Muscat or Tokay from another portfolio, but this should be simply added as an addendum to your presentation. A mix of suppliers will normally result in diluting your event and your presentation.

If you know the restaurant or have access to whoever is organizing the dinner, try to coordinate with them to have input into what will be served and which wines you wish to showcase. At the very least, make sure the distributor gives you as much advance notice of both the menu and the wines chosen so that you can prepare your presentation.

Quite often, the wine dinner is scheduled several months in advance, in which case vintages may have changed or wines are expected to be shipped just prior to the dinner. Be sure to follow up at appropriate times to ensure that a.) you will have wine vintages and varietals they wish to feature and b.) the wines the distributor ordered will arrive on time.

If you do not follow up diligently, and sometimes even if you do, it is not unusual for a wine or a shipment to be held up for some reason and not expect to arrive on time. Hopefully, this is just one new vintage or one feature, but in this case you will need to air freight at least sufficient bottles for the dinner. This is an expensive exercise and makes no economic sense, but it is good judgment in terms of PR, goodwill and smooth sailing for the dinner.

If the distributor does not provide handouts, I always provide a list of the wines, with a brief description and room to make notes. Depending upon the venue and availability, placing maps of the region or winery brochures on the table helps to personalize the dinner further.

The advice about speaking at wine dinners is a little like that for the sales staff Friday tastings: keep it interesting, entertaining and to a time limit. The audience is very different, of course, and the information you impart is packaged for the consumer, but the point is to give them a memorable experience that also translates into sales.

Formats for wine dinners can be varied, but essentially there is a reception wine given to the guest upon arrival and the attendees gather in a cocktail pre-dinner setting in a private room or part of the restaurant set aside for the dinner, giving sufficient time for everyone to arrive. This is often the time when the host speaker—importer, winemaker, winery owner, broker, export manager or national sales director—can circulate, be introduced and answer questions about this first wine. It is an informal setting and not usually conducive to public speaking.

Once the guests are seated and the first course is served, along with one to three wines served to be enjoyed with the first course, this may be an appropriate opening for you to get up and speak about the reception wine and the first course wines. Usually at this time I set the scene with background on the region, the winery and perhaps a personal, funny or endearing story about the history and people. I launch into a brief description of each wine and its compatibility with the course. It is an opportunity to give limited technical information: the difference between French and American oak, what malolactic fermentation means (in its basic sense) are examples of what guests might find informative. Discussing a particular varietal and its role in blends, if that is part of the tasting selection, is appreciated. Do not delve into technical discussions regarding the entire process of grape to wine. You will see eyes glaze over and it will all be for naught. They are at the wine dinner first and foremost to enjoy good wine, appetizing food and have fun. In the process they are hoping to make new discoveries and feel uniquely connected to the winery.

As each course is served, gauge the most opportune moment to get up again and talk about the wines. Keep the talk brief, perhaps even briefer as you proceed. If there are numerous wines, you will notice the noise level increasing parallel to wine consumed. Eventually, you will be lucky if you have their attention at all, but persevere with your prepared talk, because you are a professional and it is incumbent upon you to remember that you are performing your job and that is why you are there. However, tailoring the talk to the audience will make it a more enjoyable occasion for them. If you can see they are relaxed and having fun, be relaxed and have fun with them.

Do not become intolerant if they become bellicose; restrain your own drinking so that you do not degenerate to a level that diminishes your effectiveness or image. The wine dinner guests have paid to be there to eat, drink and listen to an expert. Circulate during courses, invite questions, comments and opinions on the wine and remember to thank them all for coming.

Trade Tastings

This subject should be divided into two very distinct areas: trade tastings and consumer tastings. They are as disparate as night and day and despite the seemingly related format have very little relation to one another.

Trade Show—Distributor

In my opinion, the most important trade style tasting is the one you do at the behest of your distributor (see Figure 12.2). Not because this necessarily produces the best results and the most lustrous sales—although it can—but because it demonstrates loyalty and a willingness to support them in their home market efforts. In addition to

Figure 12.2   A Distributor Trade Tasting in New York

direct sales, it is an opportunity to meet or cement relationships with principals and sales staff, and learn more about the trade in that area.

Pay attention to their criteria for the tasting. They can include:

- charging for the booth or table
- providing a table or section for free
- you providing the wine
- sharing the cost of the wine
- requiring you to supply a certain number of bottles
- optional wine quantities
- requiring that all wine be pulled from stock
- allowing you to bring new vintages or special cuvees
- prohibiting any wines that are not already in their inventory

Whatever the conditions your particular distributor imposes, respect them. They have most likely gone to a great deal of trouble to put an annual event together, renting space, providing food, printing booklets, dealing with the logistics of wine and people placement, inviting their top accounts and ensuring it is as successful as possible. It does not endear you to them to demand your own table at the entrance to the room, deviate from the wines they have listed in their book and generally behave like a prima donna. Everyone's needs are important and everyone has the same agenda—to sell wine.

Each venue will be different. I have done trade tastings in the grand ballrooms of fine hotels, a zoo in Phoenix, art galleries, embassies in Washington DC, meeting rooms of moderate chain hotels, tents at the base of a waterfall in Colorado, under canopies in gardens, Soho loft space in Manhattan, an Art Deco theatre in Atlanta and at the distributor's own warehouse. Budget constraints and expected attendance will often dictate the location, but the motivation is always to offer a venue and wine selection that will entice the retailer, restaurateur and occasional VIP customer to come to the event, or choose this one over another at the same time across town.

Always arrive early to allow for set-up, to find shipments that may be missing, to open and allow red wines to breathe and white wines to chill. I usually arrive an hour beforehand and if everything has gone smoothly and I have sufficient time, I can leave and grab lunch, a coffee or a walk.

Wholesalers have differing criteria for the number of wines and number of bottles at their events, depending upon space and number of participants. Usually, there are six to twelve wines, although it can be as little as two, with three to four bottles of each one to account for the number of attendees, and in case a wine is corked. These are wines that will have to be approved with the distributor's event coordinator or brand manager beforehand and should be in stock. They will need to print their booklet/price list with the exact wine and vintage, know their cost and be able to supply an immediate order. In some cases, you may have authorization to show a library wine, new vintage, special cuvee or some other item that is likely to generate interest or excitement. Think about the cost-benefit ratio of this choice. Don't show a wine just to impress if you are unable to bring it in, it's already sold or the likelihood of anyone being able to afford it is very slim.

The other housekeeping items I routinely bring with me are:

- Posters (if available)
- Shelf talkers
- Multiple copies of tasting notes/tech sheets and one laminated set
- Business cards
- Stapler (I have a small travel one)
- Packing tape with dispenser
- Pens
- Depending upon venue, something to decorate the table (e.g., flowers, grapevine, stand)
- Depending upon venue, a sign/banner with my company's name
- Any really good press that is not on the shelf talkers
- At least two wine keys (because someone will invariably borrow and not return one)
- Disposable foil or plastic pourers with collars (depending upon your inclination)
- Foil cutters
- Bottled water, if not provided
- Camera
- Maps of the countries from which your wines originate
- Wheeled bag

All events will provide dump buckets, ice tubs (and ice), tablecloths and pitchers of water, for either rinsing or drinking. Obviously, if you are in an art gallery or a tent, you won't have a wall on which to put up posters or banners. You may wish to invest in a collapsible stand for a printed, permanent cloth or laminated banner. It is retractable, folds up to fit easily in a tube and is a relatively inexpensive way to advertise your business or eye-catching vineyard scene.

I use inexpensive black and white shelf talkers to place in front of each wine to both announce any favorable review/rating/accolade and to provide an easy and inexpensive method for event goers to pick up a reminder of a wine they like. People often comment on how handy this is for them, rather than trying to make notes or gathering a larger collection of papers.

If you have background and a group of tasting notes you wish to give out to interested prospective buyers, stapling them together with your business card keeps it all together for them.

Clear packing tape, on its handled dispenser, comes in handy either to attach something to your booth/space/table or to close the boxes you have stored under your table after you have filled them with the leftover, unopened wine bottles. The boxes can either be easily transported intact to the next location for a multiple city trade show, returned to the distributor, or shipped back to your warehouse.

I sometimes place a laminated map flat on the table, which is a handy reference for people to review the regions. This is especially helpful if you represent wines from an obscure region or wish to demonstrate the proximity of the appellation to other areas or some interesting topographical feature. I also place one laminated copy of a tech or ratings sheet in front of each wine for review. If they are not laminated it means you'll have to keep replacing the sheet as wine and water is spilled on them.

Taking photos of the event in general or having someone take photos of you pouring wine behind your table provides more PR and interest to your website, personalizes you and keeps the website content fresh. Besides, it's nice for you to have a record of the event as well, especially one in an uncommon setting.

A wheeled bag can come in handy to transport any full bottles that either did not come from the distributor's own warehouse, will not be needed for the next event or you are willing to pay for to take with you. Occasionally, you may wish to swap a bottle with another participant and transport that wine out also.

Don't bother with food or crackers. There will be food provided at any tasting, ranging from freshly shucked oysters and carving stations, to cheese and bread.

The best salespeople for a wholesaler will have invited retailers and restaurateurs to the show and then steered appropriate potentials to your table and introduced them to you. This focuses their tasting and, if they respect their salesperson, they will pay more attention to the recommendation.

The attendees will most likely come around with their printed booklet and turn to the page you are listed on to start tasting your wines. They may make copious notes or they may make none. If they indicate a particular interest in a wine—asking about availability, telling you they'd like to replace another wine with this, how it will complement a dish, e.g.,—make your own notes and try to get a business card. This information is helpful to the distributor to follow up on with the trade after the event.

On occasion, you will encounter wait staff and kitchenstaff of local restaurants in place of the buyer and they will be neither in a position to make a purchase nor make a recommendation. However, the restaurant has chosen to send them and it is incumbent upon you to be polite and pour for them as well. It is the right thing to do and you never know when you will encounter them again in a more influential position.

Do not leave your table unattended, unless it is for a brief trip to the restroom, the hors d'oeuvres table or to talk with someone across the room, in which case ask the adjacent supplier if they wouldn't mind watching it for you. You never know when the premier restaurant or retail store representative will come by and you may not get another chance.

Never leave the show early and always make sure you are demonstrating as much interest and effort in promoting your wines as the wholesaler has in putting the event on in the first place. It may be tiring or boring. You may have a hangover from the night before and your feet hurt. This is no excuse. For a few hours of remaining engaged, you will reap the benefits—however large or small, concrete or intangible. If you do not demonstrate appropriate courtesy in all areas, they will remember and perhaps consider your wines less of an asset if *you* become a liability.

When you get back to the office, compile notes on the event, send appropriate information to attendees who asked, and send a list of interested trade and which wines they were considering, to your point person at the wholesaler. Don't wait on this. You will likely forget or lose cards and the trail will go cold.

Trade Show—Independent

These are a little trickier. I certainly would not recommend indiscriminately signing up for trade shows around the country. They can be very expensive, unfocused and ultimately a time waster. There are exceptions, of course, and these should be taken on a case by case basis.

Government wine organizations promoting trade within the U.S. may be conducting a series of trade tastings around the country, or an event at an embassy, for example. Consider the cost-benefit ratio again:

- Is this likely to attract the right mix or number of trade potentials?
- Are you looking for a distributor in the state or territory in which it is held?
- Is the cost for the table/booth within your budget?
- Are you able to bring sufficiently diverse wines to make it worthwhile and will they charge you per wine?
- Does this conflict with anything your distributor is already doing?
- How organized is this entity?
- What is the trade-consumer ratio?
- Are there seminars?
- What is your competition?
- Is there a theme?
- Where is the venue?
- How will it be promoted?

The better organized, more appealing and well publicized the event, the greater the probability it will attract the right numbers and quality of trade. Making sure not to conflict with other, equally appealing events in the same city, or having a series of timely seminars throughout the course of the afternoon, will also increase the attraction.

These events will invariably include a consumer component, either during or after the trade. Including them, at a fee, often helps organizers defray costs, raise funds for a designated cause or allow them to rent a more glamorous venue. They are a necessary, if not particularly personally financially beneficial, aspect and should be considered as well. If the event is primarily consumer and they are expecting fifteen hundred fee paying individuals, the wine requirement is far greater, overall and per head, than for the trade tasting. If your wine is readily available down the street or all over town, or the ratings and reviews are so high as to be a collectible must-have for the consumer, this should figure into your budgetary considerations. But, remember, if you commit to the event you commit to the consumer component. It is unacceptable to pack up and go home after the trade segment and is considered really bad form. Consumers have an expectation that their event fee includes a certain number of wineries or wines, or perhaps they are looking for your wines in particular, having read about them in the press release beforehand.

Tastings of this type are often submitted to the press and this could be another opportunity for exposure for you, either in conducting a radio interview or having your wines recommended in the food and wine section of the newspaper.

Finding a viable distributor at one of these events could make the whole thing worthwhile, so don't discount the possibility, if the format and organizational efforts have met with your approval.

If you have a distributor and you really feel this is a meaningful event, try to include them in the trip by scheduling a market tie-in, either working with a salesperson, planning a wine dinner or by connecting with trade at the show that the distributor can follow up on later.

Consumer Tastings

Anyone who has ever done an exclusively consumer show will attest to the generalization that it is a "drink fest" where an inordinate amount of wine is consumed, rather than "tasted," and the likelihood of someone remembering a wine long enough to make a purchase after the event is slim to none. There are always those who ask you to fill the glass to the rim or keep coming back for more and more "tastes," or try to cajole you into giving them the bottle to take away with them. These are usually the people who are barely able to stand and really do not need another "taste," much less a whole bottle.

Nonetheless, I have done my share of consumer tastings and I have occasionally found them to be fun, beneficial and have some residual benefit. Usually, the event space is more aesthetically appealing than the run-of-the-mill trade tasting and in an interesting locale, which certainly makes it more enjoyable (see Figure 12.3). I have also tied this in with distributor efforts again, working the market on days that bookend the event, conducting seminars and doing radio and print interviews.

Figure 12.3   Disney's California Food and Wine Festival

Dispense with tasting notes and elaborate informational tools, but shelf talkers are really helpful and appreciated for those consumers who wish to pick one up as a reminder of a wine.

Consumer wine festivals and tastings will often recommend the amount of wine to bring with you. I can assure you it will be too much. Irrespective of the number of people they are expecting, you will want to balance limiting your expenditure with providing adequate wine for diverse tastes. I would not bring more than six bottles per individual wine, and less if your range is larger than six wines. If you decide to bring twelve different wines because they represent a cross-section of vineyards you represent, then bring no more than three bottles apiece. Three to four cases of wine is really a generous allowance for this type of event and will still be appreciated.

Despite the insistence of any inexperienced or aggressive festival goers, limit the pour. The aim is not to get them inebriated and your intent is to stretch the wines throughout the day. If you run out of a popular wine or two, that is to be expected. Just make sure you have an acceptable array of wines for the remainder of the show.

If you can interest the consumer in a drawing or sign-up sheet, you may also be able to gather a data base of potential wine buyers, either by selling directly (to states that allow interstate wine shipments with the appropriate license) or to include in an email blast with news and reviews. Those who demonstrate interest can be directed to their local retailers.

The same opportunity for publicity may also apply to a consumer tasting as well, since it will be in the interests of the organizers to draw as much attention to the event as possible for ticket sales and charity tie-in.

If you decide to participate in this type of event, know what you are getting into and have fun with it. Perhaps it's an opportunity to include a partner to pour with you and go skiing afterwards, attend a gallery opening or try a new restaurant.

Making the Best Use of Press

Free advertising is one best use, and can take several forms.

As already mentioned for trade shows, the expanded benefit of such an undertaking is being able to incorporate a radio or print interview or wine review into the experience. It is free and, in addition to local exposure, can be added to the website or press kit for current and prospective distribution.

Press releases are another way to generate publicity. Not to announce you have a new brand, the latest vintage is out or such-and-such brand released a new wine (yawn). Media get humdrum releases of little importance (to anyone but you) all the time. Think about it from their perspective and the relative widespread value of the information.

- Do you have a renowned winemaker coming to town with something interesting to say or event to participate in?
- Are you hosting or speaking at a local consumer tasting that is open to the public?
- Have you just opened your business in the area?

- Do you have an innovative slant to the marketing of your brands?
- Have you "discovered" a new wine region, unknown to the general public?
- Did one of your wines achieve something exceptional? (not just 95 points in a wine publication—of far greater resonance to the reading public)

The list may spark some of your own ideas. I am not a marketing expert and you may find that hiring or consulting with a firm that specializes in this area will benefit you. But at first blush, the opportunity does present itself to market your company and its products for free.

Tailor your approach to the appropriate media outlet. Think about whether your "news" is better suited to a local, citywide, regional or national publication and read sufficiently within that publication to learn more about its tone and the writers. Is there a columnist or a specific journalist who writes about small business, wine or the restaurant scene, e.g.? Submit the press release to them, or call and let them know what you have in mind. A directed approach is often a more successful one.

High ratings and great reviews may be of limited appeal to journalists in considering a piece on your company, but they will be of considerable interest to your prospective and current distribution partners. Include the ratings/reviews/accolades in nicely organized attachments or on your price list. Keep it brief and attractive and minimize the file size (no multi MB graphics). This applies to all emails in general. It will retain the interest of your busy customers or potential customers if you have a clear and concise message.

If you have new ratings in a recognized (generally U.S.) wine publication, send an announcement to your distributors. It is a tool that makes it easier for them to sell as well, so they will welcome it.

POS—Points of Sale

POS (point of sale) material is an essential tool in the wine industry. Of these, **shelf talkers** are probably the most ubiquitous in the business (see Figure 12.4). Some of the uses have already been mentioned, but as a true "shelf talker" to promote your wines in a store, it begins to work for you to differentiate your wine from the multitude of

Figure 12.4 Shelf Talker

options on a store shelf. Eye-catching wording, color and an emphasis on a high rating (if there is one) can propel the consumer to pick up a bottle of your wine over anything else, including label design.

Case cards are another way to attract attention in a store, particularly at a case stacking display. These are stiff, sometimes glossy color or laminated cards approximately the width of a 12 bottle case of wine that is propped up behind the wines in an open case. Marketing in this case can be anything that is of most benefit to you, or fits your brand's style. Again, ratings might be the best and most effective method. Focusing on things like the organically grown origins of the wine, featuring a provocative or evocative logo prominently, highlighting particular features of the wine or the region can all be ways to promote the wine and draw the consumer in the display's direction.

Display sheets—i.e., a form of shelf talker in a laminated, full size 8 ½ x 11 sheet are very handy for stores, where they allow them, for display in racks or, in the case of Costco, in the fine wine bins. As of this writing, Costco prepares its own, standardized shelf talker with an approved rating and inserted in a plastic sheath beside the wine.

This is certainly helpful to the customer, especially since there is usually no wine steward in their stores, but it does become so uniform as to recede somewhat in view. They allowed, again as of this writing, the aforementioned sheets, tucked in behind the wines in the individual bin. I have found, to my surprise, that despite its efficacy not many people do this. Even if other wines are similarly rated, having this colorful, large sheet tends to draw the eye and the consumer's attention.

Table tents are the informational cards you often see on restaurant tables, inserted in Plexiglas sleeves, propped up in their own card base or slipped into menus, usually to announce a special glass pour, upcoming wine dinner or some promotional wine. These are usually provided by the wholesaler, or even the restaurant, utilizing your own logo, the winery label or bottle shot (which they can download from your site) and put together on a computer program. If you are asked, and you can do this inexpensively on your own, they can certainly be worthwhile. It can mean more wines poured or greater attendance at your wine or tasting event.

Brochures from the winery can be helpful and appealing, but have limited quantifiable value. They become more of a souvenir at a consumer tasting, a nice addition to a press kit or an educational piece for the salesperson.

Promotional items are another marketing medium, although they should be used judiciously or you are either wasting the winery's money or blowing your own budget. Polo shirts, hats, aprons and waiter's friends with logo, can all be attractive items to the distributor's sales people, but unless there is an abundance of them, or the winery encourages you to spread them around, I would dispense them only for specific purposes: to supportive sales people, as part of a promotional contest or as a casual wine dinner prize, to the winner of a trivia quiz question or specific ticket number. I don't think there is any value in indiscriminately passing them out at sales meetings or shipping them en masse with wine samples. The original purpose is quickly forgotten and the item becomes simply another article of clothing or a corkscrew rattling around in the bottom of a bag.

Posters are lovely, but of limited benefit. There are always exceptions to these generalizations, and one case for posters might be a signed, framed image that someone would like to hang in their office. In that case, they are usually of the iconic or sensational variety and valued for that reason rather than simply to promote a particular brand.

According to Budget

According to *your* budget and a common sense approach is the way to market your business and the wines you represent.

In evaluating wine tastings, trade shows, consumer festivals and charity events, consider also the city or state in which this will take place. Budgetary considerations then apply to:

- **Hotels**—NYC is clearly going to be more expensive than Dayton, Ohio or staying four nights more expensive than one.

- **Airfare**—across country more expensive than upstate, booking in advance less expensive than last minute.

- **In-town transportation**—will you have to take taxis everywhere or ride the train from another state, or do you need to rent a car?

- **Cost of shipping wine**—air freight, ground freight, taking in your car, checked in as luggage.

- **Quantity and value of wines**—relating to the cost to you for providing it.

- **Service charges, fees for valets, storage**—will you need help with cross-town transport of wine, assistance in and out of hotels, from hotel room to ballroom, charges for storing the wine in the luggage room or having it shipped back to you via their concierge?

- **How and whether you can capitalize with follow up**—the more you follow up the greater opportunity to make sales.

- **Expectations of your distributor in that area**—whether, e.g., they expect you to take the sales team to dinner or lunch, provide bottles for sales calls around the trade show or stay several days to work the market.

- **Tie-in with other markets**—if you can drive or make a quick flight to an adjacent city or state to work that market or attend their trade show it will provide economies of scale.

In evaluating marketing, the considerations are not only whether you can afford it, but does it result in a meaningful return. Broad market, high volume, household name brands do well to advertise in *Wine Spectator* to proclaim a new accolade or remind the consumer that they are still the standard bearer of that country's wines, but this expensive one-off method will produce limited, if any, dividends and blow the budget of most small wine companies.

Expensive, professionally printed four-color, vintage-specific POS is overkill, especially with today's publishing programs. As long as they look professional and are accurate (the right vintage for the right rating!) and omit spelling and grammatical errors, these are perfectly acceptable. Print only as many as you need for a vintage or production, because you will find that you'll be sold out of the wine and still have a stack of shelf talkers or tasting notes left.

Email blasts can be an effective way to market to both consumers and the trade and budget will dictate whether you do this by utilizing your own gathered data, pay a nominal charge for limited services or retain a firm that can provide a comprehensive service to a variety of demographics within the industry and outside it to the wine-savvy consumer. This should still be within moderate parameters. You do not want to annoy anyone with constant reminders or appear to be SPAM.

Summary

Marketing and promotion of your brands and their wines is essential in some sense. They will not sell themselves and marketing assistance is expected. However, the extent of your efforts is at your discretion. If you have a very limited budget, take advantage of all the free, or inexpensive, suggestions I made. Build up a market before you agree to a wine dinner, promote yourself and your business with free exposure, capitalize on all forms of trade and consumer interest and you will find your return is commensurate with your effort, rather than your financial outlay.

My Story

So many wine dinners and tastings, so many mistakes… Early on, in Atlanta, the city of my founding business, I was cheerfully making my lone rounds of the city when I happened upon a restaurant I had not visited before. I was at my most naïve and inexperienced at this stage and when they suggested a wine dinner, I readily agreed. From pride more than anything else, I did not query the distributor as to protocol, but plowed ahead on my own with their requests. They asked me to have the table tents and invitations printed, for which I incurred considerable expense at a professional printer, this being prior to the advent of computer publishing. I agreed to provide all the wines. There was no tie-in with any sales, no agreement that they would put the wines on the wine list or any expressed reciprocation for my generous participation.

The night of the dinner, I arrived to find that the wait staff had opened every single bottle—all 72 of them—in advance of the dinner, without any tally of dinner guest numbers. I was horrified, having provided a case of each of the six wines only from which to draw the necessary bottles, and hopeful that they would buy the rest for their wine list. Attendance was moderate, but nowhere near the numbers necessary to consume the volume of wine, none was ever returned to me (I was too mortified at this stage to ask) and no business ever resulted from this disastrously expensive exercise.

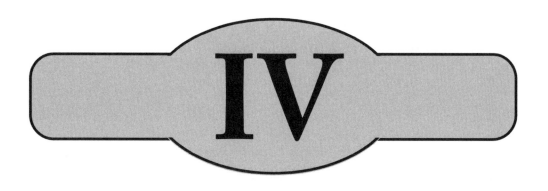

13

INVENTORY CONTROL

There are various times throughout the process from winery to consumer that you will need to be aware of your inventory levels and re-order point. Earlier, I recommended ways in which to evaluate your initial needs. This balancing act and moderate crystal ball gazing goes on throughout your wine career as you make market predictions for the sales potential for your wines.

Reasonable Levels

This will necessarily depend upon a range of factors, including:

- **Price points**—if your wines are on the high end of the scale, or conversely the low end, movement will most likely be commensurate with the cost of your wines.

- **Demand for wines of your region**—if you are on the leading edge of a new trend, or riding the wave of heightened demand, you can factor this in as one of your considerations.

- **Demand for your wines in particular**—e.g., you are hitting a great price point for the wines, find that people are responding enthusiastically to the packaging or style, this may accelerate sales.

- **Distribution**—whether your own wholesalers are hitting their numbers, sales people are responding well, there is demonstrable growth to the brand.

- **U.S. market coverage**—how many wholesalers you have brought on, which of the concentrated population bases have the wines, etc.

- **Future expectations for the wine**—how you plan on increasing exposure, what markets you may open up, putting on brokers, discount programming, starting your own distribution, e.g.

- **Ratings and reviews**—if you have had, or know you will have an outstanding review or comprehensive article in a major publication, with the likelihood that this will increase demand.

- **Your plans for personnel expansion**—perhaps you plan on hiring a National Sales Director, regional manager or sales assistance in the local market.

- **Marketing**—your efforts to promote your brand through advertising, interviews, POS and other tangible means and to what extent they increase sales.

- **Demand from foreign markets**—this is a tricky one, but worth taking into consideration. By this I mean, demand from other countries or the winery's own country. If you anticipate (or the winery has given you advance notice) that the remaining production of the vintage could go to national or foreign distribution, because they have opened up a new market, or because ironically the stellar ratings *you* have generated have filtered back to them and created demand domestically, then it is up to you to protect your current placements and future sales.

The idea is, normally, to order sufficient quantity to fill the pipeline, with a cushion, so that on one hand you won't run out and on the other, get stuck with too much product racking up storage fees. This amounts to devising your own informal formula, based on the points above (and any that relate to your individual circumstances) to determine what you need to maintain a balance.

Vintage Management

You will often hear a distributor ask you about what is new or "fresh" in your lineup. They have already presented the 2008 wines to all the prime accounts in their market and want a reason to go back and generate more sales. Or they have been supplying the same vintage for a prolonged period of time and want the next vintage as a way to stimulate renewed interest. Or because, unless the wine is a venerable, aged reserve treasure, the prevailing thinking in the U.S. is that you should be on such-and-such vintage (especially whites) at a particular point in time.

Figure 13.1   Fifty Barrels Winery

One minor consideration is when harvest occurs in your sourcing region—roughly February to April in the Southern Hemisphere and August to October in the Northern Hemisphere. Therefore, you could reasonably expect to have a New Zealand Sauvignon Blanc released in August and in the U.S. market in September, before California vineyards have even picked their grapes. But no one is going to be that fanatical about it. The release of a 2009 white in September, 2009 is more of a novelty than a guideline. However, if that same 2009 white is still available in September, 2012, there is bound to be a question. It may be drinking beautifully, even better than before and perhaps reviews will attest to its length and depth and enduring quality. You will still have people asking when the next vintage is due, with the same assumptions as expressed above and the further expectation that this next vintage will garner a similarly high rating as the last.

There is much more latitude with reds. The Cabernet may have been aged two years in oak and then left a year in bottle before its release. Therefore a 2006 wine can be a current release in late 2009. It could be such a tannic wine that a later release is anticipated and expected. Conversely, a young, bright Grenache and a light, lively Beaujolais will generally be given little leeway, because these are wines that will show best in their youth and if not suffer, at least change with age.

This is to illustrate that there is some play on either side of that vintage expectation, but in general it is perceived as more favorable to have a regular turnover of vintages and a new release each year, a bit like a coming out. This is generally managed by your ordering pattern, based on taking market conditions into consideration for your particular wine.

If your wines are enjoying routinely positive press, there is a further expectation of a regular release of the next vintage. The idea that you still have a considerable supply of the last vintage left at release time will not necessarily inspire confidence in your customers. Market conditions—recession, inflation, terrorism, decline in appeal, etc.—often cannot be anticipated, but to the extent to which you can plan and ponder the life of each vintage, the more often you will continue to provide wholesalers with positive anticipation. In fact, there are times when you are in a better position if you run out of a vintage, with the promise of the new release in days or weeks, than to still have one vintage when another arrives. Unless the previous vintage is a highly regarded icon that will remain in demand, perhaps exceeding demand for the new vintage, you will find that older vintage languishing in the warehouse until you may be forced to discount it.

The only caveat to this is that you do not want restaurants to run out of wine that is on their list or leave distributors with a lack of supply that they had counted on to fill promised orders. This is going to lose your restaurant placement and annoy your wholesaler.

Turnover

The concept of turning over the wine quickly enough to create an efficient budgetary model could be incorporated into the previous section on maintaining reasonable levels, but really deserves its own breakdown.

It is incumbent upon you to monitor the levels of your distributors' stock as well as your own. This reinforces the need for depletion reports and placement reports from your wholesalers. They should be used not only to determine if your customer is fulfilling the promises made to you, realizing the potential of the brand and providing you with valuable information about their level of sales, but also to advise you of turnover within the distributor's inventory. This is then incorporated into your own planning for reorder points to the winery—with the usual proviso that this should be weighed with other considerations germane to your individual circumstance.

If you are also distributing your own brands in your home state, then turnover is further micromanaged down to the retail level. When was the last time the restaurant reordered? How long has the same wine been on the local retailer's shelf?

Reorder Timing from Winery

If that's starting to sound like a repetition of previous sections, let me clarify for you. In addition to the juggling of market factors and conditions, there has to be consideration given to the winery's own logistical capabilities in the event of an order.

- Is the wine bottled?
- Do they have to book into a bottling queue?
- Is the wine labeled?
- Will the printer be able to accommodate your schedule or the winery's needs?
- Is it ready to be released? (releasing too early can be a mistake)
- Is the winery staffed to handle the order in an efficient timetable?
- Has the label changed to the degree that it will require a new COLA?
- Are containers backed up and require advance booking?

The length of time it will take on the water and overland are of the same importance as they were the first time the wine was introduced. Except that this time there are more people counting on you and, potentially, more to lose if you miscalculate.

Container Consolidation

This was addressed, to some extent, in the section on containers, but bears presenting from a slightly different perspective as a way to emphasize the need to manage inventory and budget by not bowing to pressure to bring in an entire container (700 to 1100 cases), when all you need is 250, or even a pallet (56) (see Figure 13.2). In addition to spreading out your invoice payments, if you need 150 cases and not 1000, it precludes the inevitability that the wines will decline before they have found homes.

Developing a relationship with a large commercially operated wine warehouse will often bring to light other customers who would benefit from container consolidation. The customer rep or warehouse manager may already know of other importers looking for the same opportunity, or having mentioned it to them, they will recall your need when someone else expresses the same.

Other opportunities to locate a container partner might be through your distributor, at a trade show or through the trade association, or equivalent, for the country of your wine's origin.

Usually, even if the regions are divergent geographical areas—even different (compatible) countries—it can be less expensive for the party who has the lesser quantity to

Figure 13.2 Fifty Barrels Winery

arrange for transport to the dock of the primary importer's load. It may even be an expense that the winery will absorb, happy to have an order now rather than wait until you need an FCL, which may be months away. There is no customary manner of handling the financial aspects of transport to port, so this is something that becomes negotiable between you and your wine supplier.

DI—Direct Import

When you achieve considerable traction with a distributor, or you have especially attractive price points, it makes sense for the wholesaler to reach a point where they wish to order from you on a DI basis. This can also become a reality if you have secured chain business, resulting in sufficient turnover to warrant having this quantity on hand. Under the three tier system, it still requires a distributor to purchase and sell the product to the chain. It is up to you as to whether relinquishing control of the container and allowing them to bring it in under their own license is worth it to you. And for the amount of business it generates, it may well be.

In aDI, the container comes from the wine source directly to the wholesaler's port and warehouse, instead of to your usual port and into your warehouse. It is also cleared with your letter of authorization as the primary source. This clearly has considerable advantages over the usual route in terms of logistics and the size of the sale. Aside from a guaranteed quantity, you also avoid the expenses associated with the container movement and any warehousing costs.

The downside is whether you wish to relinquish control over any aspect of the relationship with your supplier and the implications for the future of your relationship with the supplier (winery). You will need to be confident that this distributor will not circumvent you in any way by trying to secure orders directly from the winery, and that you put something in place to ensure that they use you as the broker in the deal. In other words, although they will be the official importer for this particular container, you retain all rights to the brand—arrangements are all made through you and payment for the wine is made directly to you.

You must also ensure you have covered the winery timing aspects (identified in the previous section related to when it will be available), so that sufficient wine is in your allocation and physically at the plant, for an order of this scale.

The expectation from the wholesaler is that you give them a discount for DI, significant enough to make it worth their while to bring in this quantity, which they must then clear and warehouse. It must certainly cover their costs (which you will not pay) and a further discount, based on what makes sense to you, for the benefit of this size order and minimal handling on your part. They may ask for extended terms, or the opportunity to pay in segments. This is certainly something to consider, especially in a difficult economy, because you have a guaranteed sale of product they have now taken possession of, and you won't incur any warehousing fees or inventory maintenance.

Summary

Maintaining inventory levels is much more than just replenishing supply when it is depleted. It is about skilful management of the dynamics of your business as it relates to the winery, balancing your needs and those of your customers, taking the individual characteristics of yours wines into consideration and planning for the future. Adopting this considered and thoughtful approach will enable you to maximize your sales potential and minimize costly inventory mistakes.

My Story

The basic message I have for this section is that I have, like everyone else, been caught with too much inventory of a vintage that became long in the tooth and had to be discounted. Conversely, I have been too conservative with wine orders that became far more popular than I had anticipated which prevented me from capitalizing on the demand.

I have taken on more wine than I should have, because "*it's the last of the vintage and the extra 200 cases will finish it up,*" or "*the next vintage won't be ready for another month.*" Bowing even to subtle pressure, or being influenced by the circumstances is almost always, for a small importer, a mistake. Whatever the winery's motivation—and there is no reason to ascribe anything other than they are thinking of their own inventory management, as well they would—if they are trying to talk you into taking more wine than you wanted, or a vintage you did not need, it is time to sit back, think about the practicality and be prepared to say, "no."

No one can predict accurately every time, but a conscientious approach will net far better results than knee jerk reactions to the moment, bowing to pressure or getting carried away with quantities without a sound basis.

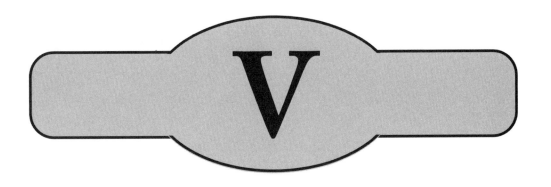

15

MARKET VISITS—WORK-WITHS AND RIDE-WITHS

Invariably, no matter what the size or capacity of your distributor, a visit to their market is required. Ostensibly, this should coincide with an appropriate time of year to work with their sales people, but it is also an opportunity to meet with the principals and cement the relationship. These market visits are called "work-withs" or "ride-withs," depending upon the inclination of the particular distributor. Perhaps geography has some bearing on this. In Manhattan, the concentration of accounts within walking distance would most likely be characterized as a "work-with" as opposed to a "ride-with." Either way, the concept is the same; you are working with the salesperson, either on foot or more usually by car and typically for the whole day. In some instances, the morning person may hand you off to another employee in the afternoon, sometimes to give both a break in the day if they have other accounts to see and pressing business. More often, it is to give more salespeople an opportunity to work with you within the confines of your visit and learn about the wines.

Overall Preparation

There are guidelines for these occasions and abiding by them will earn the respect of the distributor; not following the basics of "work-with" etiquette can brand you as someone to avoid, or at least an unwelcome supplier. It can mean the difference in sales, enthusiasm and the willingness of the salesperson to work with you again. In the world of "work-withs" and "ride-withs," the way you conduct yourself can be a make or break for your wine sales in that market.

The first step is to determine the most appropriate time for the visit and call or email far enough in advance to allow both for your preferences and an opening in their schedule. Less than six weeks would most likely result in an inability to produce both. Normally I try to set up spring visits towards the end of the prior year and autumn visits either in spring, or at least by early summer. Often the first visit, presuming it is successful, can precipitate another visit based on the enthusiasm of the salesperson for your product, or the desire of the distributor to capitalize on what they now see as a value-added brand or portfolio.

At least one month prior to the date, be sure to communicate with the brand manager, sales manager or whoever is scheduling your trip and find out whom you are working with and their contact details. An experienced and professional distributor will often have this information sent to you in an email attachment as soon as the dates are scheduled. Others are more seat-of-the-pants operators, not necessarily because they are any less professional and enthusiastic about your visit, but most likely they are short staffed and always under the gun.

When you have the information, make your first contact with the salesperson or people and introduce yourself, confirm they have all your details and tell them you are looking forward to working with them. This establishes your professionalism and also reminds them that you are in fact coming to the market, in case they were unaware or had forgotten.

This once or twice a year visit is an opportunity to offer discounts for orders placed solely during your visit. It makes the occasion a bit more special and obviously adds a sense of urgency to placing orders while you are there. This is not an expectation, nor should you feel any pressure to provide the discount. It will depend, as with every other incentive you offer, on your capacity and budget. If you do offer, e.g., a

10% discount on orders placed for that day or two days, you may find the distributor will step up to add to it. Keep in mind, also, that this is a finite period and therefore the number of cases—the amount of discount—is also finite.

Wine Dinner and Tasting Preparation

If there are wine dinners and/or tastings during your visit, determine as early as possible what wines are being poured, ensure you have them in stock and they can be picked up in time, or that they already have them in inventory. This is such a critical aspect of the arrangements and applies to your general visit as well. If the wines do not arrive in time for the dinner, it can be disastrous and will necessitate some less than desirable changes or an expensive air shipment. If you do not have the right wines to work with during the day, or sufficient variety, the trip is an expensive exercise that will not produce the desired results.

When planning a wine dinner, the chef will have certain dishes in mind and would like to select, or have you select, wines that will pair best with them. On occasion, they will even develop courses around your wines. This requires that you have information on the menu and ingredients in the dishes well in advance. I find it a pleasurable aspect to my trip planning, because I enjoy a variety of cuisine and the pairing of flavors. If you are not already comfortable with pairing wine and food, it becomes easier as you identify elements of your wines and consider how this will complement the same elements in foods. In the interim, it is always safe to assume certain standards, such as Gewurztraminer with spice, Cabernet Sauvignon with beef, Pinot Noir and Chardonnay with salmon. But it does require that you take the nuances of your own wines into consideration. Not all Chardonnays are substantial enough to stand up to a salmon dish with a heavy sauce. Not all Cabernets will go with all beef dishes. Your Cabernet might have more elements of sage and eucalyptus and a Merlot or Syrah may be better with the sauce or infused flavors the chef has in mind. The Sauvignon Blanc you represent may have powerful tropical fruit and melon; another may have grassy herbaceous characteristics and gooseberry elements.

Don't be overly concerned with the number of wines being poured. As long as you have followed the guidelines I set forth in the section on wine dinners and this is a demonstrable sales opportunity, the more wines poured, the greater the opportunity that guests will find something they like. Generally five to six is customary, but I have had as many as twelve selected by the distributor from several different vineyards.

You will also want to have all the information about the menu and wines so that you can make up a sheet for yourself to capture highlights of the wines and the order in which you will be speaking about them. I sometimes, depending upon the venue and in accordance with the salesperson's wishes, also make up handouts for the guests, so that they can record their comments about the wines. I also try to provide maps and brochures for the table, if they are available.

Wine dinners can be a bit tricky in terms of the attendance of one or more representatives from the distributor. It is expected that the restaurant will comp your meal. You are, after all, the draw for the paying attendees and you will be providing your services as the guest speaker. If the distributor has contributed the wine, most likely a representative will also be comped, but they may require payment from the rep for their meal. Only in special circumstances, where I have not provided any wine, it was a very small distributor and I derived a good deal of benefit for the event (not the least of which is good will), have I voluntarily paid for sales reps to attend. I believe it is up to the distributor to remunerate the employee as part of their expense account.

Time Scheduling

Every market visit is different in terms of what comprises the scope and makeup of the days you spend with each sales rep. A usual time span would be two to three days, perhaps coordinated by you with a trip to a contiguous market, so that you may have two days in Colorado and two days in Arizona, e.g. If the wholesaler's region is quite vast, they may ask you to spend a day each in several cities, sometimes even the whole week. I have felt a bit like a relay baton on occasion as I have worked a city or county and been driven an hour or two to the next destination where another salesperson picks me up and so on throughout a week. It has been a very effective way to cover their regions.

I have also rented a car and driven myself, or taken a flight or train between cities if the distance has been too great, such as in Texas or between New York and New Jersey.

Account Protocol

The time may consist of a day of restaurant and retail accounts, sometimes one or the other if the sales rep specializes in off-premise or on-premise, where we hope the person has been sufficiently interested and organized to plan a solid day of worthwhile appointments for you. This is not a time for ego massaging, where they take you to accounts that already have your product or where the salesperson can easily get your wines in, known as a "milk run." You should welcome the challenging accounts, the new restaurant or difficult retailer where you have the opportunity to make a placement that the salesperson might not otherwise make. This not only creates additional sales for his or her territory, but should engender good will and contribute to their enthusiasm for you and your products.

There are prized accounts they may take you to, where they are on very good terms with the buyer and have fostered a relationship that produces large and regular sales, even without your assistance. Undertaken in the right way, this is an opportunity for the sales rep to signal the retailer that they (the retailer) is important and, as a mark of respect, have brought the direct representative of the wine (you) to meet them. The retailer, if they are already familiar with the wine and carry it, can now put a face to the brand, even if it is the importer rather than the winemaker, and can ask questions and obtain more information about the wines. It is assumed that you will have been to the vineyard and can provide intimate details about the region, viticulture, winemaking techniques and other items of interest. Perhaps you will be able to tell them why this particular red has a higher percentage of Viognier than most Rhone blends, what the vintage was like in '07, or what measures the vineyard takes to be truly considered biodynamic.

If they do not already carry the wine, this is an occasion for you to make some significant sales. The salesperson, by taking you to this account, has also demonstrated a desire to promote your wines and increase your sales. They could, after all, bring almost any supplier to this account if the relationship they enjoy is a special one. They

Figure 14.1 Example of Wine Retail Shelving

have made an assessment that they believe you and your wines are worth this placement.

The *minimum* day, if conducted appropriately, should comprise approximately six to eight appointments, starting around 10am and finishing at around 6pm, with a short lunch break, unless the restaurant is also a selling opportunity where you will spend some time pouring for the buyer, or you are meeting the sales manager for lunch to discuss your portfolio.

There are many other constructs to a day, including a scenario that starts at 8am, when you are picked up at the hotel and driven two hours to the first account, and ending at 11pm when you finish the scheduled wine dinner. It is an exhausting kind of day, but I have done variations on it often and I endure whatever hours and work schedule that has been planned and executed for me, knowing that the time is finite and I will eventually get some sleep. I also respect the willingness of the distributor and the salesperson to put this much effort and time into making my trip successful.

I have met reps at gas stations off the highway or at the first off-premise account of the day and this is perfectly acceptable to me if the sales rep lives closer to the account, it is out of their way to pick me up and if I have rented a car. Most often, the rep will pick you up at your hotel and, depending upon the city and the plans for the rest of the trip, you will not need a car at all.

Expectations

It is customary, and universally expected, that you will pay for the sales rep's lunch. The dedicated professional will either plan the selling opportunity lunch for you, or make a brief and relatively inexpensive stop to refuel and be back on the street. Beware the sales rep that brings you to an expensive restaurant for an extended lunch period, where they only stock Californian wines and will never entertain representing yours. This is the opportunistic sales rep who is looking, literally, for the free lunch and once you leave there is very little post-visit sales activity.

I have been far more impressed with the rep who had me begging for sustenance at 4pm because I was lightheaded from hunger, and in their zeal to see more accounts they had forgotten to stop.

The customary number of wines to take out on these days is six to eight. Too many wines will be off-putting to the buyers, who know a large number will take a long time to taste through. However, there are sales people who may decide to pull upwards of twelve wines from inventory, keep them cool and secure in the car and have available to the accounts the wines they feel may best suit their palates or needs. In my opinion, this is a perfectly acceptable way to conduct the day. Yes, I will generally be billed back for 100% of the samples used during these work-withs, but I will also potentially benefit from the greater diversity of opportunity, as long as the samples are used to best advantage. In other words, opening twelve wines of which three to four may be poured for most accounts will result in a lot of leftover wine. Thinking ahead by the sales rep will result in gathering more people to taste at a restaurant at lunch, utilizing them at dinner or a tasting that night or making sure they are properly sealed for use the next day on the salesperson's regular route. In some instances you could also work with them yourself during the next day's work-with, but I would normally prefer to work with fresh samples since I'm only there once or twice a year and want to show the wines at optimum quality. Of course some big reds will benefit from aeration and fortifieds will be fine.

Presentation Primer

I would prefer to give you the most basic of instructions and recommendations in this section, than leave out areas with which you may not have any familiarity. So, I'll spend a little time with the ABC's of how to "taste" the account, as these were questions I had that went unanswered when I started and left me making it up as I went along.

Anticipate spending twenty to thirty minutes with each account to enable you to give the buyer an unhurried experience with the wines and allow you to relate the salient points on background and winemaking. This is a very fluid time frame, however, and there are almost as many variations on this as there are buyers. It will also depend upon what the sales rep tells you is the norm for that account or if you are running behind.

There will be the buyer who doesn't look up from his laptop and tells you rudely that he only has ten minutes and he will taste a maximum of three wines. I don't take it personally, but I do take it as a personal challenge and have started with exactly that greeting and ended up with a tour of their wine cellar's treasures in the basement and having them taste through all 6-8 wines.

I have had a buyer in Manhattan point to my sales rep and yell, "*get out*" to him as we walked through the door, and ended up with a full, leisurely tasting and a laughing conversation. It's all in the way you handle your "subject." Remember, you are there to sell wine and have traveled to the location for that purpose. If you let them know politely you are only there for the day and could they spare a few minutes, it can turn their mood around and become a pleasant and worthwhile experience. I'm not saying it will always work, but more often than not it will.

A knowledgeable presentation is one of the key elements of the tasting. Going in unprepared will annoy the buyer and make them feel you are wasting their time. Being new is some insurance against this, but there really is no excuse for lack of preparation.

If you have any time at all before your appointment at a wine store, go directly to the aisle that holds your country's section and check out the competition. Look for regions, price points and sheer quantity of offerings. All of these can be used as part of your presentation, to point out differences and deficiencies. You will not want to insult them by suggesting their selection is awful, or denigrate the competition. After all, one can assume they made these selections on the basis of their own palate and discernment. But it is appropriate to say you notice that there is nothing from such-and-such region (which you represent) or you happen to have something from a region on their shelves, but at a better price point, or more representative of the region's style, or in limited allocation. Whatever it is that will differentiate your wines from what they already sell.

If you are at a restaurant, try to look at the menu. It will tell you a lot about how your wines will pair with their dishes. Suggest that your Barbera may go beautifully with their mushroom ravioli dish, your lees fermented Chardonnay with the roast chicken, or a Sauterne with the crème brûlée. They will invariably appreciate that you have done some homework and will be open to the power of suggestion as they taste your wines.

Some sales reps will open the wine beforehand, preferring to establish whether something is corked and to allow reds to breathe. Most will allow you to open them at the first account, so be prepared with a foil cutter and wine key. The sales rep will also have these items, but it is up to you to be prepared. I also travel with a hinged closure for any sparkling wines, since the cork has expanded when released under pressure and will no longer fit. Remember to put all this in checked luggage if you fly! I can't tell you the number of times I've forgotten the wine key hidden in the folds of my carry-on, subsequently confiscated by TSA at security.

Open and pour in the order you feel suits your wines. This is normally lightest whites to heaviest reds and then dessert wines, but there may be a reason why you would open the wines by brand, such as at the suggestion of the buyer, or because you feel this is the way to understand the winemaker's intent or the region. The buyer presumably tastes different varietals throughout the day and, with appropriate explanation, will be able to adjust to tasting reds and whites intermixed.

Start opening as soon as you set up the bottles, as long as they intend to taste all the wines. Try to open all that you are sure they will taste before they are ready to meet with you and at least keep ahead of the buyer, so that you can talk without being too distracted. I am a comfortable public speaker, but I happen to be easily distracted by the process of opening the wine, even after all these years, so I find this enables my comments to flow without interruption.

I usually taste, *and spit*, the wines with the buyer when they are first opened, to feel assured they represent the expected wine characteristics, and towards the end of the day to see how they are developing. I once poured a Verdelho without tasting it and throughout several appointments I was waxing lyrical about it being *redolent with tropical aroma* and having *a luscious passionfruit palate*. Mid-afternoon someone finally asked me to try the wine with them and I discovered that there was virtually no nose and undetectable passionfruit characters. It was not corked, but it was definitely closed or possibly so slightly corked that no one was game to mention it. It was embarrassing to me that I had been so explicit about its qualities and must have left a string of puzzled buyers in my wake.

Pour enough to enable them to swirl the glass, to allow the aromas to become evident, and to get a full swallow or two. They will most likely pour the remainder out anyway. If they want more, by all means readily pour it. The aim is not to be stingy and overly frugal, but not to waste the wine either and perhaps run short at your last accounts.

Just as you take cues from the sales rep, likewise gauge the buyer's habits as they assess the wines. No one wants to be told exactly what they taste. They can decide that for themselves. Giving them some background, oak treatment, fermentation, distinctions of the vineyard or perhaps an obscure flavor they may not have encountered is usually welcome. Sometimes they want complete silence until they have finished, preferring to absorb the wines for themselves. In that case, they may have questions at the end, or inclined to reject or accept the wines on the basis of price and taste, with a view to their customers' preferences.

Allow the tasting to conclude before mentioning price. This is usually the provenance of the sales rep. It is the distributor who sets the pricing for their business and it is not your place to quote pricing, unless you have memorized the distributor pricing from previous account calls that day and simply repeat what you are aware they have established.

You do have latitude with discounts and special deals for your visit, but this is something you will be expected to support through samples or appropriate pricing on the next order, unless you have discussed it with your distributor beforehand, as outlined in the last section. It should not be sprung on the buyer or the hapless sales rep.

On occasion, a discount may make the difference between no sale and a considerable order if you can reach a particular price point, and this is something that can be discussed spontaneously, as long as it is understood that you will be supporting this discount. You or the sale rep may need to call the sales manager to verify the feasibility of this one off deal, and perhaps to verify that you have agreed to provide the necessary bill-back payment that will result from the discount.

At the conclusion of the tasting, instead of asking for an order, ask the buyer if there was a particular wine that stood out for them. Try to make a comment or two on each wine that designates them as special, either because they are very small production and there is only a finite amount available, the vineyard is certified organic, the blending varietal is unusual, the region is new, the winemaker previously made wines for such-and-such widely touted vineyard or whatever you can legitimately use to distinguish them from others in the store. Don't wait so long at this juncture that you've lost the buyer's attention or he/she has to move on. Very often, especially in less experienced sales reps, they will leave the entire presentation up to you, including asking for the order. At other times, they will know how to step in smoothly and take over, which they should since their commission is dependent upon it.

There is also the other type of sales rep, usually the completely inexperienced, or the unabashedly narcissistic (fortunately rare). They cannot help speaking incessantly during the presentation, either derailing your presentation before it has a chance to begin, or jumping in where they should just wait. On those occasions, I always wonder what they think I'm doing there. Could they not have just done all this without me? My approach is normally to diplomatically suggest, out of the buyer's hearing, that they use me to the best advantage, since this is why I have come all this way. If there is something they feel could add to the moment, based on specialized knowledge of the region, or the particular quirk of the buyer, by all means make that contribution. Otherwise, sit back, relax and let me do all the work.

If the buyer happens to be absent, called away unexpectedly prior to the appointment, or unable to taste for some medical reason, suggest to whomever is there that you leave a glass or two of particular wines you, or the sales rep, would like the buyer to taste. The glass opening can be covered in plastic wrap, if available, or at least a card of some sort placed on top to keep as much air out as possible. This is often done and can result in sales later. Not as effective as having them standing before you and tasting through the wines, but still better than leaving without any opportunity to make an impression.

I take shelf talkers with me on every sales call, either to leave it as a small reminder of the wine they tasted, or to put them up on the shelf in a retail store if your wines are already in stock. Well worded shelf talkers, hopefully with some impressive press, will inevitably boost your sales. There are too many confusing options for the consumer and this allows them to make a much more informed and comfortable decision.

One word of caution on the shelf talker with the great rating. I am especially averse to using shelf talkers of previous vintages, just because that was the one that garnered the press. I see it often in wine stores, but except when in error, I find it unethical and obviously misleading. If 2006 rated 94 and 2007, the current vintage, rated 89, you cannot leave the 2006 shelf talker. There is no reason to assume that those vintages and wines will be remotely similar, but the consumer will probably think the rating applies to the wine currently on the shelf.

Many wine buyers will eschew any wine ratings and some will simply ask you not to talk about them. But ultimately, as wine professionals, we are all aware of the impact and import of the rating and whilst the ostensible reason for leaving the shelf talker is a reminder of the brand and wine tasted, a prominent review or rating will not be overlooked (see Figure 14.2).

Ultimately, if the sale is not made then it is up to the sales rep to make contact later, assuming there has been any indicated interest. Take notes about the encounter and follow up with the rep after the visit to see if the presentation resulted in a sale.

Figure 14.2 Wine Retail Uniform Shelf Talkers

Dos and Don'ts

- **Don't drink during these ride-withs.**

  Tasting is important, of course, and should be part of ensuring the quality and integrity of the wine. But drinking during the day is another unprofessional way to turn off your accounts and the sales rep. Again, the stories I have been told of importers, brokers and winemakers who drank their way through an embarrassingly unproductive day are legion. These are sometimes individuals whose wines are considered necessary to the wholesaler's portfolio, but they are not welcomed gladly and they are not relationship building. If the distributor has an opportunity to replace their wines, they will do so.

- **Expect to wait at some accounts.**

  Either the retail or restaurant buyer is backed up, they haven't budgeted their time well or they had a medical emergency. Occasionally, they may have a cold, have just been to the dentist or simply disinclined to taste. This may be a wasted time slot in your limited day, but remaining cheerful and open to discussing the wines can also result in a sale. Never become impatient or refuse the opportunity. Take cues from your sales rep as to the benefit of waiting, the likelihood that a sale will result or how to handle the temperament of the buyer. We are there to sell a product, after all. Certainly we would like to elevate this product to something loftier than nuts and bolts and I'm sure we usually derive more enjoyment than the nuts and bolts salesperson, but our objective is still to make the sale and satisfy the customer.

- **Don't load the buyer up with material.**

  The majority will undoubtedly end up in the rubbish bin, as they only have so much room or inclination to keep information on wines they may never purchase.

- **Do ask them if they'd like a tasting note**

  Do ask them if they'd like a tasting note on a particular wine they are interested in, or will be buying. This often helps them to educate their sales staff or add notes to a wine list.

- **Try to engage the sales rep**

  Try to engage the sales rep during the day. Develop a rapport that can be built on during the year and at subsequent visits. I try to find the common denominator with each individual and ask questions about their interests, experience in the business and how long they've been with the distributor. Irrespective of the personality, there is always a way to encourage conversation and not only make the day more pleasant, but help the person you are working with become more interested in you and what you represent. You would be surprised at how many stories I've heard from sales reps about disagreeable suppliers—people who were surly, unfriendly, uncooperative, demanding, hung-over or unhelpful. These are not individuals who endear themselves to sales people who have set aside their day and made an effort to create a successful experience for them. I often wonder why they bothered to make the trip at all.

- **Do follow up with the sales rep**

  Do follow up with the sales rep after you return to your home base and let the sales manager know, via email, how you felt about the visit if it was positive. He or she can share this with the rep. Call the sales manager if you felt the rep was too inexperienced to make the day productive, or if it was a negative experience overall. Better to discuss this over the phone or in person, than commit it to writing. You will want to be diplomatic and let them know that you were reluctant to say anything, knowing that you could potentially alienate a salesperson you may work with again, but felt it was in the best interests of the company to do so. They should appreciate it.

- **Honor your commitments**

  Honor your commitments to anyone you encounter during your visit. This includes buyers, sales reps and distributor management. If you promised to send them a map, poster, brochure, find out some esoteric information or comply with a special request, they may not remember if you forget, but they will remember if you do send the requested information and it will impress them and encourage support of your brands.

Summary

Behave like a professional at all times during your work hours with a distributor and their representatives and remember the key ingredient to this encounter and the success of your work-withs—like everything else in the wine business—is the relationship you establish and foster. This does not mean you can't go out for cocktails afterwards or spend some time socializing with the sales team. It is simply important to remember to keep your eye on the prize during the time you are actually working. These are your sales rep's work hours too and no doubt they would like to make the most of them.

My Story

Market visits can be tremendously rewarding, fun and productive. They can also be excruciatingly boring, stressful and financially disastrous. I have experienced the gamut of these, but somewhere in between lies the norm and whilst still enjoyable, they are also hard work and profitable.

I have been left stranded in my hotel room by a sales rep who was unaware they were working with me that day, because the distributor failed to tell them. I've also had sales reps tell me they hadn't booked any appointments, because they didn't get any warning about my visit (I discovered they had). This is where I learned to always lay the groundwork for the visit several days in advance. In the latter example, we were still able to salvage the day because they knew the accounts they could go to without an appointment and also called ahead to set up whatever they could whilst driving. The bleakest of these examples was when I sat with a sales rep in a parking lot in a large southern city, with the car running, while she rustled through papers and her day timer looking frantically for accounts she could call amid an area ripe with retailers and good restaurants. She called two people, discovered they had no time and gave up. She drove me back to the hotel and I shortly thereafter severed ties with the distributor. This was the last of many, many chances.

On the other hand, I endured, year after year, a series of wine dinners in one particular city that were extremely stressful, punctuated with periods of boredom, but sufficiently profitable to lure me back every year. The distributor in this case was a man with no imagination and limited conversational skills, partnered with an unpredictable bipolar wife. I suffered through many strange days with them. The main focus of the visit each year comprised three nights of wine dinners which were well attended and resulted in significant sales. Many of the attendees were there to be educated about the wine and to subsequently buy, but it was also an entertaining social night for them and the evenings were late. It was often after midnight when I finished. The next day would begin early and sometimes consisted of long drives to accounts. At times I suffered from laryngitis, allergic reactions to the local pollen and lack of sleep without any consideration from my distributor, but I soldiered on secure in the knowledge that it would end and I would be able to sleep and recover when I returned home. These visits took their toll, but they did result in upwards of several hundred cases in sales with each series of wine dinners, and for a small importer this was significant. Not to do the dinners meant foregoing any sales at all with this distributor, since they considered them an integral part of the relationship. It is up to you to decide what your time and effort is worth and to respond accordingly to opportunities with which you are presented.

Conversely, my favorite visits were to a small distributor in a quirky mountain community in North Carolina and I spent many long days and nights with them driving around the different towns and conducting tastings and dinners. This distributor's fun, cheerful and endearing reps ensured that I had breaks, adequate downtime and rest, and thoroughly appreciated all my efforts, as I did theirs. Unfortunately, they were a victim of the current economy and have gone out of business. These were some of the good guys and will be missed.

16
MAINTAINING DISTRIBUTION

As already stated, it is not sufficient to make the sale and then leave the wholesale company to its own devices. You must nurture and massage and be the (pleasant) squeaky wheel for as long as you have product represented in their house. The importer who does not become a true partner in this process is the importer who will find the early efforts have been for naught and your product relegated to the close-out bin.

Support and Ongoing Communication

This can be a fairly fluid component, depending upon the distributor's needs and the dynamics of their company. At one end of the spectrum is someone who expects you to make regular visits, call and email constantly with updates, send samples of new product and vintages upon release and be prepared to offer regular discounts and incentives. At the other end you have a wholesaler who basically wants you to leave them alone to do their job and make one visit a year to work with their salespeople.

The first, needy example may indicate excessive demands based on the volume of business or, conversely, they may be the most important customer you have and comprise 30% of your business. The level of support you provide—i.e., time and money—should be commensurate with what you get back from your distributor. But initially, it is important to make known your desire to be a team player and allow the relationship to develop in an appropriate way. If you find that the orders only come when you work the market, and only to the extent of the sales you made while you are there, then this is not a partnership. Essentially, you are the only one working and the subsequent sales may not be worth the cost of the travel and incentive deals.

At that other end of the spectrum, where the wholesaler basically wants you to leave them alone, it is still in your best interests to be a contributing member of this collaboration. It is vital to provide appropriate sales tools to enable them to maximize their efforts. Leaving them entirely on their own can also result in forgetting about your portfolio.

- If you have new press, be sure to send it.
- Include them in any quarterly incentives and programming.
- Propose depletion allowances on higher volume.
- Offer to come and work the market at a suitable time.
- Let them know when a product level is low, or when the next container is expected.
- Direct them to the website where new trade tools, i.e., great press, tasting notes and shelf talkers, are available.

All of this can be conducted via email, of course, with the occasional, judiciously placed phone call. Leaving them entirely alone perpetuates a misconception that you are only marginally interested in their region and eventually they will only become marginally interested in you and your products.

Expectations

Expectations established at the beginning of the association may morph and modify as time progresses. As the relationship matures, your expectations may change as the distributor demonstrates the extent to which they will support you and order consistently.

Their expectations of you may also evolve as the wine becomes easier or more difficult to sell, as they need assistance to move an older product or require help to land a sensitive account. They may expect greater discounts for larger sales or monetary collaboration on a chain proposal, e.g.

Expectations, whether voiced or tacit, are always in play. The trick is to weigh the expectations, provide appropriate responses and maintain equilibrium in the relationship.

Retail Support and Pull-Through

The first sale is, literally, just the beginning. The wine list placement and the bottle on the retail shelf are nice starts, but small potatoes compared to what you can achieve if you continue to support the account. The goal is the glass pour, the case stack, the end cap (shelving at right angles to the main aisle shelving, facing out with the most exposure, see Figure 15.1) and the consistent orders from the retailer to your distributor. The pull-through. The repetitive sales themselves are significant, but it also confirms to your distributor that you, and your wines, are not a one trick pony. They have staying power. Assuming the wine's QPR, much of this will be accomplished by the responses you make to the retailer and the follow up with both the retailer and the distributor rep.

I have just covered, in the previous section, the value of responding to the retailer or sales rep's questions and requests, thereby establishing credibility and your interest in them. Cultivating a sales rep is also important. This is preferably the go-to guy or woman with whom you built a rapport, or the one who consistently generates the most sales in the company. These are likely to respond well to your genuine desire to support their efforts and increase sales—a win-win situation for both of you. Ensure that they always receive personalized emails and the latest news about the vineyard and wines. If they ask for samples for an approved presentation opportunity, send them. This may be the rep some distance from the headquarters and will appreciate that you sent the samples to their home rather than having to drive to pickup samples. It could be that the sales opportunity has a deadline, the release is new and not in stock and sending samples directly to the rep will save time and help them meet their goals.

Figure 15.1 Endcap Display

I'm not suggesting you foolishly eat into both your sample allowance and then your margin with indiscriminate shipments of wine to an individual sales rep. These are circumstances that stand on their own merit, after you have evaluated the person and the situation. Be cognizant of the sales rep's credentials.

- Are they a star seller or have they used up their sample quota from the main office and are looking for a way to circumvent the system?

- Did you get a good gut reaction to them during your 8+ hours together on a ride-with or did they seem to be driving around aimlessly without a plan for the day?

- Do they have a proven track record or are they new to the company and inexperienced?

Taking a chance once or twice may yield meaningful results. If not, you will have to reevaluate the wisdom of doing it again. I have experienced disappointment several times, but would still be willing to make the determination on a case by case basis and take a chance on a valuable return.

Retailers and restaurants can achieve a favored status to you, and you to them, also by establishing rapport and continuing to maintain the relationship. Perhaps it's the account you always call on when you are in the area and have taken the buyer to lunch to thank them for the previous sale or to taste them on wines away from the hustle bustle of the store. It may be the restaurant that held a successful wine dinner and attributes that to both the wines and your personality. Whatever the reason, they will support you and your wines and, aside from the benefit of spending time with someone you enjoy when you are in their market, you also have almost a guarantee that they will be receptive to your next release, new brand or something else from your portfolio. They may even save a spot on the wine list for you or ask their rep if you have something from a certain region, because they want to continue the relationship. Don't let them down if they have your wine on the list and order consistently. If you are going to change vintages, give them plenty of notice and try to save an appropriate number of cases of the current vintage for them, since this is what they selected and is in print on their list.

In addition to communication, visits and wine presentation, try to think of other ways in which you can let them know you appreciate them. It could be a winery polo shirt, apron or cap, things you have received for free from the winery. It could be something small from a trip to the wine region you know they will enjoy or an occasional lunch for the retailer. Or it could simply be a tiny allocation of something special that you can only supply to five distributors in the whole country and you have asked the rep to show it to this particular restaurant, knowing they will love it and it is perfect for their cuisine.

Diversify Portfolio Placements

Much of the time, you will want to have all the brands you represent in the one wholesaler house in the state. But there are certainly situations that call for diversification amongst distributors within the same state and can be the savviest way for you to maintain distribution. The reasons why you might consider this are:

- If the distributor is too small to take on several brands at once.
- If the distributor is too new to gauge their effectiveness.
- If you have too many brands for any one distributor to focus on them all.
- If the distributor only covers a specified area or territory.
- If certain of your brands are allocated premium and others are high volume value priced.
- If you want to evaluate the effectiveness of two or more distributors.
- If the distributor has expressed interest in only a part of your portfolio.

In most of these examples—and there can be others—the decision is yours. Make it without an emotional attachment. It is so easy to think you can check off that state and move on. You like the wholesaler, you hope for the best and in time they will do greater volume, or venture into other brands. This may happen, but it also may not. The distributor themselves may even tell you they will never be able to sell such an expensive brand in their state or they have too many wines from one region you represent. *All* your wines deserve your best efforts at representation and it is up to you to dispassionately assess your options.

Winery Visits to the U.S.

This is a far different animal than your market visits to the distributor and most definitely requires its own section.

The winery owner or winemaker will invariably decide at some point in the game that they need to come over and assist you with sales. This is said with the best of intentions, but sometimes with an inflated sense of how valuable this visit will be. For some reason, despite all your experience and familiarity with the U.S. market (and eventually, if not already, this will be true) the occasional winery owner, who is also often the winemaker, will be absolutely convinced that their brand will somehow flounder and fail without their hands on efforts, and in fact it is imperative to the success of the whole U.S. venture that they come over and shepherd its passage through the three tier system. And it requires two, extended, multi-city visits a year to accomplish this.

I welcome the "face of the winery" at most times, but usually discourage a vigneron from making this visit when the wine has just arrived or has just been launched. They are understandably chomping at the bit. It has taken months to get off the ground and the wine is finally on its way. However, this is a critical time for you—registering the brand, perhaps obtaining new licenses, getting samples out, researching more distributors, making sales and capitalizing on what may be a critical season. Once you enter the winery owner in the mix you become a travel agent and event planner and your own carefully laid plans must go on hold. There also may not be much the winery representative can do, given the limited number of markets that have the wine and whether these markets are ready for their own launch.

At the other end of the spectrum, there are winery owners you will have to coax to come over at all. They cannot find the time to leave their vineyard businesses or are so reserved that they do not feel comfortable in an unfamiliar social setting. I once represented a brand for over ten years and not once did the winery owner, who was also the winemaker, make a trip to the U.S. It was a good, solid brand from an organic vineyard, but it would undoubtedly have benefited from his appearance. If nothing else, he would have witnessed the changing U.S. palate styles and updated his wines accordingly. The wines were excellent quality, but somewhat old fashioned and sales eventually suffered.

So, whilst I encourage most winemakers/owners to visit (with exceptions, discussed later) because they do create a bigger buzz and are the actual people who have their hands in the soil and their feet in the juice—so to speak—the timing has to be right. If scheduled properly, with notice and not in the middle of summer, they will usually be very welcome and distributors will make space for them and put forth special effort to see that their time is well spent.

Initial Planning

Notice is imperative, just as it is for your own visit. Perhaps even more so, because you will need time to select the most advantageous locations, give the targeted distributor as much notice as they'll need to put on an impressive and worthwhile visit, schedule the trip and, as already said, put on your travel agent's hat. There really isn't any other alternative. Even if you tell them exactly which states and cities you wish them to visit, it is understood that they will not know where to stay, what connections to make, how long they need in each place and many other details. The Marriott downtown may not be the best choice. It could be the little inn closest to the rep they'll be working with, or the chain motel near the wholesaler's headquarters on the other side of town.

Establish at the outset how long they plan on being in the country. If it is one week, then you will be better off keeping them to one general geographical area to minimize travel and maximize working time. If they indicate they'd like to be here for three weeks, but only want to work in your home state and Manhattan, for example, this has to be discouraged. Working within your own state will presumably necessitate monopolizing all your time, unless you have a full complement of sales people, and now you have someone doubling up on a market you have already covered and their effectiveness is diminished. Perhaps Manhattan is a new market for you and there is limited potential for this brand, or it is too soon to send a winery owner, or they are overbooked. It may require a brief day in Manhattan and the rest of the time in New Jersey or upstate New York. Although you must work within their time constraints and availability, you cannot allow the winery representative to dictate the areas they will visit, and most don't try. Dayton, Ohio or Denver, Colorado may be far more attractive alternatives. You are the expert in this situation and ultimately both of you will benefit from your choice in increased wine sales.

Determine which airports they will enter and depart from. They may be at opposite ends of the country. Possibly they are arriving in New York and may be going on to British Columbia to spend time with their Canadian agent. Or arriving in LA and departing from New York to attend the London Wine Fair. This is quite common and all has to be taken into consideration when planning their visits. You won't want to have them ending up in California when they need to get back to New York the next day to take a flight to London.

I have also found it surprisingly common for less experienced winery owners to schedule a seven day visit and expect to be busy for all seven days. I do understand the desire to maximize every moment they spend on an international business trip, especially one of such short duration. But there is very little that can be done on a weekend and usually nothing at all on a Sunday, with the possible exception of a trade show, which has been scheduled and registered for months in advance. Wine dinners, advertised afternoon tastings at stores or wine bars and casual store tastings *can* be organized, but again requires a good deal of pre-trip planning and the willing cooperation of the distributor. There are some wholesalers that simply do not have the time, nor the appropriate state licensing ability, to conduct tastings on the weekend, and Saturday night is usually a restaurant's best attended night and they may be reluctant to give it up for a less well attended wine dinner.

When the trip is of longer duration, the winery representative will often appreciate a Saturday to travel from one location to the next and Sunday to rest or see something of a city.

Trip Logistics

First of all, it may appear to be an appropriately courteous action to accompany this winery representative to each location to pave the way, introduce him or her to the distributor principals and make this a smoother trip in a foreign country. In fact, as I write this it sounds as if it is absolutely the right thing to do! But unfortunately, unless you have an unlimited budget and plenty of time, the reality is that it is far more practical for you to send this person off on their own to *enhance* your efforts, not monopolize your time and incur additional expenses in duplicating the effort. Not that you cannot meet them somewhere or have them start or end their trip in your home state to discuss business or see some accounts, but to accompany them on every leg is impractical. I have found that, once I explained this to my suppliers, they are understanding and ready to meet the challenges of negotiating the country alone. After all, I have arranged for every contingency, including which airports they arrive and depart from, what mode of transportation they will be using, whether someone can or cannot pick them up, the hotels, contact details for all persons with whom they will be working and arrangements for functions. At a later date, when you are able to appoint regional managers, these are the individuals who will be best suited to escort winery representatives during their trip, and will most likely learn a great deal more about the wine and its origins in the process.

An example of the itinerary of a couple who travelled together, since both were owners can be seen in Figure 15.2; one was the winemaker, whilst the other managed the vineyard operation and marketing. There had been previous wine trips to the U.S. to other locales and this was a two week visit to supportive, secondary markets, aimed to utilize their time to best advantage with additional tastings and wine dinner. Although they had down time over each weekend, it was still quite a packed trip.

During the Trip

Much of the same protocol applies to the winery owner/winemaker/principal as it does to you, the importer, regarding transportation, the sales calls and other facets of conducting a successful sales trip. I have enormous respect for the winery/vineyard/ brand owner whose wines I have chosen to be part of a select group in my portfolio and have taken pains to ensure that we are a good fit. However, it does not mean they are fully conversant with U.S. market visit protocol and it is incumbent upon you to both advise the winery representative and, if necessary, prepare the wholesaler. I perhaps go into excessive detail on this aspect. You may benefit from reading it all, or glean what is useful to you depending upon your situation.

- In the case of **advice to the winery owner**, especially if this is their first trip, this should come in terms of expectations regarding the sales call and their particular presentation, who pays for lunch (they do), rundown of tipping in the U.S. and a general overview of the markets they will be visiting. I also try to prepare them by offering suggestions for a diplomatic presentation at an account. For instance, how not to bore or, however well-intentioned, insult the buyer!
  o **On boredom**—having the direct winery supplier at the store is normally a unique and welcome opportunity for buyers to pick their brains on a region, ask esoteric questions and generally add to the store of information. However, they do not want to be lectured or talked down to. They do not always want to be given tons of technical information and have the winery owner talk in explicit detail about their vineyard and techniques.

One Mile Winery Owner's itinerary
September, 2011

Arrive September 7th—Wednesday—LAX

Depart same day for Phoenix, Arizona (Sky airport) from LAX
Accommodations at Marriott in Old Town—short shuttle ride from airport
3311 North Scottsdale Rd, Scottsdale, AZ, 85251 (8 miles from airport)
Confirmation #83320371—King, Non-smoking—$119.00 (AAA or NRMA rate)

ARIZONA

September 8th—Thursday—work Phoenix with Superior Wine Distributing salesperson
(you will be picked up at hotel)
September 9th—Friday—work Phoenix with Superior Wine Distributing salesperson

COLORADO

September 10th—Saturday—depart for Denver, Colorado (shuttle from airport)
Accommodations at: Four Points Sheraton Cherry Creek—close to distributor and shopping
mall/restaurant area 600 South Colorado Blvd., Denver, CO, 80246
Confirmation #: 777380537—King, non-smoking—$79.00 (AAA rate)
September 11th—Sunday—free day in Denver
September 12th—Monday—work with Stellar Cellars salesperson (pick up)
September 13th—Tuesday—work with Stellar Cellars salesperson (pick up)

NORTH CAROLINA

Depart that evening for Asheville, North Carolina from Denver airport.

Accommodations at Atlantic Distributing guest house, Asheville (no expense—taken to
location by sales rep who will pick you up at airport)
September 14th—Wednesday—working Hendersonville and Black Mountain
Event at Merry Wine Market that evening (sales rep pick up)
September 15th—Thursday—working Asheville (as above)
Event or dinner that evening (TBD)
September 16th—Friday—depart for **San Diego, CA**

Accommodations at: Inns of America Suites
5010 Avenida Encinas, Carlsbad, CA, 92008
Confirmation #136655–2 Queens 'family' suite—non-smoking—includes continental
breakfast—$143.00 (AAA rate) (shuttle from airport)

Figure 15.2 Sample Itinerary

They do not want to hear a supplier drone on about their fabulous chateau in Tuscany and be shown 8x10 glossies of this magnificent palace. As this particular story was related to me, the off premise buyer declined to buy the products of the chateau owner "because *he* obviously doesn't need the money and I know other suppliers who do." A winery owner must, within reason, be just as sensitive to the situation and the personalities as you, the importer have to be.

o **On diplomacy**—the last thing a potential buyer for a wine wants to hear is how much better this particular wine is than anything else they have in the store. They don't want to have their current selection ridiculed or denigrated, nor be the recipient of negative gossip about a certain vineyard's practices, whose wines they happen to have prominently displayed in a case stack or end cap. On one occasion, to my great discomfort, I was in the presence of a winery owner who proceeded to tell the store buyer that the reason they had selected this particular Chardonnay to export to the U.S., out of the five or six they produced, was because *"the U.S. palate is not as sophisticated as the average Australian palate."* Needless to say, no sale was made at this account.

- In the case of **preparing the wholesaler** I might give them a synopsis of the winery's own expectations in regards to their market and any quirks, foibles and idiosyncrasies of the individual. Now, clearly I have made a point of establishing the importance of working with people you enjoy and with whom you can form a good working relationship. This still holds true, but that doesn't mean they don't have distinctive traits that, once conveyed to the distributor, might make for a more enjoyable and productive trip. These might be very positive attributes, such as this winemaker likes to work long hours and would really appreciate having evening events scheduled as much as possible. It may be that they have never been to the U.S. before, so it may take them a little time to acclimate, but they are excited about the prospect of helping with sales, or that English is not their first language, but they speak it fluently.

Ultimately, you will have no control over the conduct of your supplier and the success of his or her visit, but planning ahead can save some headaches and misunderstandings.

Winery Expectations of the Trip

As discussed earlier, you may have to—nicely—disabuse the winery owner of the belief that their mere presence in the market will herald spectacular sales. I don't mean to sound cynical, but you may also need to help them understand that everyone will (usually) be especially polite to them as they make their way through on and off-premise accounts, out of respect for their role and the distance they have come to see the account. The buyer may also, in their misguided attempt to compliment the winery owner, tell them how much they love the wines and suggest that they will be purchased just as soon as they can find room in their inventory, on the floor or on their wine list. This may or may not be true. However, to the uninitiated winery owner, this is a sign that everywhere they go people love and buy their wines. So why haven't you sold more?! (Yes, that has been said to me.) I believe it is far more useful to the winery owner to hear how their wines are perceived as a result of either market forces or the wine's own characteristics, and I encourage them to ask for honest feedback. Empty promises don't sell wine and don't help the brand owner understand the market or help him or her make adjustments in areas such as planting, production or allocation.

In time, as a result of your diligent efforts and if you have chosen well, the wines will speak for themselves and the winery owner will appreciate what you have done to broaden their reach in this part of the world. Their trips are a welcome adjunct, much appreciated and somewhat essential, but management of this market and the bulk of the U.S. sales will still rest with you.

Summary

Staying on top of your distribution in each market is most likely the difference between success and failure. It is certainly the difference between small and large sales numbers, between infrequent and frequent orders. Distribution, without proper cultivation, can easily fade away. Foster the relationship and maintain a balance between too little contact and too much.

My Story

Once again, I probably have as many stories as there are personalities, good and bad, amusing and disastrous.

I once had two winery owners come over at the same time, despite my best efforts to get them to stagger their trips. Due to their intense dislike of one another, my job was to make sure they were never in the same city at the same time whilst in the States! It was very early in my importing days and I only had limited markets so this was an almost impossible task. After ten days of considerable angst, things had gone about as well as I could expect. Unfortunately, they were scheduled to leave for home at the same time and I had to chauffeur them both to the airport. They sat in stony, uncomfortable silence for forty-five minutes. Following the trip, they were always in competition to see who had sold more in each of the markets they had visited. The end result to the trip was that their diligent follow up actually stimulated sales; the end to the story is that they were both much too high maintenance and I discontinued their brands.

I have also had:

- A winery owner's son who set fire to his hair whilst exploding illegal firecrackers on top of a downtown high rise roof.
- An export director who drank all the samples during the day, so that the salesperson had to make an unscheduled stop at his house in the middle of the day to pick up more samples.
- Winemakers who got lost and showed up so late to appointments or events they missed them entirely, or who slept in and missed their connections to other cities, where carefully orchestrated events had to be cancelled or rescheduled, thereby disrupting the subsequent events and segments of the trip.
- One winery owner (just one, fortunately!) who was so offensive I was asked by the distributor never to let him back to the markets he visited. He had actually *cost* them sales
- A winery owner who refused to leave the airport until someone came to pick him up, despite the fact that no one was available and he had been asked to take a taxi or shuttle to the nearby hotel.

But, quite honestly, I have mostly experienced industrious, fun, warm, dedicated individuals whose aim is the same as yours—to sell more wine and give their brand greater exposure. They may have partied late into the night, but worked equally hard during the day and never allowed their lack of sleep to diminish their cheerfully passionate presentations. Most are such assets that sales reps ask me how soon they can return.

17

WHEN IT'S NOT WORKING

There may come a time when you realize that your distributor is no longer a true partner. This may become apparent because they:

- indicate apparent disinterest in your brands by ordering less and extending the time between orders
- do not extend their commitment to your portfolio by ordering any new products as they become available
- stretch their invoice payments beyond the normal boundaries, until it becomes intolerable
- dispute invoices on flimsy grounds
- abuse sample allowances
- rarely return your calls
- create obstacles to you coming to the market
- take on other brands that seem to compete directly with yours, resulting in a loss of focus

In defense of the average, well-meaning distributor, this may be simply a business decision created from necessity. Your brands are losing focus for the salespeople, because there is something changing in the market or the price point is no longer attractive. It makes it a tough sell for them, despite their efforts. Early communication is the first order of business to nip any of this in the bud, but if you find your concerns are being deflected or repeatedly not being addressed, it may be time to consider a change.

It is important not to react from anger or with a knee jerk reaction to their lack of interest, or even if they are ignoring your statements and owe you money. Your objective is to do what is best for your brands, get paid in the process, and gracefully exit. This also means lining up another wholesaler if at all possible. Just as in the job market, where it becomes easier to find a job when you have a job, the time to find another distributor is before you leave the last one, when presumably market momentum and brand familiarity will be an asset to the new partner.

Many distributors, once you speak to them, may be agreeable to the change. It may be something they were anticipating, either at your initiative or their own. They will make this a smooth transition for you, happy that they can easily remedy a situation with products that no longer work for them or wines that don't fit their newly evolved focus.

Whether or not you have a replacement company, or if it was their decision or yours, avoiding burning bridges during this process is to your advantage. The wine world is ultimately a small place and a sales manager at one place could end up setting up their own distribution company, where they may be receptive to representing your brands if can they recall how they enjoyed working with you.

During the Transition

In most states, the withdrawal of a brand from one distributor and the appointment of another is a relatively simple procedure. There are many variations on this theme, of course, as they relate to the different state's requirements. But essentially it is a painless process. Be sure to factor in the time it will take for the state to re-register the brands or handle a new license application, if necessary. Presumably this will be shorter than the initial license application, but is something to consider.

In certain situations they will expect the remaining inventory to be picked up and transferred to the new distributor. This may be a problem, because there is no guarantee that the wine has been stored properly or that vintages are current. We can normally anticipate that if the situation has devolved into one that requires a severing of the relationship, there is very little remaining inventory. Whatever the case, you don't want it to be a deal breaker with your new wholesaler. You will certainly want to start off on the right foot with them, as you would with anyone. In this case, work out an attractive price for them or offer incentives. They will not be surprised by this turn of events and it may have happened several times before, but they will still wish to make a prudent purchase and one they anticipate being able to sell.

If all else fails, you may have to arrange for your own trucker to pick up the product and bring it back to your own warehouse. This will depend on whether:

- the product is worth salvaging
- the cost of freight is outweighed by the value of the goods
- the old wholesaler requires you to pick it up as a condition of the release

The latter is most likely in the case of franchise states, where a distributor will expect compensation or sometimes another brand in trade from the new distributor—as long as it is an attractive offer. This can really be a financial hardship for you, but something you cannot get around, unless you forego the new distribution or are willing to wait a period of time with no distribution—therefore no sales—in that particular state for anywhere from one to three years.

If you really encounter a distributor in a franchise state who refuses to release your product under any circumstance, e.g. in Georgia, there is an appeals process. Usually this requires that the distributor has failed to meet the standards set by the state and that you can prove this to be the case.

An example of a typical release letter from a distributor to the State of Georgia, with a copy to the importer, can be seen in Figure 16.1.

```
┌─────────────────────────────────────────────────────────────┐
│                  Superior Wine Distribution                  │
│                                                              │
│  Date                                                        │
│                                                              │
│  Georgia Department of Revenue                               │
│  Alcohol & Tobacco Division                                  │
│  1800 Century Center Blvd., NE                               │
│  Room 4235                                                   │
│  Atlanta, GA 30345-3205                                      │
│                                                              │
│  To Whom It May Concern:                                     │
│                                                              │
│  Superior Wine Distributing voluntarily releases the brands  │
│  Pikes Peak, Merlin's Magic and The Legacy registered to     │
│  Four Points Distributing by Mayflower Wine Imports, Inc.    │
│  This release is contingent upon pick up and payment for     │
│  any remaining inventory of Mayflower Wine Imports products  │
│  as well as the payment of any outstanding invoices due to   │
│  Superior Wine Distributing by Mayflower Wine Imports, Inc.  │
│                                                              │
│  Sincerely,                                                  │
│                                                              │
│  Thomas Beckett, III                                         │
│  President                                                   │
│                                                              │
│  cc: Mayflower Wine Imports, Inc.                            │
└─────────────────────────────────────────────────────────────┘
```

Figure 16.1   Distributor Release Letter for Franchise State

Summary

Understanding each state's position on distribution laws and moving brands *at the outset* will help considerably with the management of your brands in that state as you go forward, and how you approach the need to change distributors if that time comes. This goes back to ensuring that you take the time to familiarize yourself with all aspects of your business, regardless of whether you outsource compliance or keep it in-house. And the importance of keeping track of all your paperwork is illustrated in following story.

My Story

Over the course of many years as an importer I feel fortunate to have encountered very little difficulty transitioning away from a distributor. I believe that maintaining a cordial rapport with them throughout the entire relationship will go far to mitigate any problems, but they do occur. I encountered one situation where I had to send a particularly intractable wholesaler to collection after he refused to pay me for invoices totaling several thousand dollars. I consider a collection agency to be a pretty drastic measure and have only resorted to this option twice since 1992, because to do so is to recognize that this is an irretrievable situation and burning bridges is the only alternative. It is also expensive. In this case, he simply refused without reason and it was my last resort. Repeated efforts by the collection agency yielded no results and I was told the only option left was to sue (included in the collection agency's fees).

I came to court armed with a thick file of documentation that refuted his claims. In short order, the judge awarded in favor of my complaint and ordered the defendant to pay my invoices, plus interest, plus damages.

Before I had an opportunity to collect on this judgment, the distributor sued me for spoiled wine—the same wine for which I sued him for non-payment, a year after receipt of goods. Back I went into court, again armed with a comprehensive record file.

He maintained that he had been unable to sell any of this allegedly bad wine. Luckily for me I am a conscientious record keeper and, although this had now progressed about three years since my initial sale to him, I was able to produce a depletion report from the distributor that showed a sale of this exact wine to a large Chicago retailer. The distributor argued that one sale was all he was able to generate and only as a favor to him. I produced more depletion reports showing more sales. He tried to contest their veracity. They were originals he had mailed to me with his signature. The judge naturally ruled against him and I eventually received a partial settlement of my original claim.

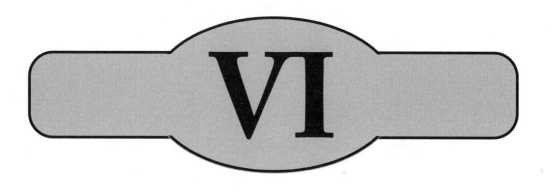

18

HOME STATE DISTRIBUTION

At some point you may want to start distributing all or some of your products in the state in which you have based your business. This has some distinct advantages:

- You benefit from the additional margin as wholesaler.
- It increases the scope of your sales.
- You are able to exercise more control over the distribution of your products.

My suggestion is to make this a step you take—at least in any significant way—after you have established a chunk of your out-of-state distribution, or you may find yourself bogged down with in-state distribution at the expense of larger volume sales. Consider the Pareto Principle—also known as the 80/20 rule. In the case of national vs. state distribution 80% of your sales will come from 20% of your customers and this is still where you should apply the majority of your focus, at least at first.

The benefits of home state distribution are still compelling, however, and the economics break down something like this in terms of **gross margin**:

FOB (your cost + 30% markup) plus wholesale (FOB + 45% markup) = price to retail

From an FOB of $150.00, your normal price to a wholesaler, you can now charge $217.50 to the retail account. Distributor markups will vary, just as importer markups do, but this is for the sake of an example. Your gross margin has just become much more attractive.

However, there are a number of expenses that are inherent in the cost of doing distribution business and must be taken into account, which will be covered in this section.

Distribution Basics

Licensing

The Federal licensing is easy. You simply check box "d" on form 5100.24 in addition to box "c" when applying for your Basic Permit. This allows you to apply for both importer and wholesaler license at the same time, whether or not you intend to use it for some time. There is no fee for either license.

The licensing requirements for your home state will be very different than those in place for you as an out-of-state importer registering brands and assigning distribution to a wholesaler. In most cases, the requirements are considerably more onerous. It can mean the difference between simple forms and perhaps a bond, to fingerprinting, background checks, several thousand dollars in fees and considerable paperwork. In other cases the paperwork is extensive, as well it might be given the fact that you are now setting up distribution of alcohol in their home state, but the fees may not be more than a few hundred dollars. Whatever the case, it is safe to assume it will be considerably less than a retail liquor license.

Facility

Decide how large you wish to become in this undertaking, which basically comes down to three choices:

1. Full-service, ramped up state-wide distribution. This will require additional licensing (beyond the one alluded to above), large storage space, a good inventory software package, additional personnel, equipment and overhead.
2. Limited, but wholly controlled distribution in your area. This will require additional licensing, but a scaled down storage space and less personnel.
3. Expansion of your sales into a local area distribution network, but outsource the services. This will not necessitate the additional licensing of your own storage facility, but successful is dependent upon the quality of the outside services you contract.

In the first example, I suggest you need a fairly hefty budget for warehouse and office personnel salaries, sales reps, insurance for both personnel and facility, transportation costs, trucks (or rentals), facility rental or purchase, forklifts, racking, utilities and so on. The starting overhead will be substantial, but if you have the right sales team it means you can ramp up pretty quickly and, assuming you have available product, enables you to realize some large volume, which may eventually outstrip your national sales. This is the most ambitious example and should not be undertaken without in-depth research and the understanding that a budget of several hundred thousand dollars will be necessary as an underpinning to your first few months of personnel salaries, expenses and plant overhead.

In the second example, distribution and storage is still under your control, but in a more economical and scaled down version. You may, for instance, have sufficient space in your own rented office dedicated to storage of a few hundred cases and be able to replenish it as needed from your main warehouse by regular delivery from a trucking company. Consideration must be given to your location and whether you are zoned for such an enterprise and if trucking companies are able to access your street, storage area, if you have a loading dock or need delivery trucks with lift gates.

In this scenario, you can select either to hire your own sales personnel or utilize local brokers as independent contractors. Distribution must necessarily be circumscribed to a manageable geographical area, from which you can easily deliver to your accounts using your own resources, rented trucks or local delivery services.

In the third example, find a good local storage facility, which will be quite different from the large, bonded warehouse at which you store the bulk of your product. It will need to be well-organized, efficiently run, responsive to fast turnaround needs and be able to deliver regularly to all the counties or towns you have designated as your distribution area. Costs will be much higher for storage than for your general, public warehouse because their main service is deliveries, but you have that second margin to absorb them. Cost-conscious case volume should be considered in this option to allow for ample availability without eating up margins in storage.

Since there will be far more stock movement in and out and smaller, finicky deliveries than the national distribution example, it is imperative that this storage and delivery facility employ people who conscientiously pack and load each wine, cross checking for vintages and correct quantities, sometimes requiring partial cases. It requires far more attention to detail and reliable truckers, also employed by the warehouse. Delivery drivers will be handling money in COD cases, so they must be trustworthy and bonded by the warehouse. These entities are available and this is actually a viable and manageable alternative when you are starting out and can be a value-added piece to your national distribution, without deviating too much from Pareto's Principle.

Taxes

In any scenario, you will now have excise taxes, applied to alcohol and tobacco, on the goods you have sold within your home state. There is a huge variance on rates between the different states, so be sure to check with your own state to factor this into your budgetary considerations. Usually these are front loaded when you bring the container into the country and then refunded when you complete excise tax forms to report which sales have been made outside your state. In the case of state distribution, of course this means you will not be refunded the tax you have paid.

Account Selection

The natural inclination is to focus on "A" accounts, followed by the "B" accounts and, if you have sufficient salespeople to cover them, the also-rans, the Mom and Pop operations or the local, out of the way places that are usually under the radar. Everyone would like to promote the fact that their wines are on the hottest restaurant lists in town. The point is that *everyone* wants to do that, and not everyone will be able to find a place in these top tier restaurants. There may simply be too many distributors for the buyer to see, lack of space or a list that is dominated by one of the big wholesalers who also supplies the well-brand liquors, or the "must have" specialty liquor. Even if you do get in, this may not be your bread and butter and will require far more attention and massaging than the quantity or value of the orders deserves (again the 80/20 rule). It is still important to have some significant accounts, since they can elevate your profile and add to the winery's cachet, but they should not be the entire focus of your portfolio. That can come later when you have established yourself as a specialized distributor of "must have" fine wines.

You would be surprised at how much you can sell to the little neighborhood restaurant, especially if it is your neighborhood and they know you. These can be opportunities for glass pours that result in a couple of cases every week, or their wine list is so small that if someone orders a Cab, chances are 50:50 that it will be yours. Even if it isn't your neighborhood bistro, it may become a place that you or your salesperson will get to know and befriend. Some local grocery or specialty stores have a nice little selection of wines and this may be your niche, since they are often neglected by bigger wholesalers.

Account Presentations

This has a lot of the elements of presentations you make on out of town work-withs, but you are now responsible for the entire presentation and assumption of risk and follow up. You, your sales rep or a broker will all have the same considerations for the presentation. Therefore reference to "you" is taken as advice to anyone filling these roles.

- Are you showing appropriate level wines for the account—i.e., the right price point, region or style?

- Have you researched the account to determine if they fit your profile focus—within your geographical scope for attention, deliveries and time?

- Do you have sufficient availability or any in stock at all, of the wines you are showing? This is not always a necessity, especially if you are generating pre-sell buzz for a hot wine or you know the restaurant or retailer will not have room for a few weeks, but is certainly something to determine and convey from the outset.

- Is your book up to date? You will need to bring a price list and leave it with them. Are the vintages you are showing the same ones in the book? Does it show all the available brands? Is the pricing current? Your book does not have to be professionally bound in 4-color (in fact it is too expensive to have this done as often as it will change) but it should be professional, accurate and updated regularly.

- Do you have a credit application (if applicable) or any other paperwork to leave with them?

- Is this an account that requires you to bring your own glassware? (I have encountered this occasionally.) If you don't, they are likely to rummage up a dirty waxed paper Dixie cup that makes the wine taste terrible!

- Have you determined whether they conduct tastings by appointment, only on the third Thursday of the month, or as a drop in any time as long as you are prepared to wait? Knowing the name of the buyer on the first visit is courteous and will make an impression, but it is more important to ensure that you know it on subsequent visits.

- Gauge the personality and traits of the buyer. If they are in a rush you should be well prepared and give an abbreviated presentation. Presumably, there will be other opportunities to develop a rapport or take more time. Talking less at first is better than talking more. They can always ask you to expand on the information, but it's a lot harder to ask someone to stop talking, and it may leave them with the impression they don't really have enough time to cultivate a relationship with you.

- *Establish credibility from the beginning*. It is much harder to regain it later. If you do not have a wine in stock, say so. If you are not clear on a price, say so. If you do not have the exact percentages on the blend, the type of oak or what the vintage was like, tell them you will find out. *Do not wing it*. It's not worth it in the end. They will not really care if you know now whether it is 15 or 20% Cabernet Franc, but they *will* care if you told them 2008 was a great vintage and they found out later it was one of the poorest in a decade.

Other Issues

Consider whether you wish to impose a minimum order quantity or will "break" cases—i.e., deliver less than a case of a particular product. When you are new and your wines are relatively unknown, it might be more appealing to have a low minimum quantity, such as two cases or a minimum order value of $250, which still allows you some economies of scale on the delivery. Some small distributors have minimum order quantities of 5 cases or $500, so you will still appear reasonable by comparison.

Broken cases are usually at your discretion (except in COD states where it is the norm), but if you outsource will require more handling and higher expense at the warehouse. You might offer broken cases on high value or dessert wines, such as Port, either of which might take the restaurant a while to deplete. In the event you are warehousing your own product, by all means accept broken case orders, as long as there is some reasonable minimum on the total order. It may even work to your advantage if the retailer or restaurant orders six *half* cases, instead of three *whole* cases. The number of bottles is the same, but you have just achieved twice the wine list exposure or shelf facings (see Figure 17.1).

At the time of an order, do not leave the account without the necessary license details as they pertain to your state (in the case of California, their ABC number and reseller certificate). Not to have these on file may run you afoul of your own licensing body. At the very least, it tells you that they are licensed to sell alcohol. To sell to an unlicensed account would most definitely incur heavy penalties for you, if not the loss of your license.

Each state has different requirements regarding payment from the account, but generally they fall into two categories—COD or 30 days. If COD is the requirement, then a check must be picked up at the time of the delivery by the truck driver. Not to do so violates state law. In the case of 30 day terms, this necessitates a determination on your part that the account is credit worthy and should be in the form of a credit application. You may find that certain high profile accounts will refuse to complete a credit application, maintaining that there is no need to do so, and personally I allow them this vanity. Accounts such as these are usually unlikely to be in any financial difficulty and, whether references are obtained or not, I suggest that you establish a maximum dollar exposure for yourself until there is a history of timely payment.

Figure 17.1   Featured Wine Display in Retail Store

Go above and beyond to make a good account happy. If they run out of a wine for the weekend and delivery is not scheduled until Tuesday, get that case to them yourself, even if it means disrupting your own plans outside normal working hours. A sales person expects to conduct evening tastings and wine dinners and catch the restaurant buyer, who may be the chef or head bartender, after the dinner hour rush.

Delivery errors are a reality, so it is important to be responsive to the customer and correct it at the earliest opportunity with a cheerful attitude. Even if it is their mistake, e.g. miscommunication between sommelier and restaurant manager, take back the goods or make the exchange. Far better to retain an account for future orders than lose them over one correctable incident.

In states where terms are extended, be prepared to go and collect the check for an account that is late, or where they tell you they will pay when you bring them the replacement for the corked bottle.

Frequent the restaurant account whenever possible, even if it is just for an appetizer, a drink or a light lunch. There is a symbiotic culture in the wine industry, especially at this level, and when they see you supporting their establishment they are more likely to support your wines.

On the other hand, try not to get sucked into too many local tastings in the early stages of your import company and your distributor model, especially before you have a sales team. It is very tempting to accept a request from an up and coming wine bar, or a friend's restaurant, to do a wine dinner or tasting. As the distributor, supplier, co-organizer and speaker, you are now far more involved with the event than if you were coming in from out of town to work with your distributor on an event they have organized. Without sufficient sales support and local infrastructure, this may well be to the detriment of your national business, which still requires the bulk of your focus. Again, the 80/20 rule applies as you consider the amount of work and return for the local event vs. the work and return on a national level. Tastings and wine dinners become an essential component of your core distribution business, but must be evaluated in context. It is flattering to be asked, but you will not lose the account or the opportunity if you tell them that you would love to do this dinner, but unfortunately you have a conflict until a date down the road when you are better prepared. Dinner or tasting guests also need to have somewhere accessible to buy the wine after the event and reasonable retail store coverage is important.

Sales Personnel

The decision often becomes whether to hire your own sales team or retain the services of independent brokers. Both of which have pros and cons and can be broken down as follows.

Salesperson—Pros

- Works exclusively for you and therefore all hours and commitment is to your company.
- All focus is on your product, instead of being spread around several portfolios.
- All products, and those you determine require increased focus, will be shown.
- Can be trained in your systems as they relate to order entry, office requirements and pitching in where necessary to make a sale happen.
- Is assigned accounts and territory according to your needs.
- Will adhere to a company philosophy and ethics as part of employment and the face of the company in the field.
- Can grow as your company grows as products are added, or if a sales team needs a leader, there is someone within the company qualified to take on the responsibility.
- Loyalty and job satisfaction are engendered with appropriate salary and benefits package and fair treatment.

Salesperson—Cons

- Initially and for some time, there may not be adequate sales potential to warrant the salary and benefits, which means running at a loss.
- If there is insufficient product—either in diversity of items or volume—to sustain a full-time employee there is either wasted salary or a disgruntled employee who cannot live on the bonus structure.
- May not be experienced in retail sales and requires time and training.
- May not know the local accounts.
- Difficult and expensive to discharge this employee should they not perform well.
- Requires adequate supervision.

Broker—Pros

- Independent contractor not subject to salary, benefits or bonuses.
- There is an established 10-15% commission based on sales and no hidden expenses.
- Since commission is directly linked to sales, will work hard to ensure a sale to a desirable account.
- Understands retail sales.
- Already familiar with and has access to local accounts.
- Whatever the limitation on number or scope, the wines can be integrated into their existing portfolio without undue concern for income.
- Has built up a sales territory and relationships that could provide immediate sales.
- Can work independently with little supervision.

Broker—Cons

- Portfolio diversity means less attention for your wines.
- Can pick and choose which wines they wish to show, based not on your needs but on their own preferences.
- The accounts they service may not be your preference.
- May choose not to involve themselves at all with accounts receivable collections, maintaining this is your responsibility and it interferes with their ability to maintain a positive relationship with the account.
- Has own philosophy regarding presentations and image, which may conflict with yours.
- Can give up your brands at any time, leaving you without a replacement and the resulting loss of business.

On the surface, it may appear to be far more advantageous to hire your own sales team, but this would be looking at the weight and number of the pros, without considering two important deal breakers of the cons—your portfolio may not sustain a full-time person or team, and you may not have the budget. These choices have to make sense for you and your situation. Local brokers are a very viable option for any small company and I can highly recommend them, when the situation is right. However, there may not be any available or reputable brokers in your area. Perhaps you put an ad in an online publication like the job section of *Wine Business Monthly*: *www.winejobs.com* for someone who is willing to work commission only. It could be someone with a second job or who is willing to forego salary for the chance to gain more experience.

When hiring an employee, I always say think about the *qualities* more than the *qualifications*. Although a well qualified and well rounded individual is the ideal, you may find that someone with a certain wine sales background is not necessarily the right fit. For example, and only as an example and not meant to be a rigid principle, sales people who have worked in wine stores *buying* product do not always make the best person out there *selling* it. A sales mentality has to be the first consideration. Wine store employees are accustomed to:

- being in one place
- working within an established range and number of hours
- having people come to them
- buying product
- selling a huge range of products from around the world

A distributor sales person has the exact opposite working environment:

- they travel around all day
- hours are fluid and extensive
- they go to the buyers to make the sales
- selling product
- the range of wines they represent is limited

I think we can skip the résumé.

Figure 17.2 © David Pike

This is not meant at all to denigrate the experience, qualifications and motivation of the wine store employee, but whilst the opportunity to be fairly independent and closely aligned with a select group of wines could appear attractive to some, they may discover they are not natural self-starters, the portfolio is too limiting and they are uncomfortable asking for the sale. On the other hand, it could be the perfect breakout chance for an individual who started with a wine store to gain experience and is grateful for the opening at an up and coming distributor to prove themselves.

A sales rep making a lateral move may not be a better choice. Yes, they have the experience, the orientation to the type of job they will be doing and perhaps even familiarity with local accounts. But why are they making the move? Were there problems with the last employer? Did they under perform or have issues with management? Or it may simply be a move from a big distributor where their sole responsibility is to wake up at 5am and stock grocery shelves to a small company where they have a ground floor opportunity to make a difference.

Are they experienced, but brash, opinionated and overly self-confident? This may have worked well at a behemoth distributor whose products are necessary to an account's survival. But if you are like me, you want this individual to be mirroring your own values of excellence and relationship building in a small, growing company and someone like this is likely to rub people the wrong way and get them barred from the account.

The point is that you will save yourself a lot of wasted time, expense and headaches if you make a little extra effort to really take a look at a candidate, ask for references and conduct a pretty comprehensive interview. Give them a trial period and see what develops.

Office Personnel

Aside from obvious salary and benefit considerations, the more sales people you have out there the presumption is the more you sell and the more you make. Not so with office personnel! They are an essential, vital part of the business and without their expertise and contribution it would be impossible to function. But too many and you will collapse under the weight of your non-revenue producing overhead.

Again, the model you have chosen will dictate the number of office staff and their roles, but going on the assumption that you have intended to take a serious run at being a distributor, you will need two people in the office to start. If you import all the wine you distribute (which is not necessarily true but the premise we'll use), you can expect the container shipments to increase as you require more wine to divert to your own distribution. This will also increase the paperwork on both the winery and retail account end. These are now the responsibilities of your integrated import/distribution office:

- Purchase orders to winery and tracking of fulfillment.
- Container logistics
- Inventory control at two warehouses and possibly a third (your office)
- Warehouse and delivery logistics

- Order processing of calls from accounts and calls/emails from salespeople/brokers
- Coordination of aspects of the salespeople or brokers roles
- Reference and credit checking of wholesale and retail accounts
- Invoice preparation and disbursement
- Accounts payable
- Accounts receivable, including phone and email collection
- Filing
- Purchasing
- Compliance, even if it is outsourced will require coordination
- Excise tax information gathering, preparation and timely submission
- Marketing and promotion, including POS materials and website
- Bookkeeping
- Shipment of samples to prospective wholesalers
- Payroll (which can also be outsourced to a payroll service like ADP)

While day to day bookkeeping should be done in the office, periodic accounting, financial statements and tax preparation are best left to your own outside professional. QuickBooks will be able to provide you with excellent tools, including financial statements, if information is input correctly on an ongoing basis. Accountant and tax professionals are accustomed to working with QuickBooks backups that can be backed up and emailed to them in compressed files when necessary. Prompts are easy to follow.

Hiring Basics

The following is my own personal philosophy and recommendations, based on years of hiring people in the wine industry and prior to that when I managed 130 employees in another industry.

For any new hire, make sure they understand what the job will entail and do not spring something on them after they have accepted the position or they will feel they have been misled. Understanding that the distribution division is in start-up mode and there will be a couple of days of inventory management each week until the company expands is different from being told the job is a full-time sales position, only to discover that three days a week you will be operating the forklift as a permanent situation. Company mission and guiding principles should be clear in your own mind and conveyed in conjunction with expectations.

I saw a job description recently that did not mince words, but really gave a clear understanding of the position. This is just an excerpt:

> *We are looking for 3–4 visionary leaders to be the future senior executives of The Company as we grow and expand our unique cutting edge business model around CA and beyond. Please do not apply if you are looking for a comfortable big company wine sales job. Right fit will be driven professional with a long term view, willing to trade some short term benefits for huge long term opportunity. The Company has all the tools you'll need for great success so your hard work is all that's missing.*

I believe in stressing a policy of cross training, to a degree, and this should be explained to each new employee, especially office and warehouse personnel. It engenders heightened team spirit and transparent understanding of expectations from the beginning. Although it is within reasonable limits to expect sales reps to also prepare their own POS material and submit detailed reports to management, the purpose of their position is to generate sales. If they are stuck on the phones in the office because someone is on vacation, it is inhibiting your growth.

The cross training should take into consideration the aptitude and experience of the employee, so that the creative marketing person is not expected to take on bookkeeping and a sales manager is not filling in for the receptionist.

Overall, specific job assignments are recommended in the office so that there is continuity and accountability, but with the need to pitch in where necessary as the work flow ebbs and flows, crossover and cross training should be part of the equation.

As the sales and paperwork increases, the time will come to consider other hires, but unless a rapid increase in sales from a specific source is anticipated, I suggest that you wait until there are unmistakable indications that workload cannot be handled by current support personnel and perhaps initially consider a part-time hire to take up the slack. Workload has a habit of expanding to fit the hours and people available, so evaluate whether this is truly adding to your bottom line in a meaningful way.

Depending upon your choice in storage, delivery and sales model, you may need warehouse personnel, drivers, sales manager, etc. Increased orders may necessitate a second order entry/customer service person. Contingent upon your growth inclination and budget, you might hire someone for marketing and another for compliance.

Outside the Single Account Model

The pursuit of an edge over the competition, especially as a startup business, can sometimes be very difficult. The behemoths have their account dominance on occasion for reasons stated earlier; the well established companies with good product and great customer relationships already have that edge over you in the single on-premise and off-premise account. What's a newbie to do? Still, thinking outside the box may be the way you can increase your volume and begin to allow you to make some inroads.

Chains, Resorts and Country Clubs

In addition to national chains, there are also statewide chains where the buyer is accessible and a relationship can be developed, much in the way you would nurture a relationship with a single retailer or restaurant. Because they are within a reasonable drive from your office you can make appointments to see them on a regular basis to make presentations. California seems to have a preponderance of chains, but there are head offices in other states and some states that have a significant number of restaurants, even if the head office is elsewhere.

- Cheesecake Factory's head office is in Calabasas, California, but there are fourteen restaurants in Florida and ten in Texas, e.g.
- McCormick & Schmicks Seafood is based in Portland, Oregon, where there are six restaurants, but there are also six restaurants in Illinois and eighty throughout the country.

- P.F. Chang's is based in Scottsdale. Arizona, but also has many locations throughout the country.

- Costco's head office is in Issaquah, Washington, but they have regional offices across the country. These regional offices make all or most of the fine wine decisions (those wines that go in the wooden bins) and many of the floor stack decisions. These regional buyers accept appointments for presentations and can be powerful allies in your distribution business. Often, if the wines selected in one region do well, they become strong contenders for other states.

- Most states have resorts and private country clubs that become wonderful opportunities for wine placements and can do a great deal of business. There are world renowned spa resorts in Arizona, and Disney's Epcot in Florida as prime examples. One of my first accounts in Atlanta was a country club that not only put several of my wines on their list, but held tastings for their members, who then bought cases of wines they particularly liked. The incentive for the club was to have good, interesting wines on their list that kept their members coming to events, and the members were able to buy wines at a low markup.

Wine Clubs

Although California is a haven for wine clubs, they are available all over the country and easily researched online. Some wine clubs are connected to stores and others only send wine and wine related gift baskets through a virtual store. Many of these have regular customers who receive monthly or quarterly offerings and are looking for constant turnover with new and intriguing wines for their client base. Wine clubs often order in increments of sixty cases each of red and white, or have tiers of wine pricing, where they might purchase fifteen to twenty cases of a top tier and up to one hundred cases of a lower tier.

Military Bases, Cruise Lines and Hotel Chains

These are all additional opportunities that are often missed, but do require a good deal of research, understanding and possibly outside resources, such as brokers who specialize in these entities. I mention it now, simply as a resource you may want to investigate a bit further down the road, once you have your core business stabilized.

Summary

In your basic distribution model your main concern should be to offer excellent customer service, a reliable alternative to the many distributors the accounts already see and QPR on your wines. Home state distribution can be a worthwhile adjunct to your import business and really take your business up a level. Try not to waste too much money on extraneous purchases in the beginning, be creative in expanding your home base and make your money work for you as much as possible with the largest return for your investment of time and wine.

My Story

My very first retail account was a local mom and pop specialty grocery store with a small wine aisle, tucked down a secondary road in a neighborhood. They offered ready made gourmet foods and high end essentials for a preponderance of local high end clientele. At first blush, this was not an A, B or even a C account. But they were close by and I got to know them from quick trips in to pick up take out food on my way home. From the first appointment they were willing to make a big commitment to my portfolio and ultimately my unknown wines from my small, new portfolio comprised 80% of their stocked wine. It became a valuable account.

A popular, busy restaurant with a casual atmosphere, excellent food and, especially for 1992, an eclectic, daring wine list was one of the first restaurants I ventured into to sell my wares. I was treated politely, but the buyer did not buy anything. For some reason, I was on a mission to make it on that wine list. I persevered through three or four tastings without a purchase. Eventually I started dropping in to do paperwork at the counter and order a glass of wine or a bite to eat as I worked. After about eight trips to the account, the buyer (who happened to be the chef and the owner) openly acknowledged that I had paid my dues and he was ready to make some purchases. He was testing me, just as accounts will test you or your sales people. Not always, of course. But this buyer knew that he was a desirable account and I was so new I might not last long enough to warrant the change on his wine list. They want to make sure you will be around for the long run and that they will not have wasted their time getting to know you and your wines. Again, this developed into one of my better accounts and the owner became a good friend. You will not necessarily have time for this much massaging and cultivation of a potential buyer, but in the first instance, the point is that you cannot afford to dismiss an account because it does not seem to fit a profile and in the second, it is important to recognize that symbiotic relationship between the distributor and the retail accounts.

19

OTHER THOUGHTS

We have now gone from the very first glimmer of thinking about importing wine, through the process of establishing and developing your business. At the end, I thought I would round out the picture by briefly mentioning, or discussing in more detail, other aspects that may come up in the course of your journey. Some of these are controversial ideas and some are simply expansion thoughts.

Think Green

Going green and preserving our resources is beyond trendy these days; it is about survival and reducing the carbon footprint on the planet. There is a plethora of organic foods in the stores these days, recyclable products everywhere, energy efficient appliances and entire homes based on alternate power sources and recycled construction materials. Businesses are recouping taxes and credits on energy efficiency and utilizing renewable resources. Therefore, the idea of thinking green is becoming more and more a part of our way of life as population and pollution explodes. In the wine

Figure 18.1   Boxed Wine

industry, being on the leading edge in this endeavor is one way to stand out and environmentally friendly at the same time. This includes seeking out biodynamic vineyards and organically grown grapes.

Tetra Paks (generally individual cartons) and boxed wines (3L as the norm) are becoming mainstream alternatives, with a considerable rise in wineries embracing this technology in sustainable packaging (see Figure 18.1). It may be an area you would enjoy exploring or might encourage your winery supplier to expand their offerings by putting some wines into this packaging. Since 2006, according to Beverage World magazine, *116 new wine products were launched in Tetra Pak cartons.* Boxed wines have increased dramatically as well. They are no longer confined to inexpensive wines of marginal quality. Premium wines are now much more prevalent in this type of container.

Internet Sales

This is a separate license, which may be issued, should your state allow it, to sell retail only online. In other words, there is no bricks and mortar store, where there would be many more concerns regarding availability of a liquor license, proximity to schools and churches and expense. This license is issued strictly to sell online from a website.

The problem with this is that you will be competing against the distributors and retailers to whom you already sell. Wineries do it, of course. If they have sufficient production, they will sell to retailers in their state and distributors out of state. But they also have a website which often has an attached wine club.

There are a limited number of states to which you may ship, often limited amounts of wines, licenses to obtain and excise tax to pay within that state. It will most likely not be a lucrative side of your business unless you decide to devote more time to building up this aspect through vigorous marketing, buying potential customer lists or compiling your own through frequent tastings and trade shows where you gather email addresses, perhaps by offering prizes for a drawing. This could also mean drawing attention away from conventional distribution, unless you assign separate staff to this function. Wines other than those you import will also round out a full offering online and make it fresh and dynamic.

If you decide to explore the idea of internet sales, my suggestion would be to offer items that will be "online only" or set up a separate website that does not conflict with your primary trade website. And remain competitive in your pricing, so that it does not undercut the majority of retailers out there. Most retailers spend a good deal of time researching prices on the internet and may either refuse to buy your wines from their distributor at the outset, if they see you have significantly undercut them, or complain if they have already made a purchase.

Clearing Wine

There is no provision to clear wine under your import license that is not label approved or intended for trade show or as bona fide samples. Those are my italics, for emphasis, but TTB makes that very clear when they require you to complete a trade waiver to clear wine that has arrived by air or outside normal customs clearance channels. They ask you to attest to this and sign the letter when submitting it for customs clearance. Not all samples will generate a trade waiver request, but more and more they are and eventually they will deny a request if they feel it has exceeded appropriate levels for sample usage.

Quite often, consumers will either buy wine in another country to ship to the States or go online to order from the website and expect it to be shipped to them. This is not allowable under Customs regulations. To be legal, and cleared by you as the importer, each and every bottle would have to be submitted for label approval to TTB and have the appropriate label affixed to the bottle. Clearance would then take place in the same manner as for your normally imported products. You would produce a COLA for your customs broker and pay appropriate duties and taxes. Clearly this would be financially prohibitive and generally impractical at the wine store end, where a customer could potentially purchase twelve different wines for a case, all of which would have to be approved and relabeled, taxes and duty collected and remitted, and fees paid to you as the importer.

There are certain provisions made by U.S. Customs for consumers to transport wine with them into the country after a trip for personal use only, some of which are a bit hazy and can be subject to duty and superseded by state laws. This is what U.S. Customs says on their website, which can be found at www.cbp.gov/xp/cgov/travel/vacation/kbyg/paying_duty.xml/

Export

This is allowed under your Federal Basic Permit obtained through TTB. There is no additional cost (at least at this writing). There is a considerable amount of paperwork, all of which is explained in detail at: *www.ttb.gov/itd/exporting_documents.shtml* to begin.

There are certificates, customs documents and drawback forms to complete and submit to the National Revenue Center (to claim a refund on taxes paid in-state). There are compliance and label laws to learn in the destination country, all of which should be investigated through that home country's wine governing body.

Alcoholic Beverages One liter (33.8 fl. oz.) of alcoholic beverages may be included in your exemption if:

- You are 21 years old.
- It is for your own use or as a gift.
- It does not violate the laws of the state in which you arrive.

Federal regulations allow you to bring back more than one liter of alcoholic beverage for personal use, but, as with extra tobacco, you will have to pay duty and Internal Revenue Service tax.

While Federal regulations do not specify a limit on the amount of alcohol you may bring back for personal use, unusual quantities are liable to raise suspicions that you are importing the alcohol for other purposes, such as for resale. CBP officers are authorized by the Bureau of Alcohol, Tobacco, Firearms and Explosives (ATF) to make on-the-spot determinations that an importation is for commercial purposes, and may require you to obtain a permit to import the alcohol before releasing it to you. If you intend to bring back a substantial quantity of alcohol for your personal use, you should contact the port through which you will be re-entering the country, and make prior arrangements for entering the alcohol into the United States.

Also, you should be aware that state laws might limit the amount of alcohol you can bring in without a license. If you arrive in a state that has limitations on the amount of alcohol you may bring in without a license, that state law will be enforced by CBP, even though it may be more restrictive than federal regulations. We recommend that you check with the state government before you go abroad about their limitations on quantities allowed for personal importation and additional state taxes that might apply.

The obvious choices for wine export would be American wines, since presumably other countries will have their own export program at the winery, just as they have exported to you in the U.S. My personal opinion is that it only really makes sense for you, as the purchaser and not the producer of the wine, to investigate exporting when the U.S. dollar is weak enough to make the exchange rate and the resulting price attractive in the export country of choice. It is something else to consider and you may find a wine that is so inexpensive it makes it worthwhile irrespective of exchange rate.

Grey Market

Everyone who deals in or has contact with this so-called "grey" area of wine importing (not to be confused with the "over 55" consumers!) seems to have a strong opinion on this. There is no "grey" area when it comes to opinions. I will attempt to dissect the meaning of this term and make sense of it.

Wikipedia defines grey marketing as *"the trade of a commodity through distribution channels which, while legal, are unofficial, unauthorized, or unintended by the original manufacturer."*

Grey marketers are licensed importers who obtain label approval for the wine through TTB, so that it is cleared lawfully through customs. The Federal government chooses not to police the legitimacy of the importer application, and has no way of determining which COLA is being submitted with authorization from the winery, nor does it seem to be an issue for them. States which require a letter to prove that the importer is the appointed agent for the brand in the U.S. will not allow a grey marketer to register the brand nor obtain a license, but this is a state by state issue.

Wikipedia goes on to say that it is commonly utilized *"when the price of an item is significantly higher in one country than another. This situation commonly occurs with electronic equipment such as cameras."*

Wherein lies the rub and is a common misconception when it comes to wine. Consumers who buy grey market goods assume they are paying less than they would if bought through "white" channels, i.e. directly authorized from supplier (winery) to importer, to distributor, to retailer. The fallacy in this thinking is that either the three-tier system is being circumvented, or the authorized importer's pricing is so high that buying grey market goods means a savings. As if the grey market somehow comprises altruistic individuals who just want to make more wine available to the masses.

You may surmise from this that I have a problem with grey marketing. Not in theory. I do have a problem with the aforementioned thinking. Some of this seems to derive from the custom of many champagne houses creating artificially high pricing in the U.S., whereas the same item may be purchased much cheaper in Europe. This encouraged unauthorized importers to purchase from Europe and sell in the U.S. at a lower price, whilst still maintaining a profit margin.

No, no white wine, just a couple cases of '64 Chateau Beychevelle
back there between the beans and diapers—five bucks each.

Figure 18.2 ©David Pike

In the case of wine, grey marketing occurs most often when a wine has achieved a high U.S. rating and is (generally) in extremely short supply. Unauthorized importers may have access to distributors in the country of origin or find the wine in Europe, e.g. where there happens to be excess supply and can be bought for a discount. When the legitimate importer has carefully allocated a limited supply of stock to customers and suddenly more wine makes its way into the market, it can make them look disingenuous and create a sense that limited supply has been falsely created. It also circumvents the relationship between the authorized importer and their authorized distributor, which can result in further disruption in the market between distributors and retailers.

I believe the common objection from importers is that they have taken great pains to source and establish wines through the origin—the winery or vineyard. They have often made several trips to the destination and spent countless valuable hours working with the winery on wine selection, pricing, labeling and so forth. The relationship has been established with the express understanding that you are the exclusive representative of their wine over here (unless it has been disclosed that the country will be divided in an agreed upon fashion). In other words, all the things we reviewed in some detail in the early chapters.

The appointed importer has warehoused product, submitted to publications (from whence the great rating derived), put in the hard yards through previous vintages and a range of wines to establish the brand and finally, one wine gets the exposure they have been waiting for in the form of a high rating or significant review. The grey marketer sees an opportunity to capitalize on all this foundation and finds a way to source just this one wine, knowing that it will sell quickly.

Normally, the only reason the price may be less from the grey marketer is when they sell directly to retail in their home market, foregoing all or part of the second margin, since there is very little overhead connected with their enterprise. Otherwise, unless the importer is gouging, the price should not vary significantly and can sometimes be greater from the grey marketer.

One complaint from consumers regarding grey marketing relates to provenance. The idea that there is no way to validate the origin of the unauthorized wine or whether it has been properly stored. When the wine passes through so many hands—authorized or unauthorized—there is often no way for a legitimate importer to determine that the wine's integrity has been maintained either. Is the wine too close to the sun baked window in a retail store? Did it sit out on the dock too long at the distributor? Are trucks always temperature controlled? Reputable, conscientious importers always try to make sure wine is properly transported and stored and make decisions regarding transport and distributor appointments accordingly, but control passes on and absolute certainty is not always possible.

My last point on grey marketing is to consider what your philosophy and mission statement is going to be in your import company. Will you disrupt the marketplace in which you sell the product? Are you sure of provenance and integrity of the wine? Does it fit your business model? I am not discouraging you from availing yourself of grey market goods. I simply pose these questions for you to ask yourself.

Summary

Negotiating through the maze of legal requirements in a highly regulated industry is cumbersome and frustrating, but worth the effort to determine that you are in compliance with the laws and regulations that affect your license, your livelihood and your good name.

My Story

Relative to the issue of grey marketing, there are two instances in which I was aware of a product brought into the country other than through my own channels, and in both cases it was the same item, a fairly priced wine with a sudden high rating and national exposure. Unfortunately, there was a finite amount of this vintage and I had to carefully monitor its access and distribution.

In one instance, the grey marketer was an importer I had known, and liked, for several years. To my knowledge, he brought in one pallet of this wine (56 cases), bought presumably from a local distributor in the country of origin, and it was quickly sold without any backlash to me or disruption to my business.

In the other instance, an importer went directly to one of my best customers, a retail chain to whom I had just sold what I told them was the last of their allocation, and attempted to sell them somewhere between fifty and one hundred cases. To add insult to injury, he tried to undercut my price, which was understood by the chain to be the best price I could offer. Fortunately for me, the relationship with the retailer was strong enough that the buyer called me. She was not happy. I looked very foolish at best and duplicitous at worst. After considerable anxiety on my part at the potential jeopardy this created for my business, I was able to explain what had occurred, and to their great credit they refused to purchase the product from this grey marketer. When I confronted this particular importer with the problem they had created for me at this account—not the issue of grey marketing overall—he dismissed me with these words *"Grow up; it's just business."* Well it may be to him, but because of the relationship I enjoyed and had fostered with this important retailer it was not "just business" to either one of us.

Conclusion

There are those who will say there should be additions, deletions, deviations and alternative explanations in this book, that they wouldn't and haven't done it this way, and I respect that. No coverage of a subject as vast and multi-layered as this can be all encompassing. This is also my story and a subjective look at my triumphs, travails and tribulations in the wine industry. In the course of this personal journey on which I have taken you, I have tried to adhere to sound, concrete guidelines of starting and running a wine import company. If you follow these principles you may not know everything, you may not be wildly successful, but I guarantee you will be way ahead of any learning curve you would encounter had you not read this book.

This is a business that, despite everything—economy, trends, regulations and competition—remains exciting, fun and rewarding, populated by interesting characters and a treasure trove of fabulous, yet to be discovered wines. I began importing wine in 1992, took a detour in 2007 by focusing on consulting and writing, but ultimately I could not stay away from the hands-on aspects of this field and began importing again in 2009. Nineteen years down the track it still has allure.

To conclude, I wish you success, great experiences and above all, remember: It *is* about relationships!

Appendixes

Appendix 1

Definitions for Acronyms and Abbreviations

ABC   Alcohol Beverage Control

ATF   Alcohol Tobacco and Firearms

B/L   Bill of Lading

CIF   Cost, Insurance and Freight

COLA   Certificate of Label Approval

DI   Direct Import

EIN   Employer Identification Number

FCL   Full Container Load

FDA   Food and Drug Administration

FOB   Free on Board

FTL   Full Truck Load

LC   Letter of Credit

LCL   Less than Container Load

LTL   Less than Truck Load

ML   Milliliter

PO   Purchase Order

POA   Power of Attorney

POS   Point of Sale (referring to materials)

QPR   Quality Price Ratio

TTB   Alcohol and Tobacco Tax Trade Bureau

License Control States

"There are two general classifications. "Control" states, 18 in number, are the sole wholesalers of **distilled spirits**, as well as the retailers in various ways in some of these States. "License" states, of which there are 32, do not participate in the sale of alcohol beverages and regulate through the issuance of licenses to industry members that do business within their states." From *www.ttb.gov*. In addition, one county of Maryland is included in this list, although the balance of the state operates as a "license" state.

Please note: many "control" states allow the sale and distribution wine and/or beer through appropriately licensed businesses, but are classified as one of the "control" states because distilled spirits fall into this category. I have not differentiated in this list, since wine importers may also decide to become licensed to import distilled spirits. For an overview of state laws and their incongruities there is an interesting table in Wikipedia, but it is not wholly accurate and I urge you to contact any state prior to doing business, as laws change through the state's own modifications or through court decisions, resulting from direct challenges to the law.

ALABAMA	MICHIGAN	PENNSYLVANIA
IDAHO	MISSISSIPPI	UTAH
IOWA	MONTANA	VERMONT
MAINE	NEW HAMPSHIRE	VIRGINIA
MARYLAND	NORTH CAROLINA	WASHINGTON
(Montgomery County Only)	OHIO	WEST VIRGINIA
	OREGON	WYOMING

Appendix 3

License Franchise States

The states listed below are those that have franchise aspects to their laws. Some states listed below may also be classified as "control" or license independent retailers, depending upon the type of alcohol (wine, beer or distilled spirits) or the county. For example, Alabama operates as a "control" state monopoly for distilled spirits only, with privately operated retail stores for beer and wine, but Mobile and Baldwin counties are franchise counties. As explained further in the section on franchise states, these laws make it difficult for any supplier (winery or importer) to terminate their contracts with beverage wholesalers. As a result, wholesalers in these territories can become virtual monopolies, but this is not always the case. Whether or not a state or a single county operates under franchise laws (and how restrictive this law may be) is an important consideration in your quest to achieve and maintain distribution and should be another reason to contact the licensing board of the individual state in which you wish to operate.

ALABAMA	MAINE	NEW MEXICO
ARIZONA	MARYLAND	NORTH CAROLINA
ARKANSAS	MASSACHUSETTS	OHIO
CONNECTICUT	MICHIGAN	OKLAHOMA
DELEWARE	MISSOURI	TENNESSEE
GEORGIA	MONTANA	VERMONT
IDAHO	NEVADA	VIRGINIA
KANSAS	NEW JERSEY	WISCONSIN

Appendix 4

Web Resources

Alcohol Tobacco Tax Bureau: *www.ttb.gov*

States contact details: *www.ttb.gov/wine/control_board.shtml*

COLAs online: *www.ttbonline.gov*

Wine institute: *www.wineinstitute.org*

Trade organizations: *www.wineinstitute.org/resources/links*

EIN: *www.irs.gov*

Exporting license: *www.ttb.gov/itd/exporting_documents.shtm*

Customs: *www.cbp.gov*

Wine Spectator: *www.winespectator.com*

Wine Enthusiast: *www.winemag.com*

Wine Advocate: *www.erobertparker.com*

Wine Business Monthly
for the online magazine: *www.winebusiness.com*
to place adds for employees: *www.winejobs.com*

Wines & Spirits: *www.wineandspiritsmagazine.com/*

Food and Drug Administration: *www.fda.gov*

FDA Prior Notice: *www.cfsan.fda.gov/~pn/pnoview.html*

Websites and Domain Names: *www.networksolutions.com*

Websites and Domain Names: *www.godaddy.com*

US Customs & Border Protection: *www.cbp.gov*

TTB (trade waiver): *www.ttb.gov/itd/importing_samples.shtml*

WSSA (Wine Shipping Co-op): *www.wssa.com*

Small Business Association: *www.sba.org*

SCORE: *www.score.org*

Burghound: *www.burghound.com*

International Wine Cellar: *www.wineaccess.com/expert/tanzer/newhome.html*

INDEX

WINE BOOK PUBLISHER OF THE YEAR
GOURMAND WORLD BOOK AWARDS, 2004

The Wine Appreciation Guild has been an educational pioneer in our
fascinating community.   —Robert Mondavi

Your opinion matters to us…

You may not think it, but customer input is important to the ultimate quality of
any revised work or second edition. We invite and appreciate any comments you
may have. And by registering your WAG books you are enrolled to receive pre-
publication discounts, special offers, or alerts to various wine events, only available to registered members.

REGISTRATION FORM

Name_____Date_____

Professional Affiliation_____

Address_____

_____

City_____State_____Zip_____

e-mail_____

What is the title of the book you purchased?_____

How did you discover this book?_____

_____

Was this book required class reading? Y/N

School/Organization_____

Where did you acquire this book?_____

Was it a good read? (circle)   Poor   1   2   3   Excellent

Was it useful to your work? (circle) Poor   1   2   3   Excellent

Suggestions_____

_____

Comments_____

_____

You can register your book by e-mail: Info@WineAppreciation.com; or snail mail
(copy and send to: Product Registration, Wine Appreciation Guild, 360 Swift Avenue, South San Francisco, CA 94080).